AGENDA
FOR
AMERICA

AGENDA FOR AMERICA

A REPUBLICAN
DIRECTION
FOR THE FUTURE

BY HALEY BARBOUR

Regnery Publishing, Inc.
Washington, D.C.

Library of Congress Cataloging-in-Publication Data

Barbour, Haley, 1947–
Agenda for America: A Republican direction for the future / by
Haley Barbour.
p. cm.
Includes bibliographical references and index.
ISBN 0-89526-721-7
1. Republican Party (U.S. : 1854–) 2. United States—Politics
and government—1993– 3. United States—Economic policy—1993–
4. United States—Social policy—1993– I. Title.
JK2356.B36 1996
324.3734—dc20 95-51389
CIP

Published in the United States by
Regnery Publishing, Inc.
An Eagle Publishing Company
422 First Street, SE, Suite 300
Washington, DC 20003

Distributed to the trade by
National Book Network
4720-A Boston Way
Lanham, MD 20706

Design by Marja Walker

Printed on acid-free paper.
Manufactured in the United States of America

10 9 8 7 6 5 4 3 2 1

Books are available in quantity for promotional or premium use. Write to Director of Special Sales, Regnery Publishing, Inc., 422 First Street, SE, Suite 300, Washington, DC 20003, for information on discounts and terms or call (202) 546-5005.

CONTENTS

Introduction

AGENDA FOR AMERICA, a foundational document of Republican thought, was written by literally thousands of people—the members of the National Policy Forum's policy councils: members of the House and Senate and their staffs, governors, and numerous other concerned citizens from around the country.

The National Policy Forum (NPF) was formed in 1993 as a participatory policy institution, and its goal is to ensure that the wisdom and common sense of the American people dominate the national policy debate. It is a Republican Center for the Exchange of Ideas, not a center for the exchange of Republican ideas. In other words, while the NPF begins with Republican principles of small government and more freedom, it seeks to include more than just Republicans in the development of ideas based on those principles—and it has. I'm pleased with all the Independents and Democrats who have taken us up on our offer to get involved in the public policy debates.

When NPF was created in 1993, we wanted to reconnect the American people with the policy process—to give them back their voice in the national debates. No other nongovernmental organization has ever undertaken such an intensive, inclusive policy process. To ensure the openness of the process, we issued a broad invitation to grassroots America to participate. We never anticipated the level of response; we heard from people from all walks of life and from all professions. Average Americans with an extraordinary commitment to meeting the nation's challenges right in their own backyards offered extraordinary commonsense solutions to our nation's problems. Approximately two hundred thousand Americans have been involved in the activities of the NPF; they have participated in sixty-four grassroots forums around the country; in policy conferences in Washington, D.C.; in focus groups, surveys, and opinion polls; and in a whole range of policy council meetings and discussions.

The 1994 publication of *Listening to America* was historic for its scope. Its contents reaffirmed our belief that good policies and ideas most often originate outside Washington, D.C. *Listening to America* was a clear statement of what Americans want: an alternative to big government, high taxes, and a regulatory agenda that stifles competition. *Listening to America* told the nation: "This is how we would govern if we were in power." The "we" in that statement is not an elite think tank, nor a special interest organization; it is the parents, farmers and ranchers, small businessmen and -women, teachers, factory workers, homemakers, and other concerned men and women who spoke up and spoke out at our forums across the country. And, not coincidentally, American voters in 1994 delivered a mandate for just the kinds of policies discussed in *Listening to America*.

In 1995, NPF sponsored a dozen Washington, D.C.–based conferences and forums on long-range policy issues, including telecommunications law reform, Superfund and the Clean Air Act, Medicare and Medicaid, trade, defense, health care reform, the Endangered Species Act, environmental enforcement and the Clean Water Act, tax reform, electric utilities, the FDA, and high technology. Each conference and forum was composed of congressional and industry leaders, policy experts, and everyday citizens who offered their ideas and proposals.

Agenda for America represents months of intensive consultation and coordination with our policy councils. Each NPF policy council cochair is a highly respected leader with recognized expertise in his or her respective area. They worked closely with each of their councils in drafting sessions and in crafting policy proposals and recommendations.

The development of all the proposals in *Agenda for America* has been an intensely inclusive process, one that has taken more than a year. The ideas and philosophy set forth in *Agenda* represent the hopes and desires of literally thousands of Americans who believe more individual freedom and personal responsibility is far more preferable than more government power and government irresponsibility.

It's important to add that *Agenda for America* is not my book. It is not the Republican Party's book. It is the result of a bottom-up process whose end product reflects the beliefs and ideas of many, many people. Probably none of those people agree with every single thing in the *Agenda*. I'll confess even I don't agree with every idea or recommendation; but that is to be expected in a participatory process, and it's healthy. In the Republican form of government, representatives of the people—even chairmen—must sometimes submerge their personal preferences to the clear will of the people.

Agenda for America is not just a book about cutting taxes or reducing government spending, it is also about changing how Washington works. It is about transforming the relationship between the federal government and the states, and reducing the role the federal government plays in our lives. It is about returning power to states and local communities and allowing Americans to take more control of their own lives and communities.

No one said it better than President Ronald Reagan: "A nation that believes in the heroism of ordinary people living ordinary lives; of tough courts and safe streets; of a drug-free America where schools teach honesty, respect, love of learning, and, yes, love of country; a vision of a land where families can grow in love and safety and where dreams are made with opportunity. This is the vision, this is the record; this is the agenda for victory."

As the NPF continues to reach out to those with ideas, we hope you will share your thoughts with us. Help us continue developing America's agenda for the next century.

Haley Barbour
Chairman
National Policy Forum

I

ECONOMIC PROGRESS *and* OPPORTUNITY

1

Taxing and Spending

Do you know that we spend more time figuring out our taxes in the United States of America than we do producing every automobile, every truck, and every van in Detroit, Buffalo, and Ohio and Kentucky and Tennessee and California and throughout America? We spend more time figuring out our taxes than the total time to produce [all] the automobiles and vans in the United States.

—Jack Kemp, codirector of Empower America, at a
National Policy Forum on
"Building a Better Tax Code: Breaking with the Past"

★

AMERICANS PAY TOO MUCH TAX to support too much government. A core objective of our agenda is to provide an alternative to the big-spending, high-taxing, overregulating government that now shackles individuals and families. Excessive and unnecessary government barriers to economic progress and higher living standards must be eliminated or reduced. We need public policies that enhance individual freedom and opportunity, and enable individuals to provide adequately for themselves and their families. To that end, we must also provide an environment congenial to entrepreneurship, innovation, business creation, and growth.

For too long now Washington has attempted to manage our economy with massive government spending programs and huge transfers of wealth engineered through the tax system. We must reduce the tax burden on our families and entrepreneurs so that we can promote economic growth and strengthen our families, which are best equipped to teach our children good citizenship and the habits necessary for economic productivity.

America has always been the land of opportunity. And the basis of economic opportunity has always been growth. When the economy grows, more jobs open up, there is more room for small business entrepreneurs with new ideas, and families' standards of living improve, allowing them to invest in durable goods and/or higher education for their children. With a rapidly growing economy we can provide jobs for everyone willing to work, along with the chance for advancement and upward mobility. All these factors join together to produce a dynamic economy and a society that can be prosperous and at peace with itself.

America is poised to lead the world into a new era of economic growth. Technological innovations that offer enormous promise for greater productivity and more high-paying jobs are coming on-stream at an unprecedented pace. To realize that promise, however, the nation must significantly change its public policies. Existing policies discourage households and businesses from engaging in the very activities on which economic progress crucially depends. Our core objective is to remove government-imposed obstacles to growth. And a major obstacle to this is the federal tax system.

Any real tax reform must replace the existing system with one that is more fair, efficient, simple, and pro-growth. It would tax all income one time, at one rate, with few deductions; grant appropriate allowances for the family; and have no regressive impact on the poor, the elderly, and families with children. As a practical matter, the new tax would be simple, visible, and easy to administer.[1] It would impose lower taxes than today's because tax reform begins with spending controls. Taxes must be limited in the interests of economic growth and progress.

All of our modern experience teaches us that lower, simpler taxes benefit our people and our economy. Most vivid were the courageous tax cuts pushed through by President Reagan in his first year in office, a model for us in 1997 and beyond. After weathering a recession necessary to wring out President Carter's inflationary policy, the 1981 Reagan tax cuts brought America ninety-two months of sustained growth (1982–90), the longest ever in peacetime. The economy grew approximately one-third in real terms. Interest rates and home mortgage rates declined. Contributions to charity increased, manufacturing output rose, and foreign private investment in the United States more than doubled.

At least as important, real, postinflation median family income in this country rose between 1982 and 1990, from $35,419 to $39,086, for an increase of 10.4 percent. Nineteen million new jobs were created between 1982 and 1989, 2.4 million in 1989 alone. And 82 percent of these jobs were in higher paying occupations—technical, precision production, managerial, and professional.[2]

The benefits were widely enjoyed. During the 1982–90 period, everyone became more prosperous. The bottom fifth of income earners had an 11 percent increase in income, the next fifth a 9.7 percent increase, the middle fifth a 10.3 percent increase, the next fifth an 11.8 percent increase, and the highest fifth a 17.9 percent increase.

Some would inevitably complain that people with high incomes did even better than other Americans during the prosperous 1980s. But the goal of government should not be to make all people the same. It should be to allow everyone to become better off. And policies of low taxes and fewer regulations did precisely this.

Some believe that the "rich" don't pay their "fair share" of the total tax burden. According to the Joint Economic Committee, in the taxable year 1993, the top 10 percent of the income earners, people who accounted for 39 percent of the nation's adjusted gross income in 1993, paid a disproportionate share—almost 59 percent—of the total individual income tax revenues collected by the federal government. Their effective tax rate was 20 percent of their income. The bottom 50 percent of income earners accounted for almost 15 percent of total adjusted gross income but paid only 4.8 percent of the total individual income tax that year. Their income taxes were 4.3 percent of their income, only slightly more than a fifth of the effective rate paid by the top 10 percent of income earners.

It really is very simple: Lower taxes and less regulation help the poor, along with everyone else; higher taxes and more regulation hurt the poor, along with everyone else. After the 1990 budget deal raised taxes, everyone became worse off. And after President Clinton's retroactive tax

DISTRIBUTION OF INDIVIDUAL
INCOME TAXES BY INCOME QUINTILE
Calendar Year 1995

INCOME QUINTILE [1]	INDIVIDUAL TAXES UNDER PRESENT LAW		PRESENT LAW EFFECTIVE TAX RATE [2]
	Billions	**Percent**	**Percent**
Lowest	-$7	-1.1%	-4.6%
Second	2	0.3%	0.4%
Third	36	6.0%	4.8%
Fourth	94	16.0%	7.9%
Highest	464	78.8%	16.0%
TOTAL, ALL TAXPAYERS	**588**	**100%**	**10.9%**
Highest 10%	$374	63.6%	18.7%
Highest 5%	300	51.0%	21.3%
Highest 1%	181	30.8%	26.8%

(*Source:* Joint Committee on Taxation)
Detail may not add to total due to rounding.

1 The income concept used to place tax returns into income categories is adjusted gross income (AGI) plus:
   (1) tax-exempt interest,
   (2) employer contributions for health plans and life insurance,
   (3) employer share of FICA tax,
   (4) workers' compensation,
   (5) nontaxable Social Security benefits,
   (6) insurance value of Medicare benefits,
   (7) alternative minimum tax preference items, and
   (8) excluded income of U.S. citizens living abroad.
   The quintile breakpoints are $11,190, $21,847, $35,629, and $57,639. The highest 10%, 5%, and 1% breakpoints are $81,276, $106,249, and $219,770.
2 The effective tax is equal to individual income taxes divided by income described in footnote 1.

hike took effect in 1993, real income dropped a whopping $709, or 1.9 percent, in a single year.

History shows that rapid economic growth helps all Americans by creating new opportunities. From 1982 to 1987, the number of black-owned firms increased by nearly 38 percent to a total of 425,000. During the same period, Hispanic-owned firms surged by 83 percent, according to the *Wall Street Journal*. Unfortunately, in 1986 the capital gains tax rate was increased by 65 percent. And, not surprisingly, that huge increase brought us four straight years during which Americans started fewer businesses each year than the year before.

AMERICA'S TAX BURDEN IS TOO HIGH

Taxes on American businesses and families are, quite simply, too high. For example, on long-term capital gains, the United States has the dubious distinction of being the number one taxer in the world. What do these higher taxes mean for America? Less investment and fewer jobs. High capital gains taxes make investing more expensive and, obviously, less attractive. And without investment, companies can't expand or even stay in business (more on this later).

The federal government has been hurting families far too much for far too long—in part through the onerous marriage penalty and in large part through the steady erosion in value of the dependent tax exemption. Where in 1948 a median-income family of four paid only .3 percent of its income in federal taxes, by 1990 that percentage had risen to 9 percent. And the dependent tax exemption was hit the hardest. That exemption fell precipitously in value between 1948 and 1990. Because of inflation and other factors, the exemption today would have to be $7,000 instead of only slightly over $2,000 in order to be worth what it was in 1948. As a percentage of income, the dependent exemption has shrunk to a quarter of its former value.

Regressive tax policies have had a real effect on our families. It is expensive to raise children, particularly if you want to do right by them. Lower taxes would help parents a great deal as they struggle to provide for their children. We have already made progress in this area. The Contract with

America's $500 per child tax credit will go far toward correcting Washington's mistreatment of America's families. Lower taxes allow families to invest in the future and in their children's future. Government's attempts to invest in human capital directly, through Washington-based programs, generally backfire because of bureaucratic inertia and the distorting effects of government subsidies. Families, on the other hand, can very effectively invest in the human capital of their children, giving them the appropriate education and training, improving their material conditions, and, in the process, adding to the general economic growth.

The current tax system is strangling America's small businesses, which are the engine of job creation in the U.S. economy.

First, high marginal tax rates disproportionately hurt smaller firms because they tend to file their taxes as individuals rather than corporations. In 1993, President Clinton's tax increase bill—the largest in U.S. history—raised the top marginal tax rate to 39.6 percent.[3] As a result, small businesses today have less incentive to expand their operations, to purchase that additional machine, and to hire that additional worker.

Second, the estate/death tax rates are so high now that many heirs of family-owned businesses must sell the business in order to pay the taxes. The result: lost jobs and fewer family-owned businesses. For instance, in a survey of black-owned enterprises, nearly one-third say their heirs will have to sell the business to pay the estate tax. While the Contract with America/Republican tax cut plans called for significant estate/death tax relief for small businesses, the long-term goal should be the outright repeal of this antifamily businesses tax.

Third, federal payroll taxes are one of the greatest inhibitors of economic expansion and job creation in the small-business sector. A majority of small firms pay more in payroll taxes than in income taxes. Payroll taxes, moreover, are by far the fastest growing federal tax burden on small businesses. Reducing the burden of payroll taxes must be part of any significant federal tax reform effort.

Cutting our punitive capital gains tax will unleash a flood of entrepreneurial capitalism and job opportunities. When we cut the capital gains tax in 1978 and in 1981, investment in new business ventures skyrocketed and the Treasury increased. The Contract with America's capital gains tax cut, it is estimated, will create 722,000 new jobs by the year 2000.[4] This tax cut would lower the cost of capital by 5 percent, thereby inducing investors to increase the capital stock by $2.2 trillion by the year 2000. This larger stock of capital would also increase total GDP cumulatively by almost $1 trillion by the year 2000. And everyone would benefit. While proposals to cut the capital gains tax rates are falsely labeled as tax cuts for the wealthy, well over half of all taxpayers with capital gains in 1992 had adjusted gross incomes of less than $50,000. Over 72 percent had incomes of less than $75,000. Thus middle-class families would benefit directly from capital gains cuts. And everyone would benefit from the spur to investment, incomes, and job creation the tax cuts would bring.

Income Tax Returns with Capital Gains, by Total Income Level, 1992

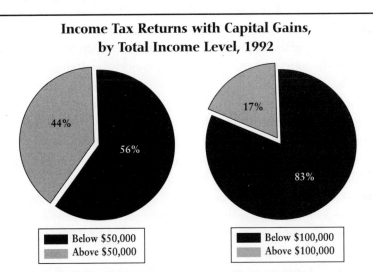

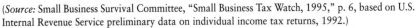

(*Source:* Small Business Survival Committee, "Small Business Tax Watch, 1995," p. 6, based on U.S. Internal Revenue Service preliminary data on individual income tax returns, 1992.)

But we must go further. Below, we examine the current tax system's failure to live up to proper standards for any tax structure: fairness, providing the real cost of government, simplicity, nonintrusiveness.

Fairness

Our present tax system is irreparably broken. Virtually no one believes our tax system is fair. The best way of looking at tax fairness is to call to mind one of the oldest, most basic principles on which this nation was founded. Throughout our history we have insisted that everyone in this society should stand equally before the law. Applying that principle in the field of taxation leads us to a just standard of fairness: If the government is to tax income, everyone should be exposed to the same rate of tax on his or her income.

For one thing, the rewards people receive from participating in the free market economy closely match what each person has contributed to it. Moreover, those rewards are not earned at other people's expense. Thus, after the Reagan tax cuts, according to the National Federation of Independent Business, the number of women-owned businesses nearly doubled (from 2.9 to 5.4 million) during 1982 to 1990, and real earnings for women rose as well. Black and Hispanic unemployment rates declined overall in the 1980s; black employment in managerial and professional occupations rose 46 percent between 1983 and 1991, and similar Hispanic employment rose 84 percent.

Unfortunately, our tax laws ignore these facts of our economic life. Indeed, President Kennedy, over thirty years ago, could have been describing our present system when he said, "An economy hampered with restrictive tax rates will never produce enough revenue to balance the budget, just as it will never produce enough jobs."

Upward-graduated income tax rates, in effect, assert that the more productive we are and the more we contribute to our economic well-being, the more tax we should pay. This though the facts are clear: High marginal tax rates crush economic growth. When tax rates were lowered in 1981, the productivity of American workers rose: the average worker produced $49,600 in goods and services in 1990, the highest level in the world.[5]

Hiding the Cost of Government

The existing system fails to tell the public what it must pay for government services. If we don't know what government costs us, we will ask for more and more. But government services and activities are not free. To provide those services and activities, government takes away resources that would otherwise be available to households to improve their living standards and to businesses to produce needed products and services. In the process, government drives up the cost and reduces the quantity of goods and services in the private sector.

Do you know, as you read this, how much federal income tax you paid last year or are likely to pay this year? Ask your friends how much payroll tax was deducted from their gross wages or salaries last year; ask yourself how much you paid in payroll taxes last year. Does anyone have even a ballpark estimate of what he or she paid in federal excise or corporate taxes last year?

Everyone in a self-governing, self-reliant society should be able to answer these questions in order to decide whether the government they're getting is worth what they're paying. But we can't. And because of that, we get too much government at much too high a cost. This lavish government costs us the valuable products and services we would otherwise have, resulting in a smaller economy that grows more slowly than it could.

We need a tax system that does a vastly better job of telling us what government costs. This is reason enough to scrap the existing system.

Complication and Intrusiveness
One of the acid tests of an acceptable tax system is that it impose the lowest possible costs of compliance, administration, and enforcement. The existing tax system is totally unacceptable on these grounds alone. Every element is extremely complicated, requiring an enormous number of man hours and hundreds of billions of dollars of manpower, machinery, and paper costs.

The complexity of the tax laws inevitably results in harsh and complex rules and regulations that ensure compliance with those laws, and their enforcement in turn generates arbitrary, often cruelly harsh penalties by the tax administrators—the Internal Revenue Service. The history of the contemporary tax system is a laboratory example of how to make tax laws more and more costly to comply with, to administer, and to enforce. Virtually every tax bill enacted in recent years has made the laws more and more complex in order to squeeze out every last dime of taxable income. The consequence has been huge increases in taxpayers' compliance costs and in IRS administration and enforcement personnel. It has also begotten enforcement procedures that ruthlessly invade our property rights; the IRS can and does seize the property of people it says have evaded paying their taxes without first going to court. No government agency should have the power to confiscate property without a finding by a court of violation of the law.

We tend to overlook that we pay for these enormous compliance burdens—over five billion hours spent in computing taxes in one year alone—by giving up products and services that we would otherwise produce. We pay for the complexity of our tax laws through lower living standards today and in the future.

It should be abundantly clear that simplifying the tax laws and reducing compliance costs go far beyond so-called tax reform. Since the adoption of the Sixteenth Amendment to the Constitution, the federal income tax has been reformed and reformed, and things only get worse. The classic case of reform gone wildly astray is the Tax Reform Act of 1986. That legislation simplified compliance only for the several million people it dropped altogether from the income tax rolls; it hugely increased the complexity and compliance costs for virtually all business-income taxpayers and for individual taxpayers who receive income from their savings and investments.

A tax revolution, not mere tax reform, is needed. We must reduce compliance, administration, and enforcement costs of tax laws rather than focus on the misbehavior of some Internal Revenue Service agents, bad as that has been. This will require replacing existing taxes with a clear, simple tax structure that taxes all income once, and only once, and at a reasonable level.

A TAX SYSTEM FOR A DYNAMIC, FREE AMERICA

To tell the people what price they must pay for governmental activities and services, the tax system must have certain attributes. Most important, taxes must be visible to the people who pay them. If we aren't aware of paying a tax or of how much we pay, clearly the tax isn't telling us anything about what we must pay for government.

We believe that tax reform should follow a series of principles aimed at keeping taxes low, fair, and nondisruptive to economic decision-making. Any tax reform should include these qualifications:

- All taxpayers should be fully informed on exactly what is being taxed, how they are being taxed, and what their true tax liability is.

- Taxes must be made as visible to the taxpayer as possible ("hidden" taxes mask the true cost of government).
- The tax system must explicitly treat all individuals equally under the law. (Deliberate differentiations in tax liabilities based on the sources or uses of income should be avoided, except in the case of capital gains. Capital gains is covered under the principle of not taxing income more than once. The capital gains tax is a double tax on the same stream of income.)
- The tax system should provide the same treatment for similar economic actions and transactions and should not be based on the attributes of the taxpayer.
- Multiple layers of taxation must be avoided and income taxed once and only once.
- Real people, not corporations, pay taxes, not withstanding that few of them are aware they actually shoulder the burden; therefore, eliminate the corporate tax and integrate it with the personal tax.
- The tax system must be simple (complexity makes the system expensive, punitive, and inefficient—a loss to the economy).
- The tax system must be neutral in economic decision-making—it should not interfere with the free economic choices of individuals, households, or businesses.
- A low tax rate must be applied across the board, thus creating the fewest distortions to the economy (high marginal tax rates damage economic growth by reducing incentives to work, save, and invest).
- No retroactive tax changes must be made, as these sap public confidence in planning for the future.
- The tax code must not impede the free flow of goods, services, and capital across borders.

Toward a Flatter, Fairer, Simpler Tax

There are presently several major alternative tax restructuring plans being considered by Congress. Although many of these plans are strikingly different, they share one important attribute: The reforms highlight the need to replace the existing system with one that is more fair, efficient, simple, and pro-growth.

They are:

Armey/Shelby Flat Tax—Majority Leader Dick Armey and Senator Richard Shelby have introduced a plan based on a 20 percent flat rate in 1996 and a 17 percent flat rate thereafter. The plan has an individual wage tax and a business tax imposed on all forms of business that allows the deduction of "business inputs" but not taxes, interest, and dividends.

Domenici/Nunn—Senators Pete Domenici and Sam Nunn have introduced a bill that proposes a fairly comprehensive consumption tax base but retains a reduced mortgage interest deduction, a charitable deduction, and exacts a deduction for higher education expenses.

Lugar National Sales Tax—Senator Richard Lugar has proposed that the present income tax system be replaced with a national sales tax. The Lugar proposal is aimed at addressing the basic problems afflicting the U.S. economy, as well as liberating Americans from the intrusive burden of the income tax.

Specter Flat Tax—Senator Arlen Specter introduced the Specter flat tax proposal in Congress in early 1995. The proposal seeks to achieve the four fundamental goals of tax reform: growth, fairness, simplicity, and deficit neutral.

Rep. Bill Archer—Bill Archer, chairman, House Ways and Means Committee, advocates pulling the income tax out by its roots and throwing it away so it can never grow back. Chairman Archer's guiding principle is to choose a new tax that provides the greatest, most productive boost for the overall economy and contains five attributes: simplicity and freedom, saving incentives, international competitiveness, fairness, and it addresses the underground economy.

Which proposal will finally be adopted remains to be seen. However, if we do it right, if the rates are low enough, and if we stop double and triple taxing, we will have the support of the American people.

In addition to limiting taxes so that they no longer penalize investment and families, we must overhaul the entire income tax structure. It must be clear and fair, and reflect the true and full costs of government. The current system's complicated loopholes hide from taxpayers the full burden of the tax system.

We must move toward comprehensive reform that will keep the government from penalizing people for investing, saving, and working hard. That remedy would be a simpler, flatter tax system for all Americans. By eliminating tax brackets and tax loopholes we can encourage hard work and investment. We can foster economic growth and help families and individuals climb the ladder of success.

With such a system, taxpayers will know that they are bearing only their fair share of the tax burden. It also will bring about extensive public savings on inefficient tax subsidies, not to mention the time and trouble involved in complicated disputes with the Internal Revenue Service. With loopholes eliminated, entrepreneurs will be able to concentrate on making the best product at the best price. This increased efficiency will produce savings for consumers, profits for entrepreneurs, and employment opportunities for workers.

Tax and Spending Limitations

We must keep in mind that any lasting and effective tax reform must begin with tax limitation and spending control. Government spending increases the pressure for higher taxes. This in turn renders tax reform more difficult. For example, the government often speaks of the "cost" of reducing taxes. To index capital gains taxes for inflation would "cost" the government several billion dollars a year, on its reckoning. But tax cuts in fact cost nothing, because they allow people to keep what they own in the first place. Therefore, in addition to a Balanced Budget Amendment to the Constitution, Congress should enact a supermajority requirement to raise taxes.

By instituting spending limitations that put the budget on a glide path toward balance by the year 2002, we will reduce the demand for tax revenues. By providing tax relief as a matter of principle, we will increase the incentive for government to economize. By taking more money out of the hands of government officials and letting it stay with workers and consumers who earned it, we will increase the funds available for commerce and investment.

Balancing the budget can work in tandem with our other goals to lower the burden of government on the American economy and so spur growth and prosperity for all Americans.

2

Regulatory and Economic Policy

JOHN McCURDY HAD OPERATED a small herring smokehouse successfully for more than twenty years. Despite having produced more than fifty-four million fillets without a single reported case of food poisoning, the Food and Drug Administration (FDA) suddenly told McCurdy that he would have to change his smoking methods. Cost: $75,000 in new equipment. Facing a hopeless choice between installing expensive equipment and fighting a legal battle with the FDA, Mr. McCurdy chose the only other alternative—he closed his business. Number of jobs lost: twenty-two.

Carol Roberts is a self-employed knitter who does all her work at home. She produces sweaters, hats, and mittens, which she sells to retailers for a small profit to help support her family. The AFL–CIO and the Department of Labor are now pushing to reinstate a ban on at-home garment work that was lifted in the 1980s. If the law goes back into effect, Carol Roberts and thousands of home garment workers like her will be considered criminals.

One federal regulatory agency is seeking to compel certain bucket manufacturers to do the unthinkable: make leaky buckets. The Consumer Product Safety Commission is planning to issue regulations to require manufacturers of industrial five-gallon plastic buckets to redesign their products. Concerned that infants could climb inside the buckets and drown, the agency studied the matter for five years and issued a 101-page report. The report noted that "industry representatives claim that they can envision no use for a bucket that leaks."

In May 1992, thirty FDA officials raided a doctor's office in Kent, Washington. After breaking down the doors, the officials—guns raised in the air—ordered the physician and nurses to stand in a circle without speaking or moving. The reason for the raid? The FDA suspected the doctor—who was known to practice alternative medicines, such as natural vitamin treatments—of using imported, injectable B-vitamins. The vitamins had not passed FDA muster.

A small pool service company in Pennsylvania is compelled by regulators to send employees to a comprehensive course on pesticides so that they can learn to open one-pound bags and put the right amount into a swimming pool. Millions of homeowners perform this routine chore themselves, without benefit of advanced training. But the Federal Insecticide, Fungicide, and Rodenticide Act (FIFRA) requires applicators of some pesticides to be "certified pesticide applicators." Chlorine is classified as a pesticide because it kills algae—hence the mandatory training.[1]

Economic growth in the twenty-first century will depend not only on letting American citizens keep what they earn through lower taxes, and on keeping the federal deficit down through controlled government spending, but also on freeing us from excessive government regulations.

American initiative is currently being smothered in a complicated system of federal regulations that engulfs almost every aspect of our lives—the food we eat, the air we breathe, the products we buy, the transportation we use, the medical care we receive, and the way we run our businesses. Regulatory policy affects both our workplaces and our homes. The scope of government regulation is enormous and has a tremendous effect on us as individuals as well as on our economy.

We emphatically recognize the need for government regulation in many areas of our lives, including those that relate to health, safety, the environment, and certain other areas, such as securities, patents, copyrights, and trade. We do not oppose federal regulation, per se. Proper federal regulatory activity is appropriate and necessary.

Many of the regulations, however, entail endless red tape but no longer provide any benefits for the ordinary citizen. When regulation increases, so does the cost. The price tag for regulation has grown much faster than its benefits. Because of these regulations, conducting business is more expensive than replacing people with computers and other machines; moreover, minimum wage and other labor laws make hiring new workers more expensive. Similarly, environmental, banking, and civil rights laws often raise the cost of equipment, require extensive record keeping and paperwork, and even drive up the cost of credit. Firms face a choice: Either pass on the cost to the consumer or scale back future hiring.

While many people are becoming more aware of the negative impact of federal regulatory policies, the debate over economic growth all too often continues to center only on the size of the deficit. Political candidates frequently are asked, "What is your plan to cut the deficit?" They rarely are asked, "What is your plan to reduce regulation?" Meanwhile, the number of federal regulations climbs steadily. It is worth noting that in 1993 the federal regulatory apparatus cost an estimated three times as much as it did in 1970. The overall cost of regulation reached an estimated $647 billion in 1994, according to a March 1995 General Accounting Office report. That $647 billion burden was more than three times the entire 1994 federal budget deficit of $200 billion.[2]

So why isn't regulatory reform a hotter issue? The main reason is that regulatory costs by their very nature are hidden from the consumer. People who know exactly how much they pay in taxes are often completely in the dark about how much federal regulatory policy takes out of their budgets. They usually have no idea that government regulations drive up the cost of the goods and services they purchase every day.

Two examples:

- The cost of a car is estimated to be about $2,000 higher than it normally would be because of government regulations.
- Building a house costs an estimated $5,000 more than it normally would because of government regulations.

To the greatest extent possible, the cost of regulation must be made transparent to the maximum number of all parties affected by them. The overall cost of regulation amounts to more than $6,000 per household. "Fifty-two cents out of every dollar that you earn goes to the cost of government taxes, mandates, and regulations," Representative Tom DeLay observed at a 1995 National Policy Forum Environmental Enforcement

Megaconference. "The government bureaucrats get to spend more of your hard-earned money than you do."

Tom DeLay is right. A shocking portion of our working lives is devoted to earning money to pay for taxes, regulations, and other government activities. Every year the average American works full-time from January until July 4 just to pay costs associated with government. That means that most of us work more than half the year for an increasingly rapacious Uncle Sam.

Although it's difficult to fully assess the economic toll of excessive regulation, we do know where regulation hits the hardest: small businesses, the job-creating engine of our economy. As an official from the National Federation of Independent Businesses put it in 1993 congressional testimony:

> There is growing bipartisan agreement about two phenomena that are taking place in America's small business sector. Number one, virtually all job growth in this country comes from small business. And number two, the burden created by federal regulation falls predominantly and disproportionately on the very people we rely on to create these jobs. [3]

Many seemingly noble regulations, including the Clean Air Act and the Americans with Disabilities Act (ADA), can have a devastating impact on small businesses such as bakeries, dry cleaners, and auto repair shops, which may already be operating on a very small profit margin. All these businesses are now regulated as "major" sources of air pollution. As such, they are required to obtain a new operating permit every five years, at an average cost of $10,000.

And owners of small businesses find themselves buried in a mountain of forms. According to the U.S. Small Business Administration, these owners spend at least a billion hours a year filling out government forms. Estimated annual cost: $100 billion.

Another regulatory peril: When the federal budget is tight—as it is now—lawmakers are tempted to require businesses to pay for services that might otherwise have come out of the government's pockets. For example, lawmakers might mandate that a private sector employer pay for a day-care center. In the jargon of Washington, this is "off budget." But that doesn't mean it's free. Somebody pays.

States and localities are also adversely affected by regulatory policy. Federal mandates can force them to spend their taxpayer dollars complying with unfunded federal mandates. These federal regulations often preempt state initiatives. They also force the states and localities to allocate scarce resources away from activities important to individual communities, and give them to activities that Washington, D.C., deems a higher priority. A recent survey of 314 cities by the U.S. Conference of Mayors estimated that the 1993 cost of such federal mandates was $6.5 billion. The three most expensive federal mandates were the Clean Water Act ($3.6 billion), Solid Waste Disposal Act ($900 million), and Safe Drinking Water Act ($600 million). These costs of course are passed along to the taxpayer. Over the next ten years, compliance will cost one U.S. city—Columbus, Ohio—up to $1.3 billion. Annual cost per household: $700.

Because they are forced to pay for federal mandates, states and local governments must cut back or ignore the activities and initiatives they and their constituents think most important.

As severe as the financial burden of regulation is, that's not all of it. After congressional Democrats pass laws mandating the regulation of an activity, they encourage excessive codification, implementation, and enforcement by federal agencies. While the laws are made by legislators, regulations are usually made by unelected regulators entrusted with "interpreting" the laws. Many of these regulators are, to say the least, zealous. With hardly anyone in Washington paying attention, they busy themselves with harassing productive citizens by handing down all sorts of mandates, edicts, and fines, often bringing to bear the full power of the federal government upon hard-working Americans.

BUILDING SUPPORT FOR REGULATORY REFORM

Republican presidents have tried over the years to hold the regulators back. But even President Reagan succeeded only in slowing the rate of increase in regulations. From 1980 to 1985, real federal regulatory spending fell by 3 percent, regulatory employment by 16 percent, and *Federal Register* pages by almost 40 percent. But the respite was brief. After 1988, the regulatory state blossomed with a flurry of new laws.

Today the Republican Congress is making some progress on the regulatory front, living up to its pledge in the Contract with America to end the insidious Capitol Hill practice of passing the buck—quite literally—to the states and localities through unfunded mandates. Shortly after the Republicans won a majority in Congress, a new Republican-backed law was passed that limits Washington's power to impose unfunded federal mandates on the states, one of 1995's most important legislative regulatory reforms.

Now, thanks to this law, lawmakers and regulators are forced to assess the financial cost of regulatory burdens before they impose them on states and localities. When the cost is too high, Congress has to have a separate vote to approve the imposition of the cost, thus making it clear to us, the taxpayers, just how much of our money lawmakers are spending with unfunded mandates. This extra step should cut down substantially on Washington's penchant for running our lives and spending our money.

But insisting on assessments of the costs of regulatory burdens is only one element of the needed regulatory reform. The merits of regulations should be judged not only on the basis of costs, but also on need and expected benefits. In other words, the public has a right to know what they can actually expect to get for their regulatory expenditures.

Environmental regulations account for one of the largest portions of the federal regulatory burden—roughly one-quarter of the total. We all favor strong environmental safeguards where they are needed. Nothing is more precious than our health, safety, and the environment on which we depend, and necessary protection of these values amounts to money well spent.

But it is important to recognize the distinction between more regulation and more protection; conversely, less regulation does not necessarily mean less protection. Not every perceived environmental risk is of the same magnitude, and large expenditures on insignificant or speculative risks can actually reduce public protection and welfare by diverting limited resources from more important environmental programs or community needs, as well as negatively affecting business development and employment. It should also be recognized that the hidden costs of environmental regulations that raise the cost of basic consumer goods, utility bills, and local taxes and service assessments fall disproportionately on poorer Americans and those with low fixed incomes, and that this by itself can have health consequences.

To achieve the maximum benefit from what we spend on environmental protection, it is necessary to carefully assess expected benefits and set priorities. For many years the scientific community and government leaders have increasingly recognized that environmental regulations promulgated in the past have often been driven by popular or political perceptions of environmental risk rather than by sound science, and by filling gaps in scientific knowledge with "assumptions" about risk used to justify more regulations. Some existing environmental laws and regulatory policies impose expensive requirements with no regard at all for whether they will achieve any significant improvements in environmental protection. Additionally, government regulations have often been adamant about the benefits of regulations or government programs even though the underlying scientific data have deemed otherwise. These misrepresentations could well hinder real environmental and scientific advances and weaken our state and local governments and businesses.

To remedy this situation, Republicans in Congress have supported legislation that would require federal agencies to conduct scientifically sound, objective, and unbiased risk assessments and cost-benefit analyses for major regulatory actions and provide full information about those analyses to the public. We believe that such requirements are clearly needed to set proper priorities and obtain the most environmental protection possible while keeping government spending and regulatory burdens under control.

PROTECTING THE RIGHTS OF THE REGULATED
Congress must also demand changes in the way federal agencies enforce the regulations. Since federal regulators have all too often sought retribution against citizens who question enforcement decisions or legally resist what might be unlawful abuses of their freedom by arbitrary bureaucrats, citizen whistle-blowers need to be protected by law.

A key to regulatory reform is to return power to state and local governments, where many federal regulations belong. The federal government should take two steps to reach this goal:

1. Congress and the executive branch should build on the legislation to restrict unfunded mandates. Specifically, they should carry forward the review set in motion by the new Constitutional Caucus in Congress. The aim of the Caucus is to bring the federal laws back in line with the original intent of the Constitution. (Most regulations are imposed under a very broad interpretation of Article I, Section 8, of the Constitution, which gives Congress the right to regulate commerce between states. Recently the Supreme Court has quite correctly called into question such interpretations.)
2. Congress should thoroughly review the existing regulatory agencies to see which ones can be operated at the state level, and make these the priorities for quick devolution.

ABANDONING DELEGATION

Another major aim should be to restore Congress itself to its constitutional limits. This is especially crucial to controlling runaway regulations. Congress increasingly has delegated the lawmaking authority entrusted to it by Article I of the Constitution to the executive branch—in most cases to unelected bureaucrats—and to the courts. When Congress passes vague mandates, bureaucrats flesh them out and apply them. The result: runaway legislation.[4]

An especially compelling example of this kind of runaway regulation comes in federal wetlands policy. Congress never has voted on a law to protect wetlands, which, by bureaucratic definition, can be a piece of land that is bone dry for all but a few days a year. Legislation from the 1970s limiting the dumping of major pollutants into a U.S. waterway has been reinterpreted by the executive branch to criminalize dumping fill dirt on a piece of dry land, making it a felony.

Changing the procedures for making regulations can help head off such abuses in the future. Elected officials should be held accountable for the abuses that stem from laws for which they voted. Equally important is the need to address current regulations that harm the economy, hinder job creation, and violate individual rights.

Two areas that demand immediate action:

The Food and Drug Administration (FDA)

The FDA is supposed to protect the public from unsafe medicines and medical devices. Instead it has become a hazard to the public health, driving up the cost of health care and, most tragically of all, keeping off the market drugs that might save lives.

The FDA has a three-phase process for approving new drugs. Under Phase I, the manufacturer must prove a new drug is safe. Under Phase II, the FDA must be satisfied that there is a correlation between the use of a product and its intended effect. Under Phase III, the company must demonstrate, through extensive field tests, the efficacy of the drug.

On average, it takes eight years and costs nearly $400 million to bring a new drug to the market during Phase III.[5] Because of this long delay, many die. Dr. Louis Lasagne, director of Tufts University's Center for the Study of Drug Development, calculates that during the seven-year delay in the approval of beta blockers (a heart medication), 119,000 heart patients, who might otherwise have been saved by the drug, died.

The FDA also exercises a stranglehold over the dissemination of factual information about pharmaceutical drugs, especially benefits discovered after the drug has been put on the market. For example, it can be a federal crime for an aspirin manufacturer to hand a doctor a pamphlet on research indicating that aspirin can help prevent certain heart problems—the kind of pamphlet routinely available in many pharmacies.

A good start toward defanging the FDA would be to allow manufacturers to use private laboratories rather than the FDA for efficacy testing.

The Americans with Disabilities Act (ADA)

The 1990 Americans with Disabilities Act, which prohibits job discrimination against the handicapped and mandates that public transportation and other facilities be wheelchair-accessible, was intended to help handicapped Americans.[6] But instead it has caused a blizzard of complaints and lawsuits, many of them farfetched. The principal beneficiaries? Lawyers. Nearly 20 percent of the forty-five thousand ADA-related complaints filed with the Equal Employment Opportunity Commission between July 1992 and spring 1995 were filed by people claiming their back problems constituted a disability. Only 10 percent alleged hiring discrimination.

A few examples:

- A dentist dismissed for fondling his patients sued under ADA regulations, claiming that his urges to fondle constituted a disability.
- An employee fired for carrying a gun to work claimed that a nervous disability caused his gun toting.
- A woman with memory problems that made her unable to perform her tasks adequately successfully sued after being fired. She claimed her memory problems were a disability. Apparently she had no problem remembering that the ADA might get her rehired!

The ADA requires that employers provide disabled workers with "reasonable accommodations" that do not cause "undue hardships" to the employer. In practice, the government and courts determine what is "reasonable." Hence the aforementioned forty-five thousand complaints in a period of roughly three years.

The ADA also mandates that state and local governments help the disabled in specific ways that may be extremely costly, even when more innovative and less expensive alternatives might be preferable. Often funds needed elsewhere must be allocated to ADA requirements.

No one is against creating an environment in which disabled Americans can enjoy useful and independent lives, but the ADA may have important flaws that render it inappropriate for that task.

One step that would go a long way toward remedying the situation would be to allow ADA issues to be handled by state and local governments. This would allow more flexibility in compliance. A city with few wheelchair-bound citizens might be able to come up with a creative solution to their problems—perhaps providing door-to-door car service for a fraction of the cost of retrofitting buses with wheelchair lifts.

THE WORKPLACE

Government has a legitimate role in defining responsible basic standards for workforce protections. Indeed the debate about workplace policy during the past fifty years has not been over *whether* workers should receive protections, but over *how best to provide* those protections. Unfortunately, worker protections have typically been dictated by the federal government. Decisions affecting workplaces have come down from Washington to the shop floor. Outside input into the decision-making process has come, if at all, from powerful special interests, particularly organized labor.

The process has been open to activists, but it has proved prohibitively complex to the vast majority of people affected by these regulations. This must change if the fine print of federal workplace policy is to mesh with promoting opportunity and growth.

In the future, the process for reaching those standards must ensure true, informed input from all knowledgeable and affected parties. To ensure that all relevant information is available, no new law or program should be enacted without first being subjected to an analysis of cost effectiveness. Cost-benefit analysis should also be used to evaluate whether current programs and requirements should be continued.

We should recognize that, in most instances, private sector initiatives are superior to government dictates and enforcement.

EMPOWERMENT

People, not the federal government, are best qualified to make the important decisions affecting their lives. Employers and employees should be empowered to make decisions about what is best for them. For example, it is time to abandon the one-size-fits-all safety programs at virtually every workplace that were the policies of earlier, Democrat-controlled Congresses.

The empowerment approach of the Congress elected in 1994 calls for the relevant parties to work out the best methods for achieving safety in the workplace. In some cases, cooperative teams of workers and managers will be formed. In other instances, the company will hire safety auditors or perform extensive self-analysis. Regulators are ordered to get out of the way of innovation, and to recognize that safety occurs at the worksite, not by fiat from Washington.

Much of what currently passes for federal workplace policy is little more than an assortment of dubious rights secured by the threat and reality of tremendous monetary judgments through the litigation lottery. Knowing that a large payoff may be looming, employees act differently than they would if expected to work out a problem themselves.

AN IMPARTIAL POLICY
Government should not choose sides between businesses and industries, or between labor and management. Federal workplace policy must be balanced and impartial.

The process of government for too long has been used as merely a means of achieving ends unrelated to the specific issue at hand. Some businesses, for example, may seek tough regulations to raise the operating costs of their competitors, as in the call by a few companies for mandatory, employer-paid health care coverage. Labor organizations may lobby in the name of safety for access to business facilities, when the real issue is union organizing. And, of course, competitors, unions, and others have been known to call in the federal enforcement agencies to bring pressure on their targets.

Laws and rules that permit these abuses have no place in a policy designed to enhance individual initiative and business opportunities in the competitive worldwide marketplace.

INCENTIVES
In most instances, incentives are preferable to mandates, and private sector initiatives are superior to government dictates and enforcement. Government interference and intervention should be held to a minimum, and invoked only when absolutely necessary.

The heavy regulatory burden imposed by the Occupational Safety and Health Administration (OSHA) and its enforcement powers have failed to eradicate accidents and unsafe conditions in the workplace. High workers' compensation insurance costs have been a greater inducement to action by employers than the threat of OSHA. While some managers cut corners, the vast majority of employers want to ensure a safe workplace. Their desire to do the right thing must be encouraged with information, advice from experts, and incentives for going the extra mile.

Workers can be given incentives as well. Many businesses have tremendously reduced the number of workplace accidents by giving employees and teams of workers bonuses for every month they go without any injuries. These types of innovations should be encouraged. Not only have the bonuses cut down insurance costs for businesses but, more importantly, fewer workers are getting hurt.

TRANSPORTATION

Our transportation policy is the uncoordinated amalgamation of various governmental actions that affect the overall cost of transportation. These governmental actions also have a dramatic impact on the relative cost of the different means of transportation—for example, the cost of a train ticket as compared with a plane ticket. The common effect of these governmental actions is that they distort the market allocation of transportation resources. A coherent transportation policy would recognize these direct and indirect effects and eliminate market distortions.

The trend toward treating transportation-related issues—ranging from infrastructure to safety—as national problems has intensified in the past twenty-five years. Not surprisingly, centralized planning has not increased the efficiency of our transportation system. Improvements have come when the federal government has stopped regulating transportation (for example, the elimination of the Civil Aeronautics Board), not when Washington has attempted to limit private industry's efforts to meet transportation users' needs (for example, the Interstate Commerce Commission's regulation of trucking). We simply do not need more five- and ten-year plans that reflect the government's conception of what our transportation system should look like.

Transportation policy should be based on market allocations of transportation resources. The market provides the single best means for individuals to invest in those transportation services most suited to their needs. For example, the government's decision that a certain percentage of the population should buy electric cars regardless of how much they cost or how well they perform should not be our controlling principle. The government should not be in the business of mandating the use of electric vehicles (or propane or methanol or compressed natural gas or any other kind of vehicles for that matter). Rather, the government should do no more than simply establish fair and reasonable regulatory and tax policy that provides a "level playing field" on which Americans can make their own decisions on the type of vehicle they want to acquire and drive.

Finally, Congress should never use transportation funding measures for special interest demonstration projects. Demonstration projects are little more than a fig leaf, a trusty gimmick for covering up naked pork-barrel spending. Government involvement at the national level should be limited, and it should never try to pick winners and losers in the transportation sector.

Some specific transportation reforms follow.

Eliminate "Patron Saint" Agencies

The alphabet soup list of agencies and departments of the federal government that were established to focus on a single means of transportation should be eliminated: Interstate Commerce Commission (ICC)—railroads; Federal Railroad Administration (FRA)—railroads; Federal Highway Administration (FHA)—highways; National Highway Traffic Safety Administration (NHTSA)—cars and trucks; Federal Maritime Commission (MARAD)—ships; Federal Aviation Administration (FAA)—aviation; and Federal Transit Administration (FTA)—mass transit. Eliminating these agencies would give the boot to the governmental patron saints for those industries that may no longer be able to compete in the marketplace.

Consolidate Safety Functions

The federal government has a legitimate role to play in ensuring the safety of our transportation system. That role should complement state and local efforts while ensuring that local restrictions do not pose an undue burden on interstate commerce. Toward that end, the safety functions of the various transportation departments and agencies should be consolidated with the safety functions of other agencies, and their regulations justified on the basis of a strict cost-benefit analysis. Such consolidation would allow better comparison of the safety costs and benefits of all industries—not just transportation-specific industries.

Develop Infrastructure Based on Need

Infrastructure development should be based on market, not government, determinations. For example, airlines, cities, and the flying public have a much greater interest in determining how many airports are needed—and where—than does the FAA. Limitations on privatizing airports should be removed. Limitations on toll roads should be removed, and the user fees generated to cover the costs of construction and operation should not be funneled through the federal government. These steps would help channel infrastructure development to those areas that transportation users have deemed the most useful—not to those industries that have the most political clout or to those districts where members of the congressional transportation committees reside.

Eliminate Subsidies

Along these same lines, the general public, including users of unrelated transportation services, should not be forced to subsidize Amtrak, mass transit, and maritime operations.

An exception to this proposition is when fiscal and environmental considerations may ease the ban on operating subsidies. For example, Amtrak is spending over a billion dollars to modernize its infrastructure between New York and Boston, and will probably not make a profit in that area for some time. As a general rule, subsidizing Amtrak operations in such an area would be unjustifiable and should be opposed. But when one considers the possible savings or impact in other areas, and that there is strong public interest in improving the transportation infrastructure in the region, this subsidy may be good for the taxpayers.

Alternatives to the Amtrak subsidy for improving the infrastructure may cost more and be less successful. Adding additional lanes to I-95 between Boston and New York would be at least as expensive as the

Amtrak subsidy. Yet, it would do less to reduce gridlock and would result in appreciably more auto emissions in an area already crowded. The cost of building a second airport in the Boston area, long under consideration but apparently delayed by the potentially greater use of Amtrak, would far exceed the Amtrak subsidy. Therefore, in this case, the Amtrak subsidy would meet the transportation problem more efficiently and in a better environmental and cost-effective manner than the airport.

The taxpayers should not have to subsidize the operation of rail passenger service. At the same time, if its operation is substantially beneficial to the public beyond the subsidy to the Amtrak passengers, the value of the general benefit should be considered in the ultimate determination of whether public funds should be used to support Amtrak operations.

In another area, to the extent that maritime shipbuilding is required for national defense, such expenditures should be made part of the defense budget and not hidden in the Transportation Department.

Eliminate Tax Distortions
Taxes that limit transportation choices (for example, the luxury tax and discriminatory tariffs on imported vehicles) should be eliminated.

Eliminate Transportation Mandates
Regulatory measures that force industry to produce government-mandated means of transportation (for example, Corporate Average Fuel Economy, electric vehicle mandates) should be eliminated.

Privatize Government–Owned Assets
Direct government-provided transportation support, such as FAA air traffic control, should be eliminated, since the users of such services can clearly be identified and charged.

Eliminate Social Engineering Requirements
Social requirements, such as affirmative action set-asides and Davis-Bacon requirements, should be eliminated because they limit market-based choice and thus make the transportation system less efficient and more costly.

Use Market Principles

Whenever the government does undertake to regulate transportation, it should rely on market-type methods. For example, it should use congestion pricing, rather than lines, to regulate delays; user fees, rather than general taxes, to cover the expenses of government-provided transportation services; and private contractors, rather than government employees, to perform nonpolicymaking functions.

At this point, when we are just dangling our feet in the waters of reform, we cannot shrink from our responsibility. We must dive in head first.

Reforming the Civil Justice System[1]

Discourage litigation. Persuade your neighbors to compromise whenever you can. Point out to them how the nominal winner is often the real loser—in fees, expenses, and waste of time. As a peacemaker the lawyer has a superior opportunity of being a good man. There will still be business enough.

★

SO WROTE ABRAHAM LINCOLN, in notes for a lecture to law students. For a very long time the Emancipator's words reflected a near-universal consensus: litigation was to be discouraged, a last resort; it was, at best, a necessary evil; the aim of the civil courts was both to redress genuine legal claims, and also—equally vital—to protect potential targets from charges that were less well founded.

How well does our present-day civil justice system live up to Lincoln's ideal of restraint, peacemaking, and scrupulousness? Consider the following lawsuits filed in recent years:

- A man who ran a footrace with a refrigerator strapped to his back and was injured won $1 million. "Men who injured themselves in refrigerator races—in which large, unusually beefy guys strap refrigerators to their backs and see who can run the fastest—argued that the warnings against carrying these appliances were insufficient." (*New York Times*, 6/3/91)
- "Luella Wilson, a 92-year-old Vermont widow, almost lost her house after lawyers won a $950,000 court judgment against her. Her crime?

She had loaned her great-nephew money to buy a car, in which he later crashed and injured others.

"He, of course, had little money, but no matter. She did. So they sued her. Lawyers call this 'negligent entrustment' without even cracking a smile." (*Phoenix Gazette,* 7/1/94)

- "When a van ran a stop light and a public transit bus hit the van's rear bumper, the only real damage was a displaced bumper and a slightly dented door. However, when the bus driver went to speak to the driver of the van, two women suddenly 'fell' out of their seats, landed on the floor, and started to moan.

  "One said, 'I think my neck is broken. Call a doctor.' The other yelled, 'I hurt my back. Get me an ambulance.' The 'falls' occurred fully two minutes after the bus had stopped.

  "A moment later, two people got on the bus, laid [*sic*] down in the aisle and pretended they also had been injured in the 'accident.' These people laid [*sic*] in the aisle until a policeman came aboard and an ambulance was called.

  "Decent people... have to pay higher insurance premiums because of crooks who file phony claims." (Columnist Ann Landers, *Arizona Republic,* 10/93)

- "Two days after the 1984 lethal Union Carbide gas leak in Bhopal, India, trial lawyer John Coale arrived by plane. Was this ambulance chasing? He said he didn't care. 'If I come in from the airport and two days later have 7,000 clients, that's the greatest ambulance chase in history.'

  "Needless to say, Coale and others filed their cases in the United States. India, you see, doesn't have a history of big awards." (*Phoenix Gazette,* 7/14/93)

- "In Texas, a plaintiff was awarded $248,000 after an 'expert' witness testified that an auto accident had caused or contributed to the plaintiff's cancer." (*Las Vegas Review Journal,* 8/9/92)

- "A Virginia special-education teacher... sued in federal court after failing to achieve the minimum acceptable score on a standardized national test—eight times. She claimed she was handicapped because the test did not accommodate her slowness in understanding written and spoken information. While a federal judge dismissed her suit, the appeals court overruled him and reinstated the claim." (*Investor's Business Daily*, 11/4/92)

- "A corporate lawyer named Frank D. Zaffere III has sued his fiancée, Maria Dillon, for breaking off their engagement.

  "Zaffere is asking Dillon, a twenty-one-year-old restaurant hostess, to pay him $40,310, which is the amount he spent while pursuing her.

  "This includes the cost of a fur coat, a ring, a car, a typewriter, and even the champagne consumed in Chicago's Pump Room. Zaffere said he was still waiting for his Visa and MasterCard bills before he could give a final account.

  "While this looked bad for Dillon, Zaffere gave her an out by offering to marry her, provided she met certain conditions, including 'faithfulness, truthfulness, and marrying him within 45 days of her receiving his letter.'" (*Washington Post*, 9/24/92)

Something has gone terribly wrong with our civil justice system, and at the heart of the problem is a philosophical wrong turn. The sad fact is that many of the most influential figures in our legal culture—including a host of prominent law professors, many officials of the American Bar Association (ABA) and similar groups, and even some judges—no longer share Lincoln's view that litigation is something dangerous and unfortunate, with more losers than winners. "We don't sue enough in this country," proclaims much-publicized Harvard professor Alan Dershowitz. "Suing is good for America."[2] Another prominent legal academic—an ethics specialist, no less—has written of a "professional responsibility to chase ambulances."[3] Even the U.S. Supreme Court, in a five-to-four 1977 opinion written by Justice Harry Blackmun, dismissed the formerly prevalent idea that encouraging litigation was against public policy and rejected the idea that a lawsuit could "somehow [be] viewed as an evil in itself."[4]

Armed with the confidence that the more lawsuits the better for society, legal activists such as Ralph Nader and a large number of the nation's crusading law school professors have spent much of the past three decades overhauling virtually every aspect of American law to make it easier and more lucrative to sue. Courts and lawmakers have greatly liberalized civil procedure to make it easier to file suits and harder to get them dismissed.

Many litigation advocates insist that, if you haven't done anything wrong, you have nothing to fear from the relaxation in litigation standards. They should tell that to the country's obstetricians, of whom an estimated 70 percent have faced legal claims (and all of whom pay astronomical malpractice premiums as a result).[5] Or to the makers of planes, sporting equipment, or vaccines—all of which get sued again and again, whether their products are good or bad. A famous Harvard study of malpractice cases found no evidence of negligent injury in more than 80 percent of the lawsuits filed against New York hospitals and doctors.[6]

A multitude of suits are filed now that in the past would not have been. At one time, for example, the organizing lawyer filing a class action suit had to be able to show a significant chance of winning on the merits of the case. But a 1974 Supreme Court decision struck down that requirement, creating a dramatic upswing in the number of class action suits.

Similarly, a relaxation in the rules governing testimony by expert witnesses has increased the incentive to sue. In cases involving medical testimony, for example, the expert witnesses once had to represent mainstream scientific thinking. Wacky scientific theories didn't qualify. A 1975 round of federal court-ordered changes, however, changed all of this. As a result, many strange suits that would have been laughable in the past now succeed. As one example, a passenger in a taxi who subsequently developed cancer sued the taxi owner. He claimed, among other things, that his cancer had been caused by a crash in the cab. A "medical expert" testified in his behalf. The result: a six-figure award to the suit-filer.[7]

An extraordinary business has sprung up to provide expert testimony. "I would go into a lawsuit with an objective, uncommitted, independent expert about as willingly as I would occupy a foxhole with a couple of noncombatant soldiers," a former head of the American Bar Association has written. Many battle-seasoned experts now advertise in the back pages of lawyers' magazines: "100% success to date."[8] One witness clearinghouse promises that if the first expert it sends over doesn't agree with the lawyer's theory of the case, it will send over a second free of charge. Another takes a share of the jury award if its expert convinces the jury. "An expert can be found to testify to the truth of almost any factual theory, no matter how frivolous," one leading federal judge has noted.[9] Is it any wonder the public perceives truth as being for sale?

Another major source of lawsuits that wouldn't have been filed in the past are the "private attorney general" and "citizen suit" statutes, popular in the 1970s, that made just about anybody a potential plaintiff—a development that would have shocked earlier authorities. Before these statutes, if a company was in conflict with state regulations, for example, the state had the right to sue. Now private citizens, who formerly wouldn't have had standing to sue, can do so. Unfortunately, many suits are filed for purely ideological reasons, to harass businesses or to impede economic activity.

Another—and perhaps the most publicized—means used by lawmakers to increase the incentive to sue is to multiply the rewards for suing (and the penalties for getting successfully sued) in the form of damages. New laws and doctrines offer better chances to collect triple penalties and punitive damages, as well as compensation for such intangible harms as emotional distress and humiliation.

And, of course, a newly enacted law can provide plenty of new grounds to sue because it is often couched in such vague terms that no one can be sure what the law requires. A law whose content is uncertain leads directly to litigation, since inevitably there will be differences of opinion on how to interpret it.

The rules about where you can sue have also changed in a way that has multiplied the number of cases that are filed in any given year. Once upon a time, you had to sue in the jurisdiction where the opponent was present. Thanks to the "long-arm" statutes of the 1960s, however, this is no longer the case. Now a business that is headquartered in one state can in many instances be sued in any jurisdiction into which it so much as sends a Federal Express package. Potential suit-filers now have the enticing option of "forum shopping." They can choose among various state courts, selecting the jurisdiction that is the most inconvenient or unsympathetic to their opponent.

Another litigation-provoking innovation of the era: the 1977 Supreme Court ruling that gave lawyers the option of soliciting new business through advertising. Advertising on television and in the Yellow Pages would have been unthinkable to previous generations of lawyers. But today Texas lawyers alone spend an estimated $90 million on advertising.

Unfortunately, more direct means of solicitation are also common. For example, a lawyer in Houston cultivated emergency-room attendants by sending them free pizzas with his business card.[10] Lawyers' agents have posed as priests to mingle among grieving families after a plane crash, and as Red Cross workers to dig out and sign up new clients after a store collapses.[11] According to a letter from the National Highway Traffic Safety Administration staff, the Nader-founded Center for Auto Safety uses the Freedom of Information Act to obtain complaint information on potential safety-related defects, which it then sells to lawyers. This information includes names of families.[12]

While the proliferation of lawsuits is a major problem in the legal system, it is not the only one. There is also the phenomenon of the vastly increased power of lawyers once the case is under way. One of the most important expansions of this power came in the area of "discovery"— that often costly and privacy-invading pretrial phase of litigation during which lawyers can compel the opponent to hand over various forms of information. This might be anything from the contents of a filing cabinet to a private, handwritten diary.

At one time, lawyers had to be able to show the relevance of the material when the demand was made. No longer. Changes in federal rules in 1970 and 1975 drastically expanded the scope of discovery. Demonstrating likely relevance before making the demand is no longer necessary. Thus discovery, in the hands of a sharp practitioner, becomes a fishing expedition. It is often embarrassing but nonetheless legal.

As might be expected, discovery is a chief area of abuse. In an American Bar Foundation survey of Chicago litigators, for example, more than three-quarters admitted using discovery for tactical purposes to inflict various kinds of costs, monetary and otherwise, on their opponents. Popular techniques in depositions—at which no judge is present— included what researchers called "harshly aggressive styles of questioning designed to make the opposing party decide he never wanted to repeat such an experience." The idea, said one lawyer, is to "see if you can get them mad," putting them "through the wringer, through the mud" so "they are frightened to be a witness and... are a much worse witness."[13] After the *New England Journal of Medicine* published a major study by a Mayo Clinic researcher finding no evidence that breast implants caused health problems in women, injury lawyers responded by using subpoenas and other discovery tactics against both the journal and the researcher.[14]

Sad to say, many lawyers today engage in outright harassment of opponents and third-party witnesses. The situation is out of control. As former Texas Supreme Court Chief Justice Eugene Cook has noted, some law firms now conduct in-house courses on what they call "sharp tactics." "These tactics," said Cook, "involve intimidation, with one lawyer telling another, 'If I get the chance, I'll sue you.' They involve a lack of civility. They mean filing motions on everything possible and running up the tab."[15]

When some members of the twelve hundred–strong American Academy of Matrimonial Lawyers expressed alarm at the rise of slash-and-burn tactics, their then president-elect, Sanford S. Dranoff, was blunt: "You all can go pick up your 'being-a-nice-guy' medals the same day you turn in your law licenses."[16]

All too often it's the lawyers—and not the clients—who are the principal beneficiaries of these lawsuits. For example, class action suits are often run outright for the benefit of the lawyers. Lawyers step forward to represent everyone who's ever bought a product from a certain company. The real object is often not to redress some wrong but to obtain high, court-appointed legal fees for the lawyer. Some lawyers who specialize in shareholder suits go so far as to keep pet clients on hand who hold a few shares in many listed companies. They turn up as the client-of-record in suit after suit. High-tech and start-up firms, whose stocks experience wide price swings, are especially vulnerable to these suits.

Lawyers also have taken advantage of this country's unique contingency fee system. This system allows the lawyers to pocket a share of the winnings—to earn millions, even tens of millions, of dollars in fees from individual cases—even when it reaches the equivalent of $10,000 or $50,000 an hour for their work.[17] (Nearly all other countries prohibit contingency fees as unethical, on the grounds that they give lawyers too sharp an incentive to overprice their cases. Even in this country the controversial practice did not become universally lawful until the 1960s.)

As almost everyone is aware, lawyers' fees in general have skyrocketed and grown to include strange services that in earlier times might have been deemed extraordinary. In the Rodney King case in Los Angeles, King's lawyers demanded $4.4 million in fees for, among other exertions, accompanying their client to a movie and to his birthday party. Lawyers in the Rena Weeks sexual-harassment case in San Francisco, which resulted in compensatory damages of $50,000 and punitive damages of $3.7 million, asked for $3.8 million in fees on top of that, including $300,000 in "fees-on-fees": time spent drawing up reasons why they should get a high fee award. In one survey, more than 60 percent of lawyers said they had personal knowledge of bill padding.[18]

Of course, given the escalating fees and expanded opportunities for lucrative business, it should come as no surprise that the number of lawyers in the United States has escalated too. The United States has 281 lawyers per 100,000 residents; Germany, 111; Britain, 82; and Japan, 11. The ABA lamely argues that this is not because we are overstocked with lawyers; rather it is because "other countries with large populations have too few."[19] Only a minority of lawyers specialize in suing, but fear of litigation drives up demand for the services of advisory lawyers. A business deal that in Europe or Japan would be handled with a short contract or a handshake is often sealed in the United States with a long and intensely negotiated contract, for fear of a later legal dispute.

Although rising caseload figures are mostly dominated by routine filings, data on the actual economic impact of suits—as measured by such indices as the amount of money changing hands—tell a dramatic story. New York officials, for example, report that malpractice payouts by doctors and hospitals in the state rose 30,000 percent over the thirty years from the 1950s to the 1980s. The overall direct costs of personal-injury law nationwide, as reflected in the cost of liability insurance, doubled in constant dollars in the ten years leading up to and including 1987.[20] They run from three to five times as high in this country as in comparably advanced democracies, as a share of our respective economies—and the gap is getting wider, not narrower.

But the public, it seems, may have become disenchanted with the esteemed profession. A recent string of celebrity trials has convinced many people that today's advocates are willing to say anything to win.

At least on the ethical fringes of the profession, entire careers can flourish on outright fraud. After one of the lawyers in a leading New York law firm cooperated with authorities, the others were convicted of a colorful array of misdeeds, such as doctoring photographs, widening a pothole with a pickax in order to blame an accident on it, and carelessly using the same supposed eyewitness in two auto accidents. At the time of one of the accidents, the witness had been detained elsewhere—in an upstate prison, where he was serving time for forgery.[21]

Ultimately, of course, fraud costs the public: The Federal Bureau of Investigation estimates that lawsuit fraud in the car-crash field alone—ranging from faked medical claims to staged accidents—costs the average American household at least $200 a year in extra insurance premiums.

According to the National Insurance Crime Bureau, insurance fraud overall costs Americans $20 billion annually.[22]

THE POLITICS OF REFORM

For decades it was virtually impossible to get litigation abuse on the agenda for reform. "Efforts to reform the system have been blocked repeatedly in the Democratic Congress—and trial attorneys have spent millions to preserve the status quo," reported *Newsweek* in 1994, estimating that in that year alone lawyers and their PACs gave at least $40 million to candidates, mostly Democrats, to block legal reform.[23] Local political observers have described the trial lawyer lobby as comparable in state-level power only to the teachers' unions—weaker in the number of warm bodies, but better endowed with cold cash.

The political fortunes of President Clinton over the years have been closely linked to those of the trial lawyers. This became clear during his 1992 campaign when a memo from a former head of the Association of Trial Lawyers of America (ATLA) surfaced, soliciting contributions with an assurance that Clinton would always oppose tort reform.[24] In a separate incident after Clinton's election, future Secretary of Commerce Ron Brown, a member of the Washington law firm that represents the ABA and ATLA, announced in a meeting: "My friends, I'm here to tell you the lawyers won."[25]

PRINCIPLES FOR REFORM

But with or without the Clinton administration, legal reform is going to be on the agenda in coming years.

Product Liability

Product liability—that field of law governing damages for claimed malfunctions of manufactured products—is a perennial hot spot of much state reform. But it should also be a major subject of federal-level action because of the overwhelmingly interstate nature of product liability litigation. Nearly all cases pit a local plaintiff against an out-of-state defendant, so state courts and governments face "beggar-thy-neighbor" incentives: the benefits of big awards are concentrated locally while the costs are spread among distant consumers and investors. Reforms should also include curbs on punitive damages, especially on multiple punitive damages against a defendant for a single design or marketing decision.

Major proposals that have moved forward include (1) joint and several liability reforms that proportionally limit payments from defendants when more than one party is sued; (2) curbs on lawsuits filed by individuals who misuse products while drunk or on drugs; and (3) "Statutes of Repose," which cut off liability for possible injuries from machines sold long ago.

Over the long term, many reformers are interested in exploring ways to restore historic principles of freedom of contract to this and other areas so that consumers can decide for themselves how much liability to demand or waive from manufacturers or others in the marketplace.

Medical Malpractice

Medical malpractice is another hot spot. This issue has great implications for the nation's enormously high health care bill. Medical care itself often suffers greatly from the perverse incentives of defensive medicine, incentives that cause health providers to duplicate tests and perform other unnecessary tests in an attempt to shield themselves from litigation. California, Indiana, and other states have shown that strong malpractice reforms can make a sizable dent in costs and protect innocent physicians from unfounded allegations.

Controls on "junk science" and dubious expert testimony are also potentially important in curbing abuse in this area. Additionally, it is essential to apply liability reform provisions to all potential defendants in claims arising from health care–related injuries. The manufacturers of medical products, providers of blood and tissue services or products, managed-care organizations, and other health care providers all are at risk of a lawsuit when a patient is injured. Addressing the liability problems in just one part of the health care sector actually may stimulate litigation in other parts perceived to have deeper pockets or greater exposure.

Control of Damages

One of the enormous differences between our legal system and that of other countries is our willingness to allow random, lottery-like damage awards, especially punitive damages. The current practice, former Supreme Court Justice Lewis Powell has written, "invites punishment so arbitrary as to be virtually random.... It is long past time to bring the law of punitive damages into conformity with our notions of just punishment, and with the traditions of other nations that also protect their citizens against arbitrary deprivations."[26]

One idea often suggested is to make punitive damages payable to the public treasury in the form of a fine, as opposed to granting a windfall to the plaintiff and, more importantly, the plaintiff's lawyers. In any case, reform should prevent lawyers from acquiring a percentage of the punitive damage award in order to alleviate incentives to seek outlandish awards.

Shareholder Class Action Suits

In the spring of 1995, the House voted by a wide margin (with strong bipartisan support from many Democrats) for a package reforming shareholder class action suits, asking courts to

- Monitor more closely whether lawyers really are representing class interests.
- Curb vague, open-ended allegations of harm by requiring clearer proof that an investor was harmed by management's knowing failure to disclose risk.
- Restrict the use of "professional plaintiffs."

"Loser-Pays" Rule

A "loser-pays" principle requires losing litigants to compensate their opponents for at least some of the financial harm done by suing. The principle helps align litigants' incentives with those of society. Hardly a radical or untried idea, loser-pays proposals take a variety of forms. For example, if a claimant rejects a settlement offer that is higher than the sum he receives at trial, he has to pay the other side's legal fees and expenses for the work that was completed after the offer was rejected. This plan passed the U.S. House of Representatives in the spring of 1995 and was enacted as a pioneering law in Oklahoma in May 1995.

Opponents of a pure loser-pays rule believe that a loser-pays rule could give an unfair advantage to a party in a case where a defendant's liability is clear. The liable defendant could be forced to pay astronomical fees and costs even if a nominal verdict of $1 were returned for the plaintiff. In such a case, the defendant may be forced to settle for an amount far above fair damages out of fear of the fees and costs assessable against the defendant after judgment.

But imposing responsibility for fees and costs on a winning plaintiff who rejected a reasonable settlement offer can avoid this unfairness. This procedure allows a defendant to offer settlement in a fixed amount at least ten days before trial. If the judgment is less than the amount of the offer, the plaintiff rejecting the offer is responsible for fees and costs from the date of the rejected offer. This procedure has been adopted as to minor court costs in the present Federal Rule of Civil Procedure 68, where it is optional for the defendant only, and in some states.

This procedure could be broadened into a reform that would require both the plaintiff and the defendant to offer settlement. If the case proceeds to judgment, however, and it is lower than the plaintiff's offer and higher than the amount of the defendant's offer, both sides could be left to bear their own costs. If the judgment is at or above the amount offered by the plaintiff, the defendant would be required to pay the plaintiff's fees and costs. If the judgment is below the amount offered by the defendant, the plaintiff would be required to pay the defendant's fees and costs. This reform would impose on each party a substantial risk for rejecting a reasonable settlement offer.

Within this reform, alternative dispute resolutions should also be encouraged. They can save billions of dollars, particularly health care dollars. Arbitration has been used successfully in litigation involving the securities industry and labor issues. Likewise, mediation has been successful in medical malpractice suits. States should be given maximum flexibility to select the dispute resolution system that works the best.

A loser-pays rule is not a total panacea, as it only applies in cases that go to judgment. But by reducing the number of cases that proceed to trial, in addition to making parties consider reasonable offers of settlement, we may help control spiraling litigation costs paid through higher insurance premiums, costs for goods and services, and taxes.

Procedural Reforms

Procedural reforms are especially powerful and promising because they apply to many areas of litigation. A key proposal would restore sanctions for wrongful litigation, which were quietly gutted in 1992 by the previous Congress at the behest of the litigation lobby. Sanctions should normally require compensating the victimized opponent for the legal costs of response. States should be urged to enact strong parallel measures against wrongful suits in their courts; many states currently lack such rules.

Another procedural reform is the early screening of cases. Reformers can build on a trilogy of 1986 Supreme Court cases authorizing stronger steps to throw out weak cases at an early stage (summary judgment). One promising reform would restore an early judicial look at class actions to screen out those with a low chance of prevailing. Reformers also need to take a comprehensive look at pretrial discovery as well, to shield innocent parties from expensive and intimidating fishing expeditions. In the meantime, states should protect or strengthen the courts' power to issue protective orders safeguarding the privacy of litigation targets that have not been charged in open court.

One simple, promising proposal is to require lawmakers to spell out the details of new laws rather than leave uncertainties to be settled in future litigation. In particular, congressional committees would have to consider, and resolve one way or the other, such recurring questions as who can sue to enforce a new law, what effect a new law has on state law in case of a conflict, and whether a new law is retroactive in effect—all frequent topics of litigation.

$250,000 Ceiling on Noneconomic Damages

There should be full and fair compensation for all out-of-pocket economic losses suffered. Included are unlimited economic damages for medical expenses, lost wages, rehabilitation costs, future medical care, or any other economic loss suffered as the result of a health care injury, and up to $250,000 for noneconomic or intangible pain and suffering losses. Ceilings on noneconomic damages do not keep people from recovering all amounts necessary to make them whole. They only limit those damages awarded for pain and suffering, loss of enjoyment, and other intangible items that often have been highly inflated.

Hold each defendant responsible only for the portion of noneconomic damages attributable to his or her own acts or omissions. Under the current rules (joint and several liability), a defendant responsible for as little as 1 percent of the total fault may be required to pay the entire award. It seems fair that defendants should remain jointly liable for all economic losses, such as medical bills and lost wages, but they should be held liable only for their own fair share of the noneconomic and punitive damages.

Limit the Amount of Attorney Contingency Fees

The contingency fee is meant to enable those with fewer resources to obtain legal representation. However, as mentioned previously, in high award cases an attorney's contingent fee is often far in excess of the amount of time and effort expended on the case. A reasonable sliding scale that reduces the percentage of these fees as an award increases would help the most severely injured patients keep more of the award they receive.

Pay Awards for Future Expenses or Losses Over Time

It is both fair and rational to pay future expenses or losses amounting to more than $50,000 over time, while paying past and current expenses in full lump-sum. Another option is to discount awards for future losses to present value, a technique often used by economists. This reform ensures that money is available for the claimant when needed.

Provide for a Uniform Statute of Limitations

There is a wide variation among the states' statutes of limitations, which is the amount of time within which a claim must be brought by an injured plaintiff. Standardizing this requirement, creating a uniform statute of limitations, makes sense for product liability cases. Standard rules should require that claims must be filed within two years from the date an injury occurred or from when a person should reasonably know the injury exists. Exceptions should allow extra time for claims for children under age six, who may not be able to communicate the existence of an injury, and for claims where an item with no therapeutic purpose is left in a claimant's body and not discovered for many years.

Reform Punitive Damages

Punitive damages should be awarded only if there is clear and convincing evidence that the injury meets the standard set by each jurisdiction. A limit on punitive damages of $250,000—or twice the compensatory damages (the total of economic plus noneconomic losses), if greater—also makes sense. Manufacturers or distributors of medical products should not be held liable for punitive damages if their product received federal government approval or met FDA's "safe and effective" product requirements and there was no fraud in the approval process. As mentioned earlier, punitive damages should go to the state as they are not intended to compensate the plaintiff, and the attorney should NOT receive the windfall.

THE SPIRIT OF REFORM

But these are just the start. Reversing the climate of litigiousness requires a cultural shift far beyond any one package of reforms. Reform must be reflected in the spirit with which new legislation on many subjects is drafted, in the nature of judicial appointments by a new president, and in the way in which regulatory agencies whose actions often affect litigation, such as the FDA and the Justice Department, go about their work. Reform will have many implications for the federal government's management of its own litigation caseload, and that of the states—whose attorneys general have on occasion become runaway litigators themselves.

It is also important for the public to understand that the financial consequences of lawsuit abuse eventually flow "from the courthouse to your
house." Although the recent efforts of Congress to improve product liability and medical malpractice laws have been enthusiastically supported by
manufacturers and medical professionals, these reforms address less than
15 percent of all U.S. personal injury cases, and they provide no direct relief
for the average American. Yet the vast majority of personal injury and property damage lawsuits in our courts arise from either traffic or "slip-and-fall"
accidents—accidents that put most Americans at risk of actually being sued.
Even more important, most accident-based claims and lawsuits are
defended under the terms of insurance policies. This is just as true for the
most complex product liability or medical malpractice suit as it is for the
simplest automobile case. As a result, the insurance industry has no choice
but to collect the funds necessary to pay most of the settlements, judgments,
and defense costs this process generates. And of course these funds are collected from the American public, which not only pays needlessly inflated
insurance premiums because of lawsuit abuse, but also pays higher prices
for all insured goods and services.

All these reforms have a common theme: Make sure that litigation remains
a way of redressing injuries, instead of inflicting new injuries. The watch-
word of our civil courts is supposed to be *accountability*—which makes it
long since time to start holding the participants accountable for the damage
they do. The cause of justice itself demands no less.

4

Health Care

I was at the largest teaching hospital in Canada, and I couldn't provide the level of care I can provide in my private office in Augusta [Georgia].
—Dr. Ranjit Dhaliwal, explaining in the
Washington Post why he left Canada

★

AMERICA HAS THE BEST HEALTH CARE SYSTEM in the world. And yet people are edgy about it. We know that the cost of medical treatment has skyrocketed—shockingly, over much of the past decade it grew twice as fast as our gross national product—and this scares us. We worry about what will happen if we get sick. Will we be able to afford the medical attention we need? Will our premiums go up? Could a major illness spell financial ruin?

A milestone in our national debate about health care came last year when Americans definitively rejected the Clinton plan. This plan, which would have created a government-run health care system, ran to some fourteen hundred pages of fine print and was so complex that nobody really understood it. But we did know two things: it would have left us less free and, in the end, less healthy. Just look at the Canadian model! And yet as a society we agonize about the high cost of medical care for our citizens.

Many of us tend to assume that the astronomical cost of medical care is a direct result of technological advances and sophisticated equipment. But this isn't always the case. These sophisticated technologies are expensive but sometimes they can actually save money. How, for example, does the cost of a magnetic resonance imaging (MRI) test compare with the costs associated with the old-fashioned alternative—exploratory surgery?

Many will no doubt be surprised to learn that the MRI can save significant amounts of money. Not only is such a test cheaper in direct health care costs than surgery, it can save the patient from pain, suffering, and lost productivity. A number of other medical advances such as laser medicine, optics, and sensors also reduce the length of hospital stays. In many instances, this state-of-the-art equipment moves certain procedures out of the hospital altogether.

If it's not the sophisticated equipment making our medical costs rise, what is it? One reason is that most Americans remain in the dark about the actual cost of their own medical treatment; we do not as a rule exercise much in the way of choice. If we want to rein in medical inflation, this must change. It will be essential that consumers know much more than they now know about the cost of medical treatment.

As the present system functions, doctors and hospitals have no incentive to keep costs down. If anything, the threat of medical malpractice lawsuits forces them to order often unnecessary tests and provide overly cautious care. Defensive medicine, as this is known, contributes significantly to medical inflation. If patients knew more about the choices being made, they might be willing to help eliminate unneeded procedures and excessive costs.

One of our most urgent concerns, given the exorbitant cost of medical care, is coverage for currently uninsured Americans. This is an issue that must be addressed. Although often exaggerated, the number of uninsured Americans is a serious problem. During the Clinton health care debate, the figure being thrown around was 37 million. Others claimed it was even higher. The Clinton figure was nearly 41 million.

A realistic number for the chronically uninsured is not nearly that high. It is only by counting those who are temporarily uninsured (people between jobs) and those uninsured by choice (mostly younger people) that we arrive at the figure cited by the Clinton administration. A 1991 study by Congress's Joint Economic Committee found that 86.4 percent of Americans were insured and that only 2.1 percent were chronically uninsured, despite their desire for coverage. Although these figures suggest that the health system works for the majority of Americans, we cannot ignore the problem of the uninsured.

There still remain those Americans who can't find the money to buy essential health insurance. Given the billions of dollars we pour into Medicaid, the number of low-income people that it does not cover is remarkable. The federal government now funds over half the Medicaid program, with the rest paid by the states. One would think all this money would be enough to cover all those too poor to buy insurance for themselves. Clearly, this program, important as it is to the physical and mental well-being of many Americans, is not being managed efficiently.

One way to improve Medicaid is to take all the money now going to it and give it to the states in the form of block grants. We have lived long enough with the illusion that Washington knows best. With the block grants and the funds each state already spends on Medicaid, and with allowed maximum flexibility, the states should be able to handle benefits, eligibility, and delivery of services more efficiently than does the federal government.

One option would be for the states to establish their own program of health insurance vouchers for poor and lower-income people. With these vouchers the poor would be able to make the same decisions about health care as everyone else. Vouchers could give them the choices they don't now have.

A voucher could, for example, be used to pay for an HMO, PPO, traditional insurance, or even an MSA (medical savings account). Voucher amounts would be highest for those with the lowest incomes, and would be phased out at higher levels. The state would set the voucher amounts and levels of income that qualify.

The problems of health care spending, however, cannot be divorced from the problems that hinder the rest of our economy. Here, as so often in politics, we forget the big picture. The big picture is that government has become a huge burden, taking far too much of our earnings and personal freedom. One reason people face difficulties paying for medical insurance—and education, housing, and many things government steps in to "help" with—is that the government already has taken the money with which we ourselves might have bought health insurance.

Government drives up the cost of medical treatment further through the burdensome costs of federal regulation. It is estimated that it costs more than $400 million to approve a new drug in the United States—thanks to the heavy hand of the Food and Drug Administration.[1] We pay again by waiting too long for new drugs and medical devices that might save human lives. On top of it all, regulatory frustrations have forced many pharmaceutical and medical-technology companies to move their operations abroad, costing us jobs and tax revenues. Pharmaceutical and medical technological achievements have had a major positive impact on the expectancy and the quality of life for Americans. Our policies should recognize that fact.

Another way in which government has had a negative impact concerns health insurance for self-employed people. While we publicly proclaim that we want everybody to have health insurance, a bizarre twist of the tax code currently makes it more difficult for the self-employed who want to purchase such insurance than it is for corporations. Employers are allowed to deduct the cost of health care coverage for their workers, and workers do not have to pay taxes on the value of their health plan. Self-employed people, however, don't enjoy this treatment. Not only is this patently unfair, it may discourage people from becoming entrepreneurs.

The 104th Congress began to address this problem. Now a self-employed person can deduct the increased amount of 30 percent of the cost of health care premiums; this will rise to higher percentages in the future. This is a step in the right direction, but the situation won't be equitable to the self-employed until this deduction is raised to 100 percent of the premium cost as a tax exclusion; the same as for employee-purchased health insurance.

CUTTING COST, NOT QUALITY

In reforming the nation's health care system, a few ideas and principles must be kept in mind.

An important first step is to ensure that all Americans who currently have insurance are able to keep it. That alone would increase the rate of coverage to well above 90 percent.

There are a range of exciting and promising ideas. While no one plan has achieved a full consensus yet, they all share one common theme: returning choice to the taxpayer and the patient.

A variety of simple market reforms will yield tremendous improvements in health care: medical coverage that is less expensive and yet more secure. These changes will leave the doctor-patient relationship intact, while allowing patients to choose among competing insurance programs.

MARKET CHOICES

Consumers must have the marketplace choices and tools that will enable them to make an informed decision about what kind of health insurance is best for them.

Our present system—in which the choices are made by a third party, either an employer or government—is outmoded. The system was developed over fifty years ago, when, in an effort to fight war-time inflation, workers were denied raises by Washington. When they threatened to strike, they were placated by a policy that allowed employers to add a noncash and nontaxed benefit in the form of employer-paid medical insurance.

A big part of medical inflation—which makes many of us scared even to go to a doctor—is the result of the phenomenon of relying totally on insurance companies to the point that, unlike with fire, car, or rental insurance, we don't even look at our bills. We don't know the price, and we don't weigh the options. We have no incentive to avoid unnecessary costs. Only twenty-one cents out of every dollar spent on health care is out-of-pocket.[2] As appealing as this might be on a certain level, it drives costs up astronomically.

The changes will guarantee that a variety of policies will be available with features that make them highly desirable both in fighting medical inflation and fostering a healthy America.

YES, YOU CAN TAKE IT WITH YOU

A system of health insurance that is not determined by the employer will have various advantages—one being that it will go where you go.

Workers presently fear that they can lose their insurance not only if they get sick, but also if they change jobs. If an employer is providing a worker's health insurance, the worker has to leave it behind when he leaves the company (though the Consolidated Omnibus Budget Reconciliation Act of 1986—COBRA—allows some to keep their existing insurance for eighteen months).

When a worker does apply for the next policy, he or she can have difficulty, particularly if there has been a serious illness or if a chronic condition exists. The result is often "job lock."

While there is much to be said for individually owned policies, Congress is not inclined to change the current system significantly. However, it could and should adopt some reforms that would help end "job lock." For example, Congress could prohibit an insurance company from imposing a pre-existing condition exclusion period on those who lose their health insurance due to a change in jobs. There would then be no waiting period before the new employer's policy took effect. But if a person has willfully let a health insurance policy lapse, the new protection would not apply.

FEWER MANDATES

Cost, of course, remains the sticking point. Some in Congress eagerly point to the increasing cost of health insurance as evidence that ever-more government regulation is needed. What they fail to note is that government regulation has in part driven up the cost of insurance. It is estimated that as many as one out of every four uninsured people has been priced out of the market by the effects of cost-increasing mandated benefits.

A great many of the mandated benefits concern matters that should be optional. Many states, for example, impose mandated health insurance benefit laws, telling what services must be covered. Among some of these: acupuncture, in-vitro fertilization, and marriage counseling. Indeed, in Minnesota hairpieces are mandated, while in Massachusetts sperm bank deposits are. The total number of mandates in the states has grown from eight in 1965 to than more than a thousand today.[3]

If consumers can choose basic policies without expensive, government-mandated add-ons, more people would be able to buy insurance. People who want to pay for special services such as substance-abuse treatment would have the option of doing so.

GUARANTEED RENEWABILITY

The biggest fear most people have about their health insurance is that it might be canceled if they become sick. They also worry that, if it's not canceled, the cost of the premiums will become ruinous.

If health insurance policies don't protect people from the risks of unbearably high medical costs, what's the point of health insurance in the first place?

But we don't need government-run medicine to fix this problem. It can be directly addressed by providing for a guarantee that insurance policies can be renewed. This provision would simply prohibit an insurance company from canceling a policy or raising premiums to an unaffected level after a person gets sick. Most states have already adopted such reforms for people who purchase individual health insurance policies. The same rules should apply to insurers who underwrite company policies.

SOLUTIONS THAT ARE VOLUNTARY

There are solutions to rising costs, many taking place voluntarily in the present workforce without costly government mandates. For example, hundreds of thousands of doctors and hospitals are now organizing themselves into systems designed to deliver patient care more efficiently. According to the American Medical Association, the number of physicians participating in managed care organizations increased from 59 percent in 1989 to 75 percent in 1993. The private sector has successfully unleashed competitive forces to drive down costs while improving quality of care. Recent employer surveys show health benefit costs were down 1.1 percent in 1994, largely due to a movement by employers to bargain with insurers and health care providers.[4]

Under the Employee Retirement Income Security Act (ERISA), large employers are permitted to provide health insurance for their employees without going through a traditional insurance company. This permits large employers to avoid costly state mandates that can raise the cost of health insurance. Small businessmen should be permitted to join voluntary purchasing pools under ERISA, which would also give them the purchasing power and joint administrative cost advantages enjoyed by larger firms.

Employers also have pushed to establish private sector organizations such as the National Committee for Quality Assurance (NCQA) to accredit managed care organizations. The NCQA issues a *Good Housekeeping* seal of approval. For the first time, health plans are receiving report cards that allow consumers to shop and compare. These market-driven consumer reports track patient satisfaction, provider responsiveness, preventive care, and other factors important to an informed shopper. In the market, information is readily available. The more information consumers have, the more intelligent their choices about the health care they want.

Controlling costs does not mean reducing the quality of care that patients receive. Coordinated-care companies emphasize preventive care, so that illnesses are discovered at an early stage when they are easier and less expensive to cure. This increases a patient's chances for survival and avoids the more costly care needed to attack a disease in its advanced stages. Providers are rewarded for meeting state-of-the-art preventive care guidelines, and consumers receive the care for a nominal copayment.

One very potent way to build added competition into the delivery of health care is the medical savings account (MSA). MSAs work on a simple principle: the higher the insurance deductible, the lower the insurance premium. Instead of paying an insurance company an exorbitant amount to cover every trip to the doctor, a person can pay only a modest amount for catastrophic insurance that covers all bills after meeting a high deductible, for example, $3,000 per year. The catastrophic care insurance can be provided in any number of ways, from traditional fee-for-service plans to HMOs or preferred provider networks. The large savings won by adopting a high deductible are then paid into an individual account for each worker, an account that he or she can use to pay medical bills below the deductible amount. At the end of the year, any leftover money in the account can be withdrawn and used for any other purpose, or saved for future medical bills.

With MSAs, workers would effectively be spending their own funds for noncatastrophic health care, so they would have full market incentives to control costs for such care. They would seek to avoid unnecessary care or tests, look for doctors and hospitals that would provide good quality care at the best prices, and consider whether the health care or service is worth the cost. Doctors and hospitals in turn would respond by competing to reduce costs.

Many companies across the country have already adopted MSAs for their workers, and have achieved dramatic cost savings as a result. Perhaps the best example is the Golden Rule Insurance Company in Indianapolis, Indiana, which offers MSAs for its own thirteen hundred workers.[5] The innovative plan has not been forced on employees: they can choose to stick with traditional fee-for-service insurance—$500 annual deductible and a 20 percent copayment on the next $5,000 in expenses. The family choosing that option faces a maximum out-of-pocket cost each year for health care of $1,500 (the $500 annual deductible and a 20 percent copayment on the next $5,000 per person, usually up to three people per family).

But those at Golden Rule who choose an MSA instead get a much more appealing deal. To cover a family, Golden Rule will buy a catastrophic policy paying all expenses over $3,000 per year; to pay for noncatastrophic care the company deposits $2,000 for the year in an MSA for the family. Instead of the maximum out-of-pocket cost of $4,500 built into the traditional insurance plan, the maximum annual out-of-pocket cost for the family with the MSA is $1,000 (the $3,000 deductible minus the $2,000 in the savings account). For individuals, Golden Rule will buy a catastrophic policy covering all expenses over $2,000 per year and deposit $1,000 for the year in an MSA for the worker, leaving again a maximum annual out-of-pocket cost of $1,000. The MSA funds can be used to pay for qualified health expenses below the deductible, with the bonus that any money left at the end of the year can be withdrawn for any use.

About 80 percent of the company's workers chose the MSA in 1993, the first year it was offered. They had an average of $600 left in their accounts at the end of the year. In 1994, about 90 percent of workers chose the MSA, and the average employee saved even more, keeping about $1,000 in remaining MSA funds at the end of the year. The plan has saved money for the company as well as for employees: the MSA plan has not gone up in price since it was first offered.

Golden Rule has now sold similar plans to dozens of small businesses across the country, with similar or even better results. MSAs are saving money for employees and employers across the country:[6]

- Offering an MSA, Dominion Resources, a Virginia utility company, has experienced no premium increase since 1989, while other employers faced average increases of 13 percent each year.
- *Forbes* magazine reduced its health costs by 30 percent.
- A health insurance marketing firm in Kansas, Thompson and Associates, sells an MSA plan that has reduced costs for small employers by as much as 50 percent.
- An insurance marketing firm in Maryland, Plan 3, has sold MSA plans to almost one hundred small businesses, reducing the companies' health costs by as much as 30 percent.
- Windham Hospital in Willimantic, Connecticut, reduced its health costs by 50 percent after adopting an MSA plan for its workers in 1993.
- Mayor Bret Schundler of Jersey City, New Jersey, recently adopted an MSA plan for city employees that costs the city less but provides better benefits to the workers than the old, traditional health plan.[7]

To realize the full potential of MSAs, federal and state tax laws need to be changed to provide the same tax treatment for MSAs as for traditional health insurance. That is, employer contributions to an MSA should be excluded from the worker's income, just as employer contributions to traditional health insurance are. Individuals contributing to an MSA should also be allowed a tax deduction for those contributions, in the same way that individual insurance purchases should be deductible.

Investment returns earned on MSA funds should be tax-free. Any MSA funds used to pay for health expenses should also be tax-free, just as health benefits paid by traditional insurance are untaxed. But MSA withdrawals for non–health care expenses should be taxed like any other income.

THE FEDS: RESEARCH INSTEAD OF REGULATION
Pharmaceutical and medical-device manufacturers should not be hindered from moving technology to the market as soon as it is safe to do so. Our burdensome regulations governing this process must be revised.

But the federal government can do more than just get out of the way: federal investment in technology research should be focused so that concrete results can quickly benefit the patient. Centers of Excellence, where multi-discipline research teams work on a single problem, have proven particularly successful at translating technological improvements into new options for patient care. Advances in treatment of brain tumors have been among the important results.

MEDICARE

People count on Medicare, which is exactly why reforming it is as controversial as it is necessary. Medicare is critically important to America's seniors and future generations of retirees. As has been widely noted, the latest annual report from the Clinton administration's Medicare board of trustees—which includes three members of President Clinton's cabinet—established that Medicare would go bankrupt by 2002 if we did nothing to save it.[8] Clearly, we need a plan to preserve, protect, and strengthen Medicare.

MEDICARE HOSPITAL TRUST FUND EMPTY IN 2002
(Trust Fund Reserves)

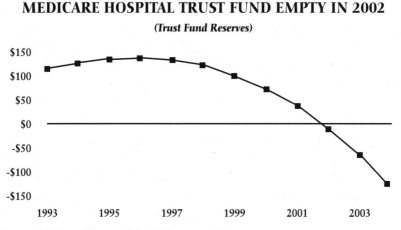

(*Source:* 1995 Annual Report of the HI Trustees, p. 13)

Why is Medicare going broke? For the simple reason that the system spends more than it takes in. According to the trustees' report, the Part A Hospital Insurance Trust Fund, which pays hospital expenses, will start going broke in 1996 by spending $1 billion more than it collects from payroll taxes, transfers, premiums, and other interest income. In 1997, the program will go another $6 billion in the red, and by the year 2000, that gap will be $26 billion. In 2002, it will be bankrupt.

In the past, Medicare financing problems have always been deferred by adjusting the program, primarily by cutting payments to doctors and hospitals or by raising taxes. However, many doctors no longer accept new Medicare patients because the payments are already so low, and a recent report by the Medicare board of trustees shows that the Medicare payroll tax (currently 2.9 percent of payroll) may have to increase sixfold, to almost 17 percent of payroll, if fundamental changes are not made soon.[9]

Relying on past experiences foolishly ignores the long-term gap that is projected to arise after the baby boom generation retires.

We can fix the problem now, or we can wait until the crisis is so severe that the only solutions available will be crushing tax hikes or slashed benefits. Without change, the trustees' report says that taxes would have to be increased immediately by 44 percent—just to prevent bankruptcy. And, without change, paying all promised benefits to today's young workers when they retire thirty to forty years from now would require increasing annual Medicare premiums paid by the elderly to almost $4,000 per couple per year. Obviously, these are not acceptable options, especially when quite mild and effective options are available today.

Not only can we save Medicare, we can improve it at the same time. The benefits package provided by Medicare is just not up to the standards of today's private plans, in no small part because the bureaucracy of the system does not allow for efficient and effective service. Medicare pays doctors and hospitals by procedure, and only about 70 percent of the costs of the services are provided under the program. Many argue that this leads to lower quality care because Medicare pays the same fees, regardless of the quality of care provided. It also reduces access to care for many patients. Medicare moreover is notoriously slow to approve new medical technologies, leaving the elderly without the latest, best treatments and care.

How can the crisis in Medicare financing be solved? And how can Medicare benefits be improved in the process? To strengthen Medicare for the twenty-first century, several principles must guide reform:

- Action must be taken immediately to preserve Medicare for current retirees and to protect the system for the next generation.
- Medicare spending must increase at a slower rate. And it can increase at a rate of 6.5 percent and put off bankruptcy for fifteen years!
- Senior citizens deserve the same choices available to other Americans. They should be able to choose from the existing Medicare program or other private sector health plans.
- Government must not interfere in the relationship that must be respected and strengthened between patients and their doctors.
- Senior citizens should be rewarded for helping root out waste, fraud, and abuse.

Republican options to reform Medicare encompass all these principles. Even though many of the new options move away from the existing bureaucratic regulatory approach, *those who want to keep their existing Medicare plan will be allowed to do so.* Unlike the Clinton health care proposal of 1994—soundly rejected by Americans—*no one is forced into any plan.* Senior citizens could still choose the existing Medicare fee-for-service program, but there would be new options as well, including the same variety of private-sector health plans now available to the nonelderly population. No longer would beneficiaries be limited to enrolling in a Medicare program

REPUBLICAN SPENDING ON MEDICARE
(in billions)

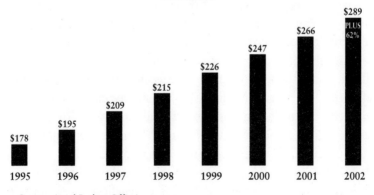

(*Source:* Congressional Budget Office)

based upon 1960s-style health insurance—no more confusing separate deductibles for hospitals, physician care, and other services. For the first time, beneficiaries could enroll in any type of approved private plan, including preferred provider organizations (PPOs), point-of-service plans (POS), provider-sponsored networks (PSNs), or a variety of health maintenance organizations (HMOs). MSAs would be available to Medicare beneficiaries for the first time. The key to reform of Medicare is to provide more choices to beneficiaries, to empower them.

What an improvement that would be over the fragmented health care that many of the nation's elderly currently receive! For instance, a 1995 report on prescription drugs and the elderly by the General Accounting Office (GAO) recently estimated that 17.5 percent of the thirty million non-institutionalized Medicare recipients are being prescribed drugs that are unsafe for their age group or that duplicate other prescriptions.[10] These prescription errors result in unnecessary hospitalizations and deaths every year and add about $20 billion to the nation's hospital bills.[11] Many managed care plans address this problem by requiring a family doctor to coordinate all of a patient's health care, reducing the likelihood that different doctors will prescribe medicines that do not mix.

These types of coordinated care plans, as mentioned above, also emphasize preventive care, so that illnesses are discovered in the early stages when they are easiest to cure. The Centers for Disease Control determined that women in HMOs are more likely to receive life-saving mammograms, Pap smears, and clinical breast exams than their counterparts in the Medicare fee-for-service program.[12] Another recent study reported that elderly HMO members with cancer are more likely to be diagnosed early.[13] This improvement in care not only saves money for the nation, it saves lives.

Because managed care plans reduce unnecessary hospitalizations and health care utilization, they can provide health services at a lower cost to beneficiaries. The average Medicare HMO enrollee incurs only half the out-of-pocket costs (including copayments and premiums) of a beneficiary under the regular fee-for-service program.[14] Managed care subscribers also face less paperwork and fewer claims forms to track.

Despite the advantages of these modern coordinated-care plans, many are not available as options to Medicare beneficiaries. Reform of the

Medicare program would make these plans available and give beneficiaries the same type of options that their children and grandchildren enjoy now. For the first time, each beneficiary—instead of the federal government—would decide who chooses the plan that best fits his or her needs.

Republicans have proposed letting Medicare grow by almost 6.4 percent a year for the next seven years. That is even faster than the private sector, which has been growing over the past five years at a rate of 6.2 percent.[15] It is certainly reasonable to think that by giving seniors private sector options, Medicare spending will fall in line with private sector growth. And even with an average annual growth rate of 6.4 percent, Medicare would have a positive balance of $300 billion by 2005, ensuring that there would be funds available as the baby boom generation prepares for retirement.

Maintaining Medicare solvency until at least 2010 is crucial as the huge baby boom generation begins to become eligible for Medicare in 2011. We must immediately begin determining how to provide a quality health care program for the elderly beyond 2011; therefore, the solution to today's Medicare issues must result in saving the program until the first edge of the baby boom generation hits in 2011 and thereafter. We can't afford to delay the impending bankruptcy for two to four years, when all focus on Medicare must be on the solution to the baby boom problem.

CHOICES FOR SENIORS

Enabling the elderly to make their own health care choices opens up a variety of exciting options, including medical savings accounts. Just as employers are now doing, the government could establish federally insured bank accounts from which beneficiaries could pay routine health expenses. Costly health expenses, such as extended hospitalization, would still be covered under a high-deductible health plan.

This proposal allows seniors to use part of the funds from Medicare to purchase insurance that would cover all expenses over a high deductible, perhaps $4,000 per year.[16] The remaining funds (about $2,000) would be saved in the MSA and would be used to pay medical expenses below the deductible. The elderly could increase the amount in their MSAs with money they are now paying out-of-pocket for health care and supplemental

Medigap insurance. The retirees could withdraw any remaining MSA funds at the end of the year and use them for any purpose.

As the previous discussion of MSAs showed, these accounts control costs and boost competition. There is every reason to believe they would work as well in reducing costs for Medicare as they have for employers who have adopted them across the country. In this way, MSAs would actually offer better benefits and higher quality care than is currently available, while at the same time solving Medicare's financial crisis. The Medicare beneficiary would also be protected in case of high medical costs.

Today, Medicare and its funds are controlled by the government. The MSA proposal would shift control to retirees—the consumers of Medicare benefits. In the process, it would not only help to solve the Medicare financing crisis, but it would also reduce costs to the elderly and actually improve their benefits. Additionally, it would allow them to profit by wise use of the funds, paying themselves an annual rebate of unused MSA funds each year. Such reform should be highly appealing to the elderly and everyone else.

LONG–TERM CARE

Health reform will not be complete without addressing the problem of long-term care, whether provided in nursing facilities or at home. Medicare does not provide long-term coverage for nursing homes, and such highly expensive care would bankrupt the great majority of elderly Americans if it were needed for any significant length of time.

"Long-term care" is the name given to that care delivered primarily to the elderly who reside in a nursing home or who receive care at home for a period of time. Currently, federal Medicaid policy subsidizes poor people who enter the nursing home by paying for their stay. While nearly half of the elderly in nursing homes are Medicaid beneficiaries, a significantly smaller percentage of the elderly on Medicare are poor.[17] The reason for the disproportionate number is that many of the elderly "spend down" their assets by transferring them to others, such as relatives, in order to qualify for the means-tested program.

The private market offers long-term care insurance, which covers nursing home care and home- and community-based care. But very few purchase it, in part because it is a relatively new product (developed in the early 1980s), but also for the same reason that many people who do not receive employer-provided health insurance choose to forgo purchasing it privately—the tax law makes no provision for purchasing long-term care insurance with pretax dollars. Early purchase of long-term care makes prices affordable.

If Washington really wants to tackle its Medicaid problem, it can start by giving the same tax break to long-term care insurance that it gives to employer-provided health insurance. Employers should be encouraged (not required) to either provide long-term care insurance as part of the overall benefits package or make it available to employees who want the option of purchasing long-term care insurance through their employer with pretax dollars. Since individuals comprise the majority of long-term care insurance purchasers, they should also get the tax break, by means of a deduction on their annual tax statement.

The need for long-term health care is not of course limited to the elderly. Traumatic brain injuries alone affect over two million Americans each year.[18] Those with mental retardation, mental illness, or other diseases also have long-term care needs. The high cost of this care could be reduced if it were delivered in the least restrictive and most cost-effective setting available.

Skilled nursing facilities are also an option for subacute care. In the 103rd Congress, virtually every major health reform measure called for studies of the increased utilization of cost-effective subacute care. But past Democratic Congresses erected legislative barriers to this type of care. Subacute care saves money, and removing the archaic Medicare statutes, reimbursement rules, and regulatory barriers presents yet another opportunity to design health care reforms that cut costs while increasing patients' options for quality care.

Medicare fraud has become a major concern among seniors. The consequences of fraud and abuse to the health care system are staggering: As much as 10 percent of U.S. health care spending, or $100 billion, is lost each year to health care fraud and abuse. Over the past five years, estimates of losses from these fraudulent activities totaled about $418 billion—or almost four times as much as the cost of the entire savings and loan crisis to date.[19]

Fraud is high because of the economic incentives in the Medicare system. With Medicare paying the bills, neither doctors nor patients have much reason to make sure that Medicare money is being spent wisely. While stronger penalties should apply to those who defraud the system, the real key to eliminating fraud is giving seniors financial incentives to do so. Seniors should receive a reward when they find an error on their medical bill. In addition, they should be given more control over their health care dollars and how they are spent, as medical savings accounts would do.

As we have seen, the market is not the problem in health care, it is the root of the solution. By giving the consumers of medical care the power to make their own health care choices, costs can be checked without trampling on peoples' freedom to make crucial decisions about their health and their lives. Harnessing the virtues of the market—fundamental fairness and freedom—is crucial to any effort to reform health care.

5

Environment

What is our cry? Our cry is not to dismantle the Clean Water Act, not to repeal the Endangered Species Act, not to repeal wetlands protection in America. Our cry is simple: put some common sense into it. Target the remedy to the problem, and do it in a way that respects people and jobs and property rights.
—Louisiana Rep. W. J. "Billy" Tauzin, at a National Policy Forum conference on Environmental Enforcement

★

A SANE ENVIRONMENTAL POLICY for the twenty-first century must provide effective protection for our environment, while respecting the legitimate needs and rights of our citizens. People should not be relentlessly harassed by bureaucrats when they are doing nothing more harmful than trying to earn a living. At the same time, we do not want citizens or businesses robbing future generations of their heritage by harming the environment.

Our present system of environmental law and regulation is not only obsolete, refusing as it does to recognize scientific advances that change the overall environmental picture, but it also lacks in commonsense application, especially when it comes to considerations of merit and cost.

Current environmental policy is not based on these commonsense considerations. A few examples will illustrate this point:

- The owner of United Truck Body Co. had to spend $10,000 in legal fees to prove his innocence to the Environmental Protection Agency (EPA), which sued various businesses in the Duluth, Minnesota, area in an effort to get companies to agree to pay for cleanup of a local Superfund site. The offending company, before it went out of business, re-refined waste motor oil from several businesses in the Duluth area. Because the company had gone out of business, the EPA searched through old records to identify any other enterprises that might have had any business with the refinery. United Truck Body had done very little business with the refinery over the years but was nonetheless forced to dedicate considerable time and expense to proving its innocence to the EPA. Now, eight years after the EPA began its expensive bureaucratic process, actual cleanup has just begun.[1]

- Another small business owner spent $30,000 in legal fees fighting problems that were not his doing. Mr. Yee, who came to the United States as a refugee from Communist China, has been forced to defend his business against EPA Superfund officials who are taking action against him even though he had nothing to do with the pollution that was present on the property when he bought it. He purchased the property in good faith. Neither the previous owners, the bankers, nor the realtors ever told Mr. Yee of any pollution problems with the property, and now Mr. Yee is in danger of losing his business.[2]

- Locating and assessing responsibility among companies in a dispute over a Superfund site cost the citizens of Hutchinson, Kansas, a community of 40,000, approximately $500,000. The city will also have to pay $50,000 a year to install monitoring wells. All of this expense is "real money" to Hutchinson's citizens and represents only part of the cost. Banks won't lend money for the purchase or improvement of property because of perceived Superfund liability, and all real estate activity is in limbo because of litigation and falling real estate values.[3]

We are faced with an environmental policy in dire need of reform. This is going to require clear thinking instead of the appeals to emotion that now masquerade as thought about environmental issues. We are confronted with the claim that all who "care" about the environment must necessarily support every single piece of legislation and regulation that bears a "green" label. Insultingly, we're told that if we so much as harbor a reservation about some arcane provision of the Clean Air Act, we are in favor of forcing people to breathe dirty air.

Emotionalism of this type serves us ill. It obscures the truth that today environmentalism need not be an either/or proposition. In fact, we are not forced to choose between a booming economy and a safe and clean environment. We can have both. Indeed, anything less cheats us as a society.

A new environmental policy will require that we reconsider some of the fundamentals. For example, a chief flaw of current policy is that it is built on a sustainable development concept. This represents a scarcity mentality. The sustainable development model postulates a static quantity of scarce resources that must be carefully husbanded. However, we know that in many cases scientific discoveries have changed the equation. For example, the scarcity of copper was once a major worry. But now silicon (in the form of fiber optic cables) often replaces copper. Our energy supply fluctuates; a gallon of gasoline is now cheaper than a gallon of bottled water. Because of our reliance on the sustainable development concept, we have a tendency to control output, to restrict material and energy use instead of ensuring that residuals are not dumped on the property of others. We have focused on emissions reduction rather than pollution prevention.

Of course, in talking about our environmental policy, we don't want to overlook the many positive things we as a society have done since the first Earth Day in 1970. To do so would be unfair. Earth Day effectively publicized the degree to which our environment had deteriorated. Many Americans at the time did breathe dirty air because of belching smokestacks. Raw sewage and waste were routinely dumped into our rivers and lakes.

As a result of Earth Day and similar activities, Americans reached a national consensus that, in our increasingly wealthy society, environmental neglect was no longer acceptable. Succeeding years saw congressional environmental bill after bill enacted with minor, if any, opposition. We became a nation of environmentalists—a term used advisedly, given some of the abuses imposed in the name of environmentalism.

Although the planning was often poor and the regulation heavy-handed, many laws nonetheless proved effective. Sewage was removed from most of America's rivers and lakes, and basic manufacturing industries and coal-burning power plants upgraded emissions control technology. Automakers began manufacturing more efficient motor vehicles, and vehicles began burning cleaner fuels. Recycling has reduced the amount of material put into the waste stream. The scale and simplicity of the problems in those days meant that they could be addressed through the use of uniform central government command and control regulations.

Not surprisingly, the quarter of a century since the first Earth Day has seen the establishment of a huge edifice of environmental laws and regulations. Unfortunately, the presumption has been in favor of government to solve problems. Business is often portrayed as an evil foe. Balance and common sense went out the window.

This should not have happened. The National Environmental Policy Act (NEPA)—the mother of all our environmental law—implicitly recognized the need for balance. NEPA stressed "the critical importance of restoring and maintaining environmental quality to the overall welfare and development of man." But it further charged the federal government, in cooperation with state and local governments and public and private groups, with creating and maintaining "conditions under which man and nature can exist in productive harmony, and fulfill the social, economic, and other requirements of present and future government operations in America."

Cost-benefit standards were implicitly mandated. NEPA called upon Congress to authorize and direct "*all agencies* of the federal government" to "identify and develop methods and procedures... which will ensure that *presently unquantified* environmental amenities and values may be given appropriate consideration and decision-making *along with* economic and technical considerations" (emphasis added). In short, man's activities and economic needs were not deemed irrelevant.

Somewhere this idea has gotten lost. The idea that man's economic needs were to be considered was dropped. Further, a lack of scrutiny meant that many well-intended pieces of legislation had disastrous consequences. One of the primary examples is Superfund. Enacted in 1980 with the laudable goal of cleaning up hazardous waste sites, Superfund has had a devastating effect on many businesses. As written, Superfund requires that the government determine "potentially responsible parties" for any given Superfund site and make them pay for the cleanup.

Who could argue with that? We all want to clean up hazardous waste. Unfortunately, Superfund has been used to force companies that are responsible for a small fraction of the damage in a major site to pay the entire cleanup bill. In addition, retroactive liability means that a company might suddenly be handed a devastating bill for a site on which it long ago conducted operations that, at the time, were not known to be hazardous. Indeed, the Superfund law often results in companies or individuals, who never did anything more than simply own the site or part of it, being forced to pay for cleanup, even though everyone admits they had nothing to do with the pollution. Superfund is "deep pocket" jurisprudence at its worst.

And the situation is getting worse, not better. Increasingly, the federal government, facing a tight budget, tries to force more and more costs of environmental legislation onto businesses or state or local governments. Needless to say, the cost of environmental legislation has already been enormous for our society. Since 1970, the cost to the U.S. economy has been estimated at more than $1 trillion.[4] Current costs are in excess of $150 billion per year.[5] This is nearly 3 percent of our gross national product. Superfund alone has cost over $60 billion in public and private moneys in the fifteen years of its existence, although less than a quarter of the sites have been cleaned up.[6] But dollars don't tell the whole story. The Environmental Protection Agency, established in 1970, has assumed a level of detailed control over our economy that dwarfs the control ever granted to any economic planning agency. One could argue that the United States has subjected its economy to Ecological Central Planning.

The Government's Role
There are at least five areas where the centralized command-and-control approach is failing us in our efforts to achieve and maintain a clean and safe environment. Without question, positive action in these areas would improve our environment by strengthening and streamlining the government's role in environmental policy.

Prioritize based on cost-benefit and risk analysis. One failure of the centralized command-and-control approach has been its lack of prioritization based on cost-benefit and risk analysis. Indeed, some federal environmental laws prohibit consideration of cost. As a consequence, EPA has become obsessed with "chasing the last molecule," regardless of the minuscule health risk involved and regardless of the excessive costs required to obtain relatively limited benefits. Far greater environmental benefits could be obtained by working on environmental challenges that do not involve the cleaning up of that last few percent.

For example, although emissions from American cars produced today have been reduced by 95 percent over the past two decades, the federal Clean Air Act has practically forced California and some northeastern states to adopt a new vehicle adaptation that could add as much as $2,500 to the cost of a car. That is in addition to the average $1,500 worth of emissions control equipment already included in today's cars. These new requirements are designed to reduce the remaining one gram per mile of emissions by one-half. The incremental cost of removing the remaining 5 percent would be twenty times more costly than eliminating the first 95 percent.[7]

In another example of misplaced priorities, federal and state regulators are proposing extremely expensive and unrealistic means to control certain emissions from bakeries. As a consequence, many bakeries, particularly in the Northeast, are ceasing operations. Although bakeries contribute only one-tenth of 1 percent of the entire inventory of the pollutant, volatile organic compounds, the regulators are requiring that certain bakeries install catalytic incinerators, each of which costs $250,000. Many bakeries are small businesses that simply cannot afford that kind of non–revenue-producing expenditure.[8]

Base environmental efforts on peer-reviewed sound science. Instead of utilizing an approach that is based on peer-reviewed sound science, the centralized planning approach has led to demands that government spend huge amounts of money to address a "crisis" or correct a problem before scientists fully understand its extent—or even its existence. Activists who insist on the crisis method believe in science only when it predicts grave negative trends. Science, thus applied, serves only to find some evidence that mankind, or some activity of mankind, *might* endanger the earth, and then a new law or regulation is necessary. The fact that scientific uncertainty makes it difficult to define the danger, much less to act prudently, is not considered; nor have those activities sought to use science to examine the risks of *over-* versus underregulation. This has produced a growing divergence between activists and many scientists, a divergence that to date has had little impact on policy.

Indeed, action has been taken to "protect the environment" even when there was strong scientific evidence that no action was needed. For example, an exhaustive, decade-long study of acid rain (the National Acid Precipitation Assessment Program, known as NAPAP) cost $570 million. None of us wants to dismiss potential environmental threats, but this was a hefty price for a study, especially as it found that "there is no evidence of widespread forest damage from current ambient levels of acidic rain in the United States." Then, as if paying for the study weren't enough, Congress chose to ignore its findings completely, passing an also-expensive but indeed very "politically correct" acid rain program before the NAPAP study was even completed.

As the acid rain saga suggests, sound science and objective analysis aren't always paramount when policy is being made. The role of politics cannot be underestimated. Environmental policy is highly politicized and antibusiness in orientation. Indeed, extreme elements in the movement like to portray people in the private sector (farmers, industrialists, miners, ranchers, fishermen, and other business people) as selfish and greedy. On the other hand, people in the public sector—their own clique—are seen as self-sacrificing people who care only for the well-being of society, often at great expense to the taxpayer.

Require regulatory accountability. In recent years, increasing budget deficits and taxpayer resistance have made it extremely difficult and inappropriate to increase direct federal spending; thus, pressures have mounted to seek environmental improvements via off-budget gimmickry. The primary means for advancing environmental goals to date—federal regulations—create little direct costs to the government. Instead, the costs are borne by state and local governments as unfunded mandates, by businesses as regulatory burdens, and by property owners as "takings."

It should be emphasized that nearly all of this cost is then passed through to American citizens in higher taxes and higher consumer prices. People become poorer without knowing whom to blame.

Off-budget spending has received far less scrutiny than direct spending or tax measures and thus is even less efficient than normal federal programs. This lack of analysis means that programs can have extremely low value and still be promoted by the agency. The wastefulness of such programs and the lack of interest in their impact on business, property owners, taxpayers, and consumers was one of the major triggers of the voter revolt in the 1994 election. Bureaucrats and others have attempted to defend such expenditures by claiming they create jobs, but this is surprisingly naive. At best, government spending shifts jobs—from blue collar factory workers to environmental lawyers, for example—with no net gain.

Determine environmental policy where the problem exists. Efforts to redress environmental issues at the lowest possible level of government have been discouraged or ignored. Since the creation of the U.S. Environmental Protection Agency in 1970, policies and legislation enacted to remedy environmental damage have continued to rely on top-down federal programs and, not surprisingly, have discouraged local action by the businesses and residents most affected.

That the foundations of EPA would be flawed is not surprising; EPA was created in an era when the United States was still wedded to "progressive" policies. Congress knew exactly what to do about any problem: Enact utopian national legislation, create new bureaucracies to implement them, staff them with America's "best and brightest," and watch the improvements occur. Environmental policy became political policy and—too often—uniform federal command-and-control regulatory policy. If such policies failed to deliver, the quick response was more of the same—toughen the laws, eliminate all "loopholes," and spend more tax dollars. Consequently, America enacted laws that were long on rhetoric and short on rationale.

Worse, the problem was compounded by a pernicious trend toward an ever more litigious society. Today, every word in legislation becomes a pretext for an increasingly oppressive regulatory state, one in which any effort to grant local communities or private sectors flexibility is seen as evidence of backsliding, or treason against the public interest. For instance, Superfund's absurd and unjust liability rules—specifically retroactive, along with joint and several—are best viewed as a way of gathering in more financially solvent parties into the class of potentially responsible parties—a form of "deep pocket" jurisprudence. It bears no similarity to a reasonable system of environmental justice.

Instead of the government spending huge sums of money in attempts to get citizens and companies to sue each other to achieve cost recovery, we should encourage reasonably flexible enforcement of environmental regulations at the local level. Environmental self-audits and corrective action within the private sector should be encouraged instead of penalized. Responsible businesses and citizens who conduct environmental self-evaluations and disclose potential nonintentional violations should not create or expand their liability. Over a dozen states have enacted self-audit proposals.

Respect private property. In addition to the lack of faith by the federal government in the ability of state and local governments to deal with environmental issues, the current administration has shown a marked lack of respect for private property rights. This is unacceptable, because the key to good environmental practices has been private property rights.

Private property gives individuals direct responsibility for a part of the planet, while providing them with the authority to protect it. Private property resolves the "Tragedy of the Commons," making it possible for individuals to conserve resources without worrying that the resources would be consumed by others. Moreover, private property creates incentives to develop better means of protecting and nurturing the environment over time. The vast improvement in our ability to manage natural resources, farmlands, domesticated species, and aquatic species all stems from this critical linkage of innovation and reward.

In contrast, consider the plight of the Soviet Union. There, everyone in principle owned everything; the resources were managed for the good of all. Yet, when the Iron Curtain parted, we found no Garden of Eden but rather a landscape of desolation and destruction resulting from an unchecked lust for economic development that swept aside all other values.

Several examples of recent federal taking of Americans' private property are given in *Agenda's* chapter 6 on Resources and Energy. Many of these takings have occurred without the owner being compensated. Fortunately, the Supreme Court, in the 1994 *Dolan v. the City of Tigard* case, ruled that taking property without compensation violates the takings clause of the Constitution's Fifth Amendment. That amendment specifies that private property shall not be taken for public use without just compensation. "We see no reason," Chief Justice Rehnquist wrote, "why the Takings Clause of the Fifth Amendment, as much a part of the Bill of Rights as the First Amendment, should be relegated to the status of a poor relation in these comparable circumstances."

Clean Growth

Balancing our concern for the environment with our need for economic well-being will be one of our major challenges as we stand on the threshold of the twenty-first century.

We believe that the heavy-handedness of America's environmental policy was a factor in the voter revolt of November 1994. Many voters, having had ruinous personal encounters with the environmental regulators, want change. Their experiences have told them that a one-size-fits-all policy doesn't work. They know from firsthand experience that current policy discourages private, voluntary efforts to protect the environment.

Our policy must protect both the environment and the citizen. We must recognize that economic growth is key to improving the environment. Superfund, the Clean Air Act, and the Clean Water Act all require rethinking. A speech at a 1995 National Policy Forum conference given by Speaker Newt Gingrich offers guidance. The Speaker called for "bold, new, entrepreneurial, scientifically based approaches to giving our children the best planet, the best country, the finest environment in the world in a way that makes sense and is economically affordable."

An important part of the new policy is that it will empower millions of people to protect their environment instead of leaving the power in the hands of thousands of bureaucrats who are as bent on saving their jobs as saving the planet. Normal people—not just bureaucrats—care about the environment, and it is time to recognize this.

One of the most crucial shifts will be toward more local solutions to problems. Today, in a drastic change from the 1970s, we are no longer dealing with a small number of uniform national problems generated by a small number of specific substances but rather with hundreds of trace contaminants generated by thousands of minor sources such as local bakeries and dry cleaners.

Localizing the issue is thus of paramount importance. It is necessary to recognize that the appropriate measures to remedy the problem of automobile exhaust fumes may be different in Montana from those required in downtown Los Angeles. Similarly, the per capita–based costs of meeting EPA drinking water standards may vary from city to city, being minimal in bigger cities and insanely expensive in small towns. Some regulatory areas call for national standards, but few benefit from national remedies.

In certain fields, national uniformity has become a straitjacket. It limits the creativity that local and state jurisdictions and businesses might otherwise bring to bear on problems. These rigidities have fostered an arrogance on the part of regulators that has led many Americans to question not just the means but the objectives of environmental protection.

Policy is currently based on political solutions, and coercion is all too often the tool in enforcing these policies. Voluntary solutions are shunned, and we are told to look to government. This logic requires that *all* economic activities having environmental implications be regulated. And since all economic activities have environmental consequences, well, therefore, more regulations. If we continue down our current path, we are headed for what might be called eco-serfdom.

Environmental problems do exist, and environmental concerns are important. But rather than separating man from nature, environmental policy should rely as much as possible on the natural incentives of private individuals cooperating through voluntary associations. Policy should empower millions of individuals to protect their environment, rather than thousands of bureaucrats to protect their political turf. It is beyond question that if the billions of individuals on the earth do not wish to protect it, the planet is beyond hope. No amount of coercion will save the planet if the average person truly wants to destroy it. Fortunately, the simple fact is that people everywhere desire a better life, and a better life includes a safe and clean environment.

6

Resources and Energy

When rats' homes become more important than American citizens' homes, when a child of an American family is put at risk of fire to save a rat's home, I suggest it's time for us to reform some laws. I suggest we have gone too far. We have got some agencies out of control.
—Louisiana Rep. W. J. "Billy" Tauzin at a National Policy Forum conference on Environmental Enforcement

★

AMERICA IS BLESSED BY A WEALTH of natural resources. We have land that is as fertile as it is beautiful, large mineral reserves, productive waters, and rich and varied plant and animal life. We are also blessed with abundant reserves of energy-producing resources, such as crude oil, natural gas, and coal. These resources have been a source of national strength as well as national pride. But if these resources are to be protected and utilized without derailing our country's prosperity, we need to establish sound, reasoned natural resource policies founded on good science, common sense, fairness, and a respect for individual freedom.

Our current policy is not based on these principles. Especially missing is the principle of common sense. A few examples will suffice:

- In late October 1993, fires swept through Riverside County in Southern California. These fires burned 25,000 acres and destroyed twenty-nine homes. Many of the homes were destroyed because their owners had been prohibited by the U.S. Fish and Wildlife Service from creating fire breaks to protect their homes; fire breaks might disturb the habitat of the Stephens kangaroo rat. When that species of rat was listed as endangered in late 1988, 500,000 acres became heavily regulated and over 50,000 acres were put off limits to human disturbance.[1]

- In 1973, Margaret Rector, now in her seventies, purchased fifteen acres of unimproved land on a busy highway west of Austin, Texas. This was an investment for her retirement. In 1990, the U.S. Fish and Wildlife Service listed the golden checked warbler an endangered species. Prior to that time, Ms. Rector had put her land on the market to sell, but the warbler listing had halted all activity. Her land is in limbo. She continues to pay taxes on land she can't use or sell. Moreover, the assessed value of her land dropped from $830,960 in 1991 to $30,380 in 1992 because of the endangered species. Ms. Rector believes that "If the government wants our land for public use, then they should pay us for it."[2]

- Ben Cone of eastern North Carolina has owned and managed 8,000 acres of timberland since 1982. Mr. Cone, and his father before him, had managed this land as a wildlife habitat and had not cut much of the timber over the years. In return for these responsible management practices, the U.S. Fish and Wildlife Service has declared that no trees on 1,121 acres of Mr. Cone's land may be cut because of the presence of the red cockaded woodpecker. The economic loss to Mr. Cone is approximately $1.5 million. In response to the government's order in connection with the 1,121 acres, Mr. Cone has begun a massive clear-cutting program on the rest of his land. He is going from almost no timber sales to 200 to 300 acres a year. Thus, the actions of the government agency charged with protecting endangered species are directly leading to reductions in habitat needed for the endangered red cockaded woodpecker.[3]

Stewards of the Land

America's natural resources, as some of these incidents show only too well, have been mismanaged through unnecessary regulations and misguided policies. These have been put into force by elected representatives and self-appointed environmental extremists who have little stake in the region's economic or community life. As is often the case, an "absentee" landlord is partly at fault. This time the absentee landlord is Uncle Sam, who owns more than 30 percent of the land in the United States and tries to administer too much of it from Washington. Career federal employees insulated from economic upheaval generally lack any real feeling for the land they regulate.

Our current system of land management is fundamentally flawed. The United States manages its massive land holdings through four huge agencies that are themselves subsumed in two separate cabinet-level departments. They are the Department of Agriculture's National Forest Service (191 million acres); the Department of the Interior's Bureau of Land Management (272 million acres); the Fish and Wildlife Service (92 million acres); and the National Park Service (83 million acres). Needless to say, this organizational mishmash is often unsympathetic at the local level.

The American people, however, *as private property owners* dependent on the land for economic survival, particularly throughout the western United States, have been faithful stewards of the nation's resources. Natural resources can be protected, refurbished, and even enhanced without unnecessarily inhibiting people from earning a livelihood. Unfortunately, centralized management of natural resources has gravely damaged the economic well-being of entire regions of our country.

Americans are further concerned that federal agencies can use and abuse their power to discourage or prevent home-building, grazing, farming, mining, timbering, and oil and gas extraction. The economic impact can be devastating. In recent years, for example, timber sales from national forests have been reduced by 60 percent, thanks to legal and regulatory gridlock. Ironically, the timber harvesting that some seek to prohibit is essential to preserving the health of our national forests.

Although the forests themselves prosper when we do sensible things— like removing diseased timber—some of the more extreme environmentalists scream bloody murder at the very idea of this kind of benign intervention. The Endangered Species Act has become a powerful tool in the hands of those who want to stop growth or any use such as is historically found on farms, ranches, and forests. One of the reasons the act is so invasive is that species-listing decisions aren't always based upon proven scientific standards. Nor do they consider the needs of human beings—hence the kangaroo rats episode.

We favor an intelligent policy of species conservation, but believe it's high time to inject some common sense and scientific review into the debate. To put human families out of their homes for the kangaroo rat is just plain wrong.

Any discussion of our natural land resources must deal with an important subject about which the Republican perspective is even more blatantly misrepresented than in species preservation. We're talking, of course, about out national parks.

We recognize that parks like Yellowstone, the Grand Canyon, and Yosemite, to name a few, are the crown jewels of our National Park System. Nobody in his or her right mind wants to close these magnificent parks. Such parks should and do receive our highest level of support. When Republicans call for a review of some of the 369 units in our national park system, it's not in order to close any of our nationally prized parks. But some units are small operations, and they may be marginal at best.

A commonsense approach to natural resource stewardship should begin with these principles:

- Natural resource management decisions should be based on sound science verified by independent scientific peer review.
- Natural resources can be used responsibly and be protected at the same time. Environmental protection must be balanced with regional economic considerations, giving specific consideration to local jobs and regional economies.
- Federal natural resource management is often inefficient and incapable of the flexibility needed to adjust to local circumstances. Federal regulation should be minimized.
- Local users of resources are the best stewards because they have a greater incentive—economic dependence on the resource—to ensure

that the resources remain productive. Local management and decision-making authority should be encouraged wherever possible.

- Every proposed federal action or policy must take into account its impact on people and regional economies prior to its implementation.
- Those who use or benefit from public natural resources should pay a fair share for what they use or receive.
- When government seizes private property through its actions, no matter how noble the purpose, it must abide by the Fifth Amendment to the Constitution and pay "just compensation" to the private owner for what it takes.
- The federal government should focus its resources on protecting nationally significant areas of outstanding resources.

To put these principles into effect—to return to responsible stewardship of America's natural resources—we recommend several specific actions.

Endangered species. The Endangered Species Act has become one of the most potent tools environmentalists have used to gain control of public and private lands. For the act to protect animals without endangering farmers, ranchers, and loggers, it needs to be scientifically sound, economically rational, and respectful of private property rights. The listing of species should be based on objective scientific standards subject to independent scientific peer review.

Public access to all information submitted to determine a candidate for listing must be available from beginning to end of the deliberative process.

If the government bars activity on private property for the sake of saving an endangered species, the government must compensate the private landowner for that land's value. The Constitution's Fifth Amendment is quite clear in stating that private property shall not be taken for public use without just compensation. Private landowners must be given reasonable opportunities to comply with the regulations, as well as incentives to work cooperatively with the government to protect listed species. Prohibited activities must be defined in a way that avoids arbitrary enforcement.

Consultations with affected parties on federal actions need to be prompt and accurate, and federal permit applicants should be guaranteed meaningful participation in the process. The recovery plan should be the focus of all management and regulatory efforts on behalf of a species, including considerations of social and economic impacts, relative risks, costs, and alternative recovery strategies. Efforts to impose centralized federal control over the land must be stopped. For example, the National Biological Service, established administratively by the secretary of the interior in 1993, gathers, analyzes, and disseminates information on biological resources on public and private lands, ostensibly to facilitate federal land management. In reality, it may only be an excuse to regulate the land even further.

Federal land ownership and management. As stated, the federal government owns almost 30 percent of the total land mass of the United States. The current federal land management system of this huge acreage is fundamentally flawed, not because of its purpose or motivations, but because centralized command and control policies do not, and cannot, work in a free society. The system requires a comprehensive overhaul.

To repeat: The four major civilian federal land management agencies control massive amounts of land. The Department of Agriculture's National Forest Service controls about 191 million acres of land. The Department of the Interior's Bureau of Land Management controls 272 million acres, the Fish and Wildlife Service controls 92 million acres, and the National Park Service controls 83 million acres. The existence of four huge land management agencies in two separate cabinet-level agencies is a historical accident that Congress should rectify. These agencies should be merged.

A federal land-reorganization commission, similar to the Defense Base Closure and Realignment Commission, should be established to examine and make recommendations on the management of federal lands. The Base Closure Commission studied American military facilities and then made closure recommendations to the president and Congress. An independent analytical approach to reviewing lands would inevitably lead to certain land transfers from the federal inventory. Conflicting jurisdiction can be eliminated through consolidation and streamlining. Surplus lands could be offered for regional, state, or local use.

Among the policy options that such a commission could examine would be contracting with environmental conservancies to manage certain lands on a trial basis. Further options must include some regionalization of these management options to permit those most closely connected with the land—not federal employees with no direct dependence on the land—to control these decisions. Regional management compacts, with state and local representatives who have the most direct contact with the managed land, can and should do a better job of managing land and resources than far-off centralized regulators.

To bring hope and a sense of "reenfranchisement" to those who live on and near federal lands, we must trust our citizens enough to involve them in managing our—and their—natural resources.

National parks. The 369 units of the National Park System include our nation's "crown jewels." These crown jewels should continue to receive the highest level of support. However, the Park Service must refocus on its fundamental purpose of conserving park resources and managing them in a manner that will "leave them unimpaired for the enjoyment of future generations," as stated in the 1916 federal law that established the National Park Service. Responsibilities (and parks) not consistent with that mission should be eliminated.

Some national parks fail to meet the criteria for units of the National Park System and should be transferred. Those areas lacking national significance or having only limited special appeal should be transferred to state park systems or other entities. The expensive land acquisition, operation, and maintenance costs of these marginal parks rob our nation's real jewels of the funds necessary for their protection and enjoyment.

Individuals using America's parks, forests, and recreation areas should pay reasonable fees for the privilege. These fees must take into account the cost of administering and protecting those areas in today's market. The fees should help offset the cost of those services. The government cannot continue to subsidize fully all activities on federal lands. All users should bear some of the cost, regardless of locale or extent of use. Thus for example, visitors to the Grand Canyon as well as users of off-road vehicles on federal lands should expect to help support the maintenance of these lands.

Wilderness. Wilderness designations should not be abused to lock up economically productive lands. Prior to designating any land as wilderness, Congress should ensure that economic and public-use values are balanced against potential wilderness values. Current wilderness lands, moreover, should be evaluated to determine whether they continue to meet the criteria for wilderness designation.

Timber. Appropriate stewardship and care of privately and publicly owned forest resources can best be achieved by providing economic incentives and a rational forest management plan. In recent years, timber sales from national forests have been reduced by 60 percent due to legal and regulatory gridlock. Without these programs, local communities that depend on timber harvesting would simply die—as has been dramatically shown throughout the Northwest the past few years. And the rest of the country would see the price of timber products—from paper napkins to pencils to housing—skyrocket.

Restrictive federal forest management policies, such as reduced timber sales, severe timber-harvesting restrictions, and cumbersome administrative appeal processes, must be reversed. The harvesting of diseased or downed timber must be permitted to go forward. Scientific management that incorporates timber harvesting as a factor in protecting the health and vitality of a national forest must be recognized as an essential element of federal forest management policy.

Without some relief, the forests themselves will continue to die from federal mismanagement. Along with the death of forests are the deaths of the mills, industries, and communities involved with, and dependent on, viable, dynamic management of these resources.

Grazing. Those involved in federal grazing actively manage lands within their allotments and are an integral part of the life of the West. Federal grazing fees should be set at equitable levels, based on the gross value of production for cattle, taking into account the improvements ranchers make to the land. To ensure that local residents are involved in management decisions, grazing advisory councils of local land users and owners, elected officials, and residents should be established to allow them to participate in regional decisions.

Wetlands. The federal government has tended to overregulate wetlands, yet Congress has never clearly defined what a wetland is on a "sound-science" basis. As a result, "wetlands policy" is fraught with case-by-case inconsistencies that are unfair, unreliable, and unpredictable.

Market-based approaches, such as mitigation banking (wherein people can sell credits gained from creating new wetlands to people who have suffered for wetlands losses), should be pursued. These approaches provide fair-market-value compensation to both parties and ensure that overall wetlands acreage does not diminish.

One agency should manage wetlands regulations to eliminate bureaucratic turf battles among agencies, subjecting citizens to expensive delays. The agency responsible for wetlands administration must be required to publish clear guidelines for compliance, and to a timely resolution of applications. Issues should be addressed all at one time, rather than requiring applicants to undergo a sequential series of corrective actions. This sequence-driven approach wears down the parties and breeds contempt for the entire system.

Finally, when the government determines that a wetland on private property is so valuable that it must bar activity to preserve that land, the owner must be justly compensated.

Hard-rock mining. While the Mining Law of 1872 may need updating, incentives in current law to discover and develop mineral resources should be maintained. Individuals should continue to be permitted to explore and stake claims to mineral resources on federal lands. Patents for ownership to valid claims should be issued upon payment of current fair market value for the surface lands. A royalty that permits a reasonable opportunity to earn a profit should be set for extraction of publicly owned minerals.

Water rights. As an underlying policy, the federal government should cease its attempts to take over the states' historical control over water rights.

In some instances, regulatory policies that are locally based, economically sound, and environmentally sensitive are better than centralized control of regional water policies. Regionally based regulatory water policy, such as the Chesapeake Bay system or the Colorado River water system, can protect natural resources and serve regional objectives. The federal government must stop reserving the right to manage a project in its entirety, giving only lip service to local and regional concerns.

Private Sector Development

Land isn't our only overregulated natural resource. We are also overregulating our energy industry, which has its own separate cabinet-level overseer: the Department of Energy (DOE). The department was created in 1977 when Americans were frightened about oil embargoes and the depletion of our resources. It was supposed to deal with these issues.

Oil imports are now up to approximately 50 percent, but the DOE seems only to have added to our energy problems. It has multiplied bureaucratic controls over energy industries, and many of its regulations have been egregiously counterproductive. Price controls on domestic petroleum led to a rise in imports. And the effort to convert American coal and oil shale into oil through the mercifully short-lived U.S. Synthetic Fuels Corporation was a costly boondoggle. Cumbersome energy efficiency standards for household appliances were also established.

While we all recognize that energy is essential for our survival, we must also recognize that the array of complex federal laws and regulations have in general reduced America's effectiveness in finding, producing, refining, transporting, and marketing domestic oil and gas. The additional costs of complying with federal mandates can make—and have made—domestic resources less attractive than imported supplies. As a result, we become dependent on foreign sources, some far from friendly, for our energy needs.

This in fact has already taken place. U.S. consumption of domestic crude oil has declined drastically since the oil price collapse of 1986. Oil production in 1993 was 26 percent below that of 1985, while U.S. demand was up 11 percent over the same period. Imports fill this growing gap. People who argue that this is due to diminished domestic resources don't take the real facts into consideration: The United States has an estimated 200 *billion* barrels of oil and more than 1 *trillion* cubic feet of natural gas. At today's level of consumption, this is a sixty-two–year supply of oil and a sixty-eight–year supply of natural gas. In addition, academic institutions have identified additional geologic structures deep in the Gulf of Mexico with potential hydrocarbons equivalent to those in the Middle East.[4]

And yet we have reduced domestic production, artificially, through regulation. In 1992, for example, the oil and gas industry spent almost as much time and money complying with environmental mandates as it did exploring for oil and gas. Although the industry has consistently complied with a seemingly endless array of environmental regulations over the past thirty years—in 1992 alone, according to the American Petroleum Institute, the exploration and production segment of the industry spent $1.6 billion on environmental protection measures—nothing seems to satisfy the environmental extremists and their allies in the federal bureaucracies.[5]

Compliance with many of the federal environmental requirements produce minimal environmental benefit and do not respond to any particular identified risk. Many require bureaucratic record keeping, monitoring, and reporting. These requirements add to the cost of energy to the American people with, again, relatively little or no tangible environmental benefit.

Among the federal environmental laws affecting the industry are the Clean Air Act; the Comprehensive Environmental Response, Compensation, and Liability Act; the Resource Conservation and Recovery Act; the Clean Water Act; the Safe Drinking Water Act; the Toxic Substances Control Act; and the Endangered Species Act.

And unless something changes, the cost of regulation will escalate. To comply with environmental requirements, the total cost of supplying light petroleum products to consumers will increase by six to ten cents per gallon by the year 2000. Industry experts predict that a $37 billion investment will be required during this decade to meet environmental requirements for refineries and products. The total book value of U.S. refineries is presently $31 billion—$6 billion less than the cost of environmental compliance. There are 187 petroleum refineries operating in the United States today. A total of 120 refineries shut down in the 1980s.[6] These shutdowns, as those in the timber and mining industries, have thrown thousands upon thousands of Americans out of work.

The Environmental Protection Agency (EPA) estimates that enforcing standards for the emission of organic hazardous air pollutants could close thirty additional refineries with capital costs estimated at $207 million and annual operating costs of $110 million. And what is the benefit of such eco-vigilance? By the EPA's own calculations, the potential savings in life is minuscule.

Coal is our most abundant and most secure fuel for generating electricity. In fact, two-thirds of U.S. electricity is generated at coal-fired plants. The development of state-of-the-art coal utilization technologies has made it possible to mine and use our most abundant natural resource in environmentally sound ways. Full use of our domestic coal resources is essential in supporting our nation's energy security. The federal government should encourage coal utilization through responsible environmental policy, as more fully explained in chapter 5, Environment.

Nuclear energy must continue to play a major role in providing power for the United States. The U.S. nuclear program is the largest in the world in terms of operating units in service, generating capacity, and kilowatt-hours produced, with 109 reactors licensed to operate at seventy-five sites in thirty-two states. Clearly, nuclear energy is already a critical part of our electricity supply system and is necessary to our economic well-being.

The nuclear power industry can claim credit for producing $73 billion in total sales of goods and services, 417,000 jobs, and $14 billion in federal, state, and local government tax revenues. Nuclear power currently provides about 20 percent of U.S. generating capacity.

It is of foremost importance to the future of nuclear power in the United States that operating reactors continue their high levels of safety and reliability. International indicators confirm the industry's significant improvements in all areas of plant performance.

Three other major factors are important to the future use of nuclear power: the need for baseload electric generating capacity, the economic competitiveness of nuclear generation, and the development of an integrated spent nuclear fuel management system.

- As we enter the next century, the United States will require new baseload generating capacity. That capacity will be provided by large power plants that are designed and operated at essentially full power to meet the nation's demand for electricity. By the year 2000, 36 percent of baseload capacity will be more than thirty years old. Most credible electricity forecasts show that the United States will require significant additional new generating capacity by 2010, even at the slow projected growth of 1 to 2 percent.

   Nuclear energy must help provide this necessary generating capacity. U.S. nuclear plants are operating at record levels of safety and reliability and are contributing significantly to America's environmental protection needs, particularly in reducing atmospheric emissions.

- Second, the industry is taking initiatives to improve the regulatory process, that is, to allow each utility to retain the management responsibility for its facilities' safety, reliability, and efficiency. The nuclear industry has made significant progress in developing a new licensing and design certification process for new nuclear power plants. Appropriate constraints in litigation in the licensing process are key to economic common sense.

- The survival of the commercial nuclear energy industry in the United States is increasingly hampered by the lack of an integrated system for handling spent nuclear fuel. The DOE, which is responsible for nuclear waste disposal under the terms of the Nuclear Waste Policy Act of 1982, is continually frustrated in its efforts to structure a workable, long-term program for spent fuel storage and disposal.

   Since 1983, the consumers who use the electricity produced at our nuclear power plants have been paying a fee of one-mill-per-kilowatt-hour to fund federal management of spent nuclear fuel. Such consumer payments and obligations, with interest, now total approximately $11 billion. Electricity consumers have held up their side of the deal, but the Clinton administration has not.

More and more nuclear units will be forced to try to build additional on-site storage and, in the process, navigate through a minefield of state and local political opposition. More and more companies will be forced to explain to their state regulators why consumers should pay twice for spent fuel management—once to the federal government and again for expanded storage capacity at the plant sites.

In summary: We must review and overhaul our energy policies in order to have safe and reasonably priced energy supplies in the twenty-first century.

To this end we offer some recommendations:

Eliminate the Department of Energy. The function of the DOE with respect to the petroleum, coal, electricity, and nuclear industries is vague, and its research activities are redundant. All these programs should be phased out and the Federal Energy Regulatory Commission (FERC) should become a truly independent agency. The petroleum reserves and the power-marketing administrations should be sold to the private sector.

All of the department's defense-related activities should be transferred to another agency, possibly the Department of Defense. Its remaining activities should be transferred to the appropriate federal agency, privatized, or abolished.

Federal oil and gas resources. The responsible development of America's oil and gas resources should be encouraged. Energy security as a continuing national goal cannot be ignored or deferred. We must make energy security a national objective. For example, the coastal plain of the Arctic National Wildlife Refuge (ANWR), with its evidence of immense oil and gas reserves, should be opened to oil and gas exploration.

Oil and gas exploration in the ANWR is sought after by Alaskan citizens who depend on natural resource activities for their livelihoods. Careful development of these reserves with full environmental safeguards can both secure economic prosperity for the people of Alaska and ensure adequate energy for the nation as a whole.

Past efforts to develop Alaskan oil assets have proven that it can be done without lasting harm to the land mass. Movement of oil across Alaskan land, for example, has been incident-free and, in some instances, beneficial to the wildlife that exists near the pipeline.

Deregulate electric and gas utilities. Although we tend to take it for granted, electricity is essential to the way Americans live and work. Not incidentally, electric service is a significant element in the cost of doing business and, thus, its price affects our nation's competitiveness.

The generation, transmission, and distribution of electricity has traditionally been a closely regulated endeavor. It has been generally assumed that generating electric power and delivering it to homes and businesses was most reliable and cost-effective when handled by a single company. So-called natural monopolies utilities are obligated to provide electric service to anyone in a given area. In exchange, the companies are given exclusive franchises (by state and local governments). This system has worked well for years. But now, with technological advances, substantial competition is possible and indeed desirable in the industry—particularly in the construction and operation of power plants.

Certain laws enacted in recent years have been very effective in increasing competition in the generation and sale of power. For example, the Energy Policy Act of 1992 has increased competition among power suppliers by requiring utilities to provide access, under certain circumstances, to transmission lines for buyers and sellers to transport power. In 1995, the FERC proposed a regulation that would require all utilities to provide this transmission access by a certain date to all eligible buyers and sellers in the wholesale, interstate markets.

The net benefits of electric utility deregulation have been estimated to range from $80 to $100 billion per year.[7] That is almost $400 per year for every man, woman, and child in the United States. But more needs to be done to realize the full potential of competition and customer choice. All willing buyers and sellers of electricity should have nondiscriminatory access to transmission and distribution, and all utility and nonutility generators should be deregulated. The FERC's open access transmission initiative addresses only wholesale sales. Several states are considering allowing retail customers the same privilege.

As competition increases in power sales, and as customers and power suppliers receive open access to each other, the need to regulate the prices of such sales will disappear. The deregulation of electric power may occur through federal and state regulatory action, but it might require legislative action as well.

The competition among power sellers should be fair and equal. This means that government should get out of the business of supplying electricity. Federal agencies that market power should be dismantled and their assets sold to the highest bidders. State and municipal power agencies should not enjoy federal subsidies (such as exemptions from taxes) that their privately-owned counterparts do not enjoy. To use an overused metaphor, this playing field needs to be leveled.

Federal statutes that artificially constrain potential competition should be repealed. These include the Public Utility Holding Company Act of 1935 (PUHCA), which limits the kinds of products and services that may be offered by certain utilities, as well as the geographic markets in which they may compete; and the Public Utility Regulatory Policies Act of 1978, which forces utilities to buy power from certain power plants. Market forces may necessitate renegotiating many existing contracts; the government need not and should not interfere in this process. PUHCA repeal should precede other actions to increase competition so the few companies that are covered by the PUHCA are not disadvantaged by the broader deregulation efforts.

With these and other changes, the benefits of market competition will be brought to the electric service industry, to its customers, and to the economy. This means that customers—individuals and businesses—will be able to choose their power supplier and enjoy the fruits of competition among those suppliers. The result will be an increased supply of electricity at prices consumers can afford to pay.

Restructure tax policy. Federal tax policy should be structured so as to help revitalize the domestic oil and gas industry, increase jobs and tax revenues, and reduce our dependence on foreign energy. Production by new and existing marginal oil and gas wells should be encouraged. Ordinary and necessary expenses incurred in oil and gas exploration and production should be appropriately recognized as current deductions.

Nuclear energy. With nuclear energy providing about 20 percent of the electricity generated in the United States, the government's regulation of the industry must be based on reason and fairness. For instance, it has been almost a decade and a half since the enactment of the federal Nuclear Waste Policy Act of 1982, and we have very little to show for it. Utility ratepayers have been assessed $11 billion in accordance with that act, and yet the federal government lags far behind in meeting the required establishment of suitable nuclear waste facilities. The regulation of licensing and design certification procedures for new nuclear power plants should be simplified and standardized.

Renewable energy. Renewable energy resources can make a substantial contribution to American energy and security. The development and advancement of competitive renewable energy technologies are in the national interest. These resources include hydropower, photovoltaic, solar thermal, wind turbine, geothermal, biomass, and ocean energy. With demand for electricity expected to climb 26 percent by 2010, these renewable resources will be important to our future.

Direct government support for the development of renewable energy technologies may be difficult to sustain objectively, but Congress should at least eliminate legislative and regulatory roadblocks to the private sector's investment in developing these resources. Congress, for example, can deregulate small hydropower facilities and thus encourage investment in them.

In general, federal policies should be changed to include greater reliance on cost-benefit analysis, risk assessments to establish objective priorities, peer review by competent scientists, and flexibility in application. Regulatory accountability should be required so that we are provided with honest measurements of the impact of regulation on the economy and the taxpayer. Property rights must be respected. Further discussion of these issues is included in *Agenda's* Environment chapter (chapter 5).

America's natural and energy resources are varied and abundant. We believe we have set forth economically and environmentally sound ways to use these resources so as to benefit all Americans. In particular, we believe that our many commonsense recommendations, if promulgated, will result in the best possible utilization of our vast resources.

II

REVITALIZING FAMILIES, INDIVIDUAL SECURITY, AND RESPONSIBILITY

———————————————

7

Welfare and Federal Housing Policy

If you look at one factor that most correlates with crime, it's not poverty,
it's not employment, it's not education. It's the absence of the father in the
family.

—Former U.S. Attorney General William Barr

★

OUR WELFARE POLICY HAS BEEN A DISASTER. Liberals insist
that we don't actually spend all that much on it. Yes, they admit that the
system might benefit from some tinkering. But, they inevitably add, the only
people who speak against welfare are people who don't want to help the
poor. They are wrong. What they adamantly refuse to acknowledge, either
through genuine blindness or sheer demagoguery, is that welfare is harmful—in many, many ways.

Only two decades ago, those who warned that the deterioration of family
life would undermine civil society were apt to be dismissed as worrywarts,
if not kooks. Today, on the contrary, their insight is downright trendy.

Americans spent $324 billion on welfare in 1993, the last year for which
figures are available. The federal government spent more than $234 billion
of this; much of the rest was state expenditures on services mandated by
Washington. The United States disbursed $71.5 billion in monthly welfare
checks. Another $36 billion went for nutrition programs. Housing assis-
tance took $23.8 billion. Seven medical aid programs cost $155.8 billion,
and teen education programs cost $17.3 billion. Two dozen or so other pro-
grams for job training and social programs made up the remainder.[1]

Since 1965, Americans have "invested"—to use a word popular in certain circles—some $5.6 trillion in the fight against poverty. By any honest measure, this is greater in constant dollars than the cost of waging World War II. Welfare costs in 1992 and 1993 exceeded defense spending for the first time since the 1930s.[2]

Yet if American taxpayers were convinced that spending more money on welfare would help poor people, they would willingly provide it. But more money won't help, because it hasn't in the past. It has only brought an epidemic of dependency. We are beginning to recognize that government's response to poverty, except in the remarkably successful efforts to alleviate it among the elderly and disabled, can foster a "refugee mentality" among subsidy recipients. It destroys the initiative and self-reliance necessary to attain economic independence.

We who demand welfare reform do not do so because we don't care about people on welfare, but precisely because we do care about them. They are the victims of this disgraceful federal welfare state that entraps them. And their children are the prisoners of the war on poverty.

Heroically, though not altogether successfully, we have reduced the level of material poverty, especially when the value of in-kind assistance (such as housing costs) is taken into consideration. In 1990, the per-capita expenditures (adjusted for inflation) of the lowest income quintile of the U.S. population exceeded the per-capita income of the median American household of 1960. Malnutrition and hunger are rare. Indeed, people defined by government standards as poor average almost the same consumption of protein and vitamins as affluent people. Nearly 40 percent of the officially poor own their homes.[3]

Material poverty may have declined but it has been supplanted by what sociologists call "behavioral poverty." This unlovely term refers to the absence, in several million American households, of the habits, values, and patterns of conduct that make possible healthy and prosperous lives. Unfortunately, welfare is probably one of the root causes of behavioral poverty, which in turn breeds more such poverty. People who were raised in welfare families are three times more likely than other adults to go on welfare.

We believe that behavioral poverty is the reason our society is seeing a drastic decline in what economists call "labor force attachment." In 1960, before welfare became pandemic, nearly two-thirds of households among the lowest income quintile of the population were headed by people who worked. By 1991, that percentage was down to about one-third, and only 11 percent had household heads who worked full-time throughout the year.[4]

There is no mystery in these figures. The more we make personal effort optional, the less we will get of it. The classic study on this issue was conducted a quarter century ago by the Office for Economic Opportunity. The study, conducted between 1971 and 1978, was intended to demonstrate that generous welfare benefits would promote, rather than reduce, work effort. It showed exactly the opposite. The test cases, known to policy wonks as *SIME-DIME* for the Seattle and Denver Income Maintenance Experiments, demonstrated that an income guarantee produces a drastic reduction in work effort.

More recent research indicates the same. For example, an August 1993 study conducted by Dr. June O'Neill of Baruch College, now director of the Congressional Budget Office, backed up SIME-DIME.[5] A 50 percent increase in monthly Aid to Families with Dependent Children (AFDC) benefits and food stamp benefits, the study found, led to a 75 percent increase both in the number of people enrolling in AFDC and in the number of years they spent in that program. In short, as benefits rise, personal effort falls.

But a drastic reduction in labor force attachment isn't the only catastrophic result of welfare. AFDC, one of the most significant welfare programs, started out as a way to help widows and orphans but it has become, to put it bluntly, a guaranteed subsidy for illegitimacy. Approximately 4.5 million families receive AFDC, more than half of which will remain dependent for more than ten years, if we don't change the system.

But that isn't all. According to another study,[6] high AFDC benefits appear to contribute to the unemployment of young adult males by some 50 percent. Perhaps that is because they share indirectly in the AFDC benefits to women and children; perhaps it is because that benefit makes them economically irrelevant to household support. More ominously, perhaps it is because many of these young men themselves grew up in welfare households, which tend to lack role models and discipline.

Indeed the real horror of the welfare state is an intergenerational dependence that destroys society's most important unit: the family. However well-intended welfare might have been, we are burying our heads in the sand if we don't admit that today in America our government advocates welfare policies that are antifamily. AFDC is one of the worst offenders. AFDC inadvertently promotes single-parent households—a particularly thought-provoking phenomenon in light of a 1991 study of 13,986 inmates, which found that 43 percent grew up in single-family homes.[7] (Thirty-nine percent had lived with their mothers; 4 percent had lived with their fathers.)

Although welfare families are families at risk, we can't leave this subject without talking about the American family in general—rich families, poor families, and middle-income families. It is not only welfare families that suffer from illegitimacy; it is not only welfare families that are headed by single parents. Out-of-wedlock births—even the term rings old-fashioned!—and single-parent families are well on their way to becoming the accepted norm in our society.

Not only has the stigma of illegitimacy weakened among middle-class families, but divorce is now often viewed as the norm: "Hey, if you don't like being married, you can pick up and leave" seems to be a prevalent mindset. There are 1.3 million divorces each year in the United States. But divorce is often the recipe for economic catastrophe for a family.[8] Families fall into dependency as a result of divorce. Many recipients of AFDC are among the "newly poor," that is, families whose middle-class way of life came crashing down amid the ruins of a marriage. And along with that sudden economic dependency, children of divorce often experience the problems associated with illegitimacy. One example suffices: Children in divorced families are twice as likely to fail in school.

The pattern that devastated many black communities in the past three decades is now being replicated in other neighborhoods. First, the already weakened stigma against illegitimacy disappears. Then out-of-wedlock births and single-parent households become an accepted norm. That releases young males from their traditional roles as husbands and providers. Their work ethic withers, or it is never inculcated in the first place. Both joblessness and underemployment rise sharply. All the while, the absence of strong role models leads to violent and antisocial behavior. What was once a poor community becomes a welfare wasteland.

This is a nightmare scenario, but it is not at all unrealistic. That is why Congressional Republicans have brought to the floor of the House and Senate the most far-reaching welfare reform legislation in memory. This effort has combined two complementary approaches to the problems outlined here.

Both approaches start from the axiom that the present welfare system cannot be fixed with further tinkering along the lines of the 1988 welfare reform, which actually led to a significant increase in public assistance rolls.

We believe a seismic change is in order. We believe that compassion and practicality are necessary, but above all we believe in upholding the American family as a unit capable of inculcating its children with the qualities that make them able to lead challenging and independent lives.

We offer proposals—for families that now rely on welfare and for American families in general:

Both approaches challenge the basic premises of the welfare mess. These premises are (1) that welfare should be a legal entitlement; (2) that welfare must be available indefinitely, without time limits; (3) that little can be done to reverse the trend toward single-family households resulting from out-of-wedlock births; (4) that dependency can be reduced while welfare is made more attractive with side benefits like job training and child care; (5) that a multiplicity of programs is necessary to serve the needs of poor people; and (6) that the federal government knows best.

Hence, today's real welfare reformers propose to (1) end the entitlement status of AFDC and related programs; (2) impose time limits for welfare eligibility; (3) stop subsidizing illegitimacy; (4) enforce work requirements; (5) replace an array of federal programs with a few simple block grants to the states; and (6) return decision-making regarding welfare to state and local government, which is to say, state and local taxpayers.

Within that consensus agenda, there is considerable room for debate. One approach would federally mandate a reform agenda for the states, especially with regard to illegitimacy. Another approach gives priority to prying control of welfare out of the hands of official Washington, on the theory that, to make reform last, it must be shaped and implemented on the local level.

We consider these approaches two sides of the same coin. However it lands at the end of the legislative process, it will represent the hard currency of real welfare reform: an unprecedented campaign against behavioral poverty. Over the long run, the success of that endeavor will be crucial for a renewal of family life in America.

Our vision for the farther future must contain more than today's necessary strategies to make welfare work better. Indeed, we must question whether public assistance programs designed for the middle of the twentieth century can, or should, be adapted to the radically changed circumstances of the century ahead. At some point, we will have to at least try, on the state level, entirely new approaches to helping the needy.

One approach sorely in need of testing is to entirely replace the current pattern of aid from government to individuals with a system based on local private institutions. Using public resources, those entities would deliver the services, as well as the cash, that now flow through government channels. In most cases, they would be religious organizations, which we have thus far discovered are the strongest institutions to hold together low-income neighborhoods. The result would be a melding of government support and private philanthropy, material assistance and ethical rejuvenation. All of which, we would contend, are essential components for the revolutionary changes we seek.

We might even look into the idea of replacing welfare, in special cases, with loans. That would be particularly appropriate in cases when a single-parent household falls into dependency as a result of divorce. Here, the problem is not behavioral, but rather a sudden economic blow that dislocates a family's finances. In place of the rigidity of AFDC, a repayable loan program might well be more appropriate.

The challenge of renewing family life is not restricted to any one segment of our population. It faces us all, whatever our familial status, for the consequences of family breakdown ravage not just households but entire communities. We all pay the price—literally and figuratively—because there is hardly a social pathology alive—from violent crime to drug abuse and falling test scores—that is not directly related to the decline of the American family.

Our focus thus far upon poor families, whether on welfare or in danger of it, should not obscure the larger picture of our familial future. The most important pro-family policy is always economic growth. As the 1988

Republican platform put it, "From freedom comes opportunity; from opportunity comes growth; from growth comes progress." That means for everyone.

Now, when it comes to defending the family, officials across the political spectrum talk a good fight. What used to be a marginal position—that the stability of the home is the foundation of public order and economic progress—has somehow become a consensus position. Everyone professes to want the same result, although there remains enormous disagreement about how to reach it.

And with good reason. One threshold question is the extent to which the family life of the American people is even the business of government. And if so, at what level, and to what degree?

We start with this not entirely arbitrary prescription: Because strong families are indeed the foundation of a strong society, the protection and promotion of family life is a valid, in fact a necessary, task of government. At the same time, we have little reason to assume that the practices and procedures of Big Government, which have brought ruin to so many aspects of American society, would do otherwise when focused upon the American home. In other words, we recognize both an obvious need for policies supportive of the family and the equally obvious reason to approach them with caution.

Indeed, much of what we envision as a pro-family policy by the government is negative: Government should simply stop doing things that undermine or discourage family life. Why, one might ask, was there no perceived need for a pro-family agenda in, say, 1952? The answer is that, back then, government was not actively hostile to the traditional two-parent family. It did not onerously tax most families, did not penalize marriage in the tax code, did not subsidize single parenthood, did not use public schooling to undermine parental values and authority, and did not fund organizations inimical to parental rights.

When all that changed—and the details of governmental offenses against the family, as well as against common sense, are too familiar to need repetition here—families fought back. Hence the remarkable upsurge, beginning in the mid-1970s and accelerating to the present, of what for want of a better term is called *social conservatism*.

We have seen a consensus, crossing ideological lines, that a tightening of divorce laws would be in the best interest of practically everybody, but especially of children. We contend that this is not a federal enterprise but note that thoughtful men and women of both parties in state legislatures are already considering ways to promote family unity and discourage the casual dissolution of family structure.

We believe that it is crucial that the components of the liberal "nanny state" that infringe upon the autonomy of the family should be dismantled. A radical reform of the federal tax code is a good place to start. We believe that America's families will benefit from adoption of (1) a balanced budget amendment to the Constitution, (2) the regulatory reform revolution, and (3) replacing the current tax code with a simple and pro-family method of collecting revenue.

This triad is a liberation for American families, whatever their current economic status. While it does not take the place of the hard decisions that lie ahead about AFDC, food stamps, and the rest, it does explain the larger context—the philosophical, if you will—in which welfare reform must be pursued. Rightly understood and rightly undertaken, welfare reform is a labor of love.

FEDERAL HOUSING POLICY[9]

While noble intentions may have ruled at the outset, when America launched its first federal housing assistance programs in the 1930s, the result of the government's involvement in the field of housing has become a massive and pervasive human as well as budgetary problem. The stark evidence can be seen in the infamous cases of the public housing projects in Newark; St. Louis; Chicago; Washington, D.C.; and other cities.

Our housing policy is a failure on a number of levels. Public housing is the most obvious disaster. Many complexes, as everyone knows, are demonstrably hellholes. Families become hopelessly trapped in public housing for several generations. Some families, especially in the older housing projects, have lived there for as many as four generations. Public housing is a major financial drain on every taxpayer as well.

Another level of budget disaster lies in the privately-owned subsidized housing—the so-called Section 8 housing. Here the government helps individuals and families by providing rental assistance in various forms of cash payments directly to the owner of a housing project. This, too, increases the burden on the American taxpayer.

We believe it's important to reconsider eligibility for government help with housing. We also believe that there are two categories of citizens who have a moral claim on us for housing: the low-income elderly and the handicapped, those who through no fault of their own are financially unable to provide themselves with a "safe, decent, and sanitary" place to live. Americans are quite willing to ensure that people in these two categories have housing. But beyond this, we must reexamine the fundamental assumption of *all* our subsidized housing programs. Low-income housing isn't the only aspect of our government housing programs that requires a review. We must think about our housing policies overall, as they relate to special loans and tax breaks for middle-class citizens.

We must ask some basic questions:

- Starting from the premise that one of the bedrock goals of the American citizen is to own a home, what role, if any, should the federal government play in achieving this goal?
- When some individuals cannot afford to purchase a home, or elect not to, what role should the federal government play either in creating new "affordable" housing or, alternatively, giving financial assistance to enable people to pay market prices?
- To what extent, if any, can taxpayers afford to continue to support others in paying for a place to live?
- To which individuals, if any, should we provide taxpayer assistance so that they can find and pay for housing?
- Our current policy—everything from housing for very low-income families to ensuring loans to middle-class veterans—is enormously complex. Federal housing assistance is now provided across a wide spectrum of agencies. In addition to the Department of Housing and Urban Development (HUD), housing programs in one form or another can be found in the Department of Agriculture, the Department of Veterans Affairs, the Department of the Treasury, the Department of Defense, the

Department of the Interior, the Department of Transportation, the Department of State, the Department of Human Services, the Federal Home Loan Bank System, the Federal Deposit Insurance Corporation, the Federal National Mortgage Association, the Federal Home Loan Mortgage Corporation, and most recently the Resolution Trust Corporation. Many of these programs are redundant, overlapping with the other programs.

Federal involvement in housing is very expensive. At the moment, HUD spends more discretionary funds than any other federal entity in housing subsidies. Its growth of 9 percent per year in discretionary spending is exceeded only by the Commerce Department's 12 percent increase. HUD's discretionary-assisted housing outlays have grown from $165 million in 1962 to an estimated $23.7 billion in 1994![10]

By the end of fiscal year 1994, HUD had assumed a total of $223 billion in unexpended budget authority—one quarter of a trillion dollars you and I owe—in obligatory future Section 8 payments, all of which have been appropriated in prior years. Since 1980, this rate of growth has more than tripled overall domestic discretionary spending. Fully 10 percent of all domestic discretionary outlays are devoted to housing assistance, compared with the 4 percent it consumed in 1980 or the less than 1 percent of the 1962 budget.[11]

How did we get into this fix? The housing problems of the 1930s produced a housing policy that led ultimately to the vast array of programs we have today. In 1932, the financial collapse of the banking industry resulted in widespread unemployment, and Congress responded by creating the Reconstruction Finance Corporation. The idea was to grant federal loans to private enterprise, which in turn would provide housing to low-income families. During the same time, Congress created the Federal Home Loan Bank System to ensure that savings and loan associations would be able to borrow money at below market rate.

Between 1932 and 1934, a series of legislative reactions to the economic problems in the country gave rise to the belief that more federal support was necessary because many homeowners were defaulting on their loans. At that time banks were only offering short-term credit to home buyers, but very high periodic payments were required and many people simply couldn't keep up with their payments. Congress moved to ease this problem—to stabilize the housing credit markets and protect homeowners—by creating several new credit and regulatory agencies, specifically the 1934 Federal Housing Administration (FHA).

While these efforts proved beneficial, they could not help individuals who did not have the money to buy a home. In 1937, as today, there are some people who simply can't get together the capital required for home ownership. To remedy this perceived problem, the United States Public Housing Authority was created, thus establishing the concept of providing apartments for low-income families. This milestone legislation marked the beginning of a new era in housing policy and one which has proved to be a costly generosity on the part of the American taxpayer. The anomaly created by this legislation was that, in many cases, the families who received assistance in the form of brand-new public housing apartments had better living quarters than the taxpayers who paid for them.

Our concept of the role of government took another giant step in 1949 with a new National Housing Act. It proclaimed the goal of a "decent and suitable environment for every American family." (The act originated over concern that many American homes lacked indoor plumbing.)

But, of course, government's involvement in housing didn't stop there. When the Department of Housing and Urban Development was created in 1965, the federal government's mission was defined neither in terms of providing housing units for those who couldn't save enough money for a down payment on a home, nor in providing public housing apartments for low-income families. It became a much larger mission, and one the federal taxpayer would find increasingly painful to fund. Housing policy became a form of social engineering, directing not only where people should live, but what kind of places they should live in, who could live there, and how much they should pay in rent. Federal government personnel became the decision makers of how we house each other. This was the first law that made housing seem like an entitlement.

A whole new idea of the role of government in the housing market had developed by the beginning of this decade. Government had become even more expansive. The Cranston-Gonzalez National Affordable Housing Act of 1990 stated: "The Congress affirms the national goal that every American family be able to afford a decent home in a suitable environment." It became liberal dogma that federally assisted housing is assistance in some form to some segment of the population to provide some individuals with some place to live.

In 1974, when Congress launched a new program that would radically change the delivery of housing, the government dug itself deeper into an ever-more-expensive hole. The Housing and Community Development Act of 1974 further eroded the stability of public housing by creating the Section 8 subsidy program. This forced public housing authorities to compete with private enterprise. Prior to 1974, the federal government had financed a reasonably large number of leased housing programs to assist lower-income families through the use of interest rate subsidies. The 1974 statute made leased housing the primary vehicle as opposed to home ownership aid, conventional public housing construction, or the interest rate subsidy programs. The government opted to finance the most expensive form of housing subsidies—the projects themselves.

Under the newly designated Section 8 program, HUD contracted directly with the owners of existing housing and newly constructed facilities and agreed to pay the difference between a specified rent and a percentage of the tenant's income, which was tied to the project itself. The program was to be administered by HUD-area offices, by local public housing agencies, and by state housing finance agencies through a series of contractual relationships. The problem with this new program was that the tenants moved out of public housing and into brand-new units, some with swimming pools and balconies, yet they paid the same rent as before. This left the poorest of the poor in the public housing projects, a condition that exists today. It also left the taxpayer paying for apartment projects which in many cases had more amenities than their own homes. It was like buying Pontiacs for people who couldn't afford to buy a car.

In the original Section 8 program, two categories of projects were to be assisted and provided by the owner, for example, "new construction" and "substantial rehabilitation." Each year, between 1974 and 1982, Congress appropriated vast sums of money to support these programs. And each year, the new funding levels depended not on whether the housing was needed, but rather on political considerations. The Democrat-controlled Congress gave in to pleas of low-income housing advocacy groups who depended on this continued funding to justify their existence.

In 1981, to encourage the development of low-income housing, Congress enacted the Economic Recovery Tax Act. Under this act, tax benefits were given to real estate developers and owners who provided housing for low- to moderate-income individuals. This measure was used in conjunction with Section 8, and with the two combined, the production of new housing projects grew significantly.

In 1983 Congress finally agreed with the Reagan administration that the Section 8 program was too costly. The Housing and Urban-Rural Recovery Act of 1983 repealed the authorization for Section 8—for example, new construction and substantial rehabilitation—but left other moderate rehabilitation and elderly projects (Section 202). Most importantly, conservatives switched from project-based assistance under Section 8 to housing vouchers and certificates, or a tenant-based subsidy program. The tenants could choose their own apartment with a voucher or certificate—they finally had a choice!

In 1986, Congress enacted the Tax Reform Act, which did away with the tax incentives. Instead, it created the Low Income Housing Tax Credit. But since Congress had repealed Section 8's new construction and substantial rehabilitation, the only housing program that could be used with the tax credit was the Section 8 Mod Rehab program, created in 1978 and later defunded. After much lobbying by housing advocacy groups, the housing tax credit program was expanded to work with other programs, and is still being used today. This program should be abolished since it is costly and a remarkably inefficient way to produce housing.

As this housing history shows, our housing policy has evolved into a federal policy—to provide subsidy. The word *subsidy* can mean a lot of things: it can mean federal funds that are used to pay for the construction and/or rehabilitation of dwelling units; it can mean tax benefits in the form of income tax deductions to individuals and entities; it can mean bonds that are exempt from income taxation; it can mean federal funds to pay an owner of a project the difference between the market rent and what the occupant of the dwelling can afford; and it can mean direct payments to individuals who need economic assistance to pay for the cost of housing. There are other, more esoteric subsidies. But no matter the name or form, the funds come from the income of the taxpayer.

The primary problem in providing federal housing for particular segments of the American public in most markets has little to do with the available supply of housing. Rent controls and overly restrictive zoning ordinances have the effect of substantially altering market forces and should be abolished since they tend to distort the supply of housing in local markets.

But that aside, the primary problem in housing has to do with the difference in the price that private enterprise commands for housing and the price people can afford to pay. At its core, all of the issues concerning the availability of "affordable, decent, and suitable" housing become discussions about wealth, or the lack thereof, which inevitably leads to discussions about poverty and welfare, to whether individuals should be *entitled* to housing. We assert they should not.

The uncontrolled growth of housing subsidy programs puts an inordinate burden on the American taxpayer, who is made to pay the costs of new dwellings for individuals who, in many cases, could become self-sufficient. Subsidy programs that provide project-based housing assistance of any nature, individual housing voucher subsidy programs, HUD grants for housing production and rehabilitation, federal grants for community economic development, and all public housing programs should be consolidated into a single program. This includes all federal government housing programs in any agency. The solution to the "housing problem" is not more taxpayer money. The solution is to lower taxes, streamline programs, and make rational decisions about who should be housed at the trough of public funding. And this decision should be up to the taxpayer. This is best accomplished at the state level—not in Washington.

The uncontrolled growth of the federal role in housing must be stopped.

We offer some proposals.

STREAMLINE PROGRAMS
Home Ownership

All programs that offer insurance for single-family housing should be consolidated into a single program to be administered by a single agency. It should take over all insuring activities of VA, FMHA, HUD, and any other federally sponsored programs. Single-family, federally insured mortgage activities should be restricted to providing insurance for first-time home buyers on homes that sell for less than two times the local medium income and who are not served by private mortgage insurance.

The two government-sponsored agencies, the Federal National Mortgage Association and the Federal Home Loan Mortgage Corporation, are redundant and should be merged into one. These two entities are separate merely because of their existing constituencies. If consolidated, they would substantially reduce the potential exposure to the Treasury and the taxpayers.

As a means to stimulate home ownership, the interest portion of mortgage payments has been deductible from income and considered an important tax benefit. If we move to a flat tax or move away from income tax completely, this deduction may no longer be necessary. The reason is simple: If taxpayers get to keep more of their money out of the federal tax coffers, they will have more money to pay for housing—or whatever else they may choose.

The tax code has been used as a social engineering tool of liberals to manipulate housing supply and demand. While we strongly support the philosophy that families should be encouraged to become homeowners, using the tax code for this purpose is bad policy.

Local land-use regulations and zoning laws unnecessarily drive up the cost of housing as do local property taxes. We believe all forms of taxes on home ownership should be reduced and private property rights elevated to higher standing.

Section 8

We must reduce the federal obligation on the existing project-based Section 8 contracts. Thus the owners of Section 8 projects should have the right to cancel their Section 8 contract and be relieved of all government regulation. To protect the tenants, if an owner elects to cancel, all tenants in that project must be given Section 8 certificates. For nonelderly projects, the housing voucher should have a three-year, nonrenewable term and should be funded in an amount equal to the amount of subsidy currently being funded. The tenants can stay in the unit they occupy or they can seek other housing. For projects that house elderly and handicapped tenants, the housing certificate should be for the life of the tenant and should be funded in an identical manner as nonelderly tenants. Owners should be encouraged to make certain their tenants don't have to relocate.

For owners who don't elect to cancel Section 8, we believe the government must honor its commitments and continue to fund the Section 8 contracts until the agreed-to expiration date. The funding levels for the rents should be adjusted annually to reflect trends in inflation and local market conditions. These adjustments should be tied to a nationally recognized consumer price index, as adjusted for local market conditions, and not governed by subjective determinations of federal government officials. All remaining contractual project-based Section 8 funding should be consolidated into a single trust fund and managed by the Department of Treasury with oversight of the projects delegated to state housing finance agencies.

We should consolidate all governmentwide funds that provide rent subsidies into a single Housing and Economic Development Fund, then allocate the incremental new funds for these programs to the states in the form of block grants. Decisions on how to use the new funds should be left entirely to the discretion of state and local authorities. Ultimately, the block grants should be used to provide housing only to the elderly and the disabled.

For programs that are deemed mandatory—such as programs for the elderly and handicapped—or those that have as their base a government contract—such as Section 8—sufficient funds should be allocated to ensure their present viability but no new funding should be forthcoming. Programs that can be managed by state governments should be distributed to the states with sufficient funding until they can be eliminated or fully converted to other state programs. Any programs that have unfunded projects should be canceled immediately and unused appropriations returned to the Treasury.

Federal authorities should not determine how to prioritize the use of housing funds. States should decide whether to use the funds to modernize public housing or create additional housing rental assistance certificates, for whatever purposes innovative state and local officials and citizens find may suit their local housing demands.

The Federal Housing Administration

The Federal Housing Administration (FHA), created in 1934, insures mortgage lenders against the risk of default. It is essentially one of the world's largest insurance companies, operating with little change since its creation. Under its basic Section 203 programs, FHA has insured over 50 million home purchases. It covers mortgages with loan to value ratios of up to 97 percent, and maturities of up to thirty years. Maximum loan amounts vary by market area, with maximums currently ranging from $67,500 to $151,725.

FHA has been part of HUD since HUD's creation nearly thirty years ago, and it accounts for roughly half of HUD's approximately thirteen thousand employees—and probably at least 50 percent of its headaches. Since the private sector provides the bulk of single-family mortgage insurance and is a rapidly growing industry, FHA should compete with private mortgage insurers by becoming privatized and restricted to providing insurance only on those projects or houses that private mortgage insurance industry turns down.

By the summer of 1994, as project sponsors defaulted, some $7 billion of FHA-insured multifamily mortgages, almost a fifth of its total multifamily portfolio, had fallen into HUD's hands.[12] Foreclosure is expensive, and HUD incurs sizable debt service and management costs as a landlord. The best way to whittle down that dead weight is to auction off mortgages at market value. On March 28, 1995, HUD conducted an auction, and to the surprise of many, took in far more than it anticipated. It auctioned off 177 nonperforming multifamily mortgages on unsubsidized properties in the Southeast with unpaid balances totaling $907 million, from which it realized $710 million.[13]

The FHA should be privatized and in the future be limited to providing "gap": financing vehicles to finance multifamily apartment projects. These activities should be limited to giving assistance to elderly and handicapped tenants and should operate in conjunction with private forms of financing.

Furthermore, FHA should develop risk-sharing arrangements with mortgage bankers, commercial banks and thrifts, and state and local housing finance agencies to provide credit to the most difficult segments of both the single-family and multifamily market as defined by state agencies.

Public Housing

The area of housing policy requiring the most immediate attention is public housing. While Uncle Sam provides the money, local housing authorities own and control the projects. Our long-range goal should be to eliminate federal involvement in public housing completely. State and local governments should assume absolute control over, and responsibility for, the housing authorities in their jurisdictions. Until responsibility and funding are vested in one entity, the fiscal nightmare will worsen, and the housing stock will continue to deteriorate.

To accomplish this transition, the federal government must repeal the statute requiring that tenants pay 30 percent of their income for rent. This process of attracting income-earning tenants rather than welfare recipients already has begun; in February 1995, the New York City Housing Authority, the nation's largest, announced it would begin to give working people preference over welfare recipients. Currently, only .8 percent of the authority's applicants are working families. We must also repeal the statute that prohibits all but union members from working on projects. As a priority, we should enable tenants, nonprofit groups, and other interested parties to manage and buy units, thus returning to the original American dream of home ownership and creating a stable and more prosperous society.

Oversight and control of all public housing authorities should be transferred to state agencies, which would have the authority to deal with the project in any manner they deem reasonable, including selling, demolishing, or rehabilitating. States would have the authority to recapitalize projects and bring in private investors. Individual public housing authorities, state housing finance agencies, or for-profit managers would act as management agents for each of their projects.

And, above all, the choices for Americans concerning where they wish to live should not be controlled by a central government—those choices should be exercised individually and based on the realities of the free market. Individuals—not the federal government—are the solution to the housing problems.

8

Crime and Criminal Justice

When we neither punish nor reproach evildoers, we are ripping the foundations of justice from beneath new generations.
　　　　　　　　　　　　　　　　—Alexander Solzhenitsyn

★

CRIME AND PUNISHMENT are two morally linked concepts that have become almost totally disconnected in our society. The state, no longer the august dispenser of justice, has been transformed over the past thirty years into the Great Rehabilitator. While a vocal segment of our society embraces a "treatment" model for prisons, some judges now appear to regard themselves not as finders of fact or arbiters of the law but rather as ministers of healing.

And what is the result of these seemingly humane developments? A more humane society? More justice for our citizens? Unfortunately, exactly the reverse is true. Look at contemporary America. Since 1961, we have witnessed a doubling of the murder rate, a quadrupling of the rate for rape, and a quintupling of the robbery rate. Our cities are less safe than ever.

Vicious felons are released again and again into our communities, as ordinary citizens watch in amazement. Seventy percent of the violent crimes in this country are committed by only 6 percent of our population—yet for some reason we cannot keep people in prison where they belong. We read of murders committed by people who were freed from prison years before they had served their sentences. The system is being used to coddle a criminal class while the courts are flooded with frivolous suits. Throughout

America, innocent people suffer and die because the connection of crime to punishment has been severed.

As for the criminals, they not only do not respect the law, they do not fear it. They know the loopholes and the "technicalities" by which our courts often set the guilty free. They are only too aware that the federal government has erected barriers to the pursuit and punishment of wrongdoers. One of the worst of these barriers is the infamous "exclusionary rule," which dictates that "tainted" evidence, no matter how crucial, cannot be used to convict.

The good faith exception to the exclusionary rule needs to be expanded to ensure that when police gather evidence in the reasonable belief that their actions comply with the Fourth Amendment, that evidence will be admissible in federal trials even if it later turns out that an unintended violation of the Fourth Amendment occurred.

For example, a search of an automobile "incident" to a valid arrest of the driver is one of the number of warrantless searches that the Supreme Court has previously held to be valid under the Constitution. So, when the police search a vehicle incident to an arrest and find drugs in the car, that is a valid search. But if, unbeknown to the arresting officers, the arrest warrant is technically invalid for any number of reasons, the drugs found in the car can be deemed tainted evidence and are not allowed to be used to convict the criminal. Certainly, it is not right for the criminal to go free on this technicality. Liberal lawyers are fond of reminding us that such absurd situations are "the price we must pay for our precious liberties." But the republic functioned quite well for its first 170 years without the exclusionary rule, which in fact is a gross distortion of the Fourth Amendment's proscription against "unreasonable searches and seizures." The Fourth Amendment says nothing about excluding evidence on a technicality. This last idea was the contribution of lofty liberal legal experts and misguided judges.

A sense of futility has developed. Every now and then, noting in the polls that voters are alarmed by crime, Washington flies into a righteous frenzy with another crime bill full of tough talk, hefty grants, and big promises. Among the more futile of Washington's assaults on crime are the occasional gun control bill and Bill Clinton's unfulfilled promise to put "100,000 more officers" on our streets. The crime bill signed by President Clinton on

September 13, 1994, is another example of federal government overspending while refusing to tackle the real problem. This particular crime bill, for example, includes funding for basketball leagues and even issues federal requirements governing youth basketball participation. No wonder our citizens continue to feel unsafe. No wonder criminals scoff at the law.

Although crime is primarily a local matter, the federal government does have a role to play. Unfortunately, today the U.S. Department of Justice has strayed from its constitutional warrant to prosecute serious federal crimes, especially violent crimes such as terrorism and organized crime, in favor of promoting a liberal agenda. We find teams of Department of Justice lawyers leaning on businessmen about racial quotas, engaging in protracted congressional redistricting cases, and bringing the full force of government to bear against nonviolent abortion protesters who are acting in good conscience.

During the civil rights struggle of the fifties and sixties, the Department of Justice played a crucial and noble part in prosecuting those who practiced racial discrimination. That era, however, is largely past. Today's ideological crusades by Justice lawyers have more to do with fashionable political positions than with justice.

One example is the use of the "independent counsel," created by Congress in the aftermath of Watergate to prosecute certain specified executive branch officials. This system has reversed accepted procedures in the criminal justice system. Congress targets one or more defendants who are alleged to have committed real or fancied crimes. Then an independent counsel is appointed, unsupervised by the Justice Department, who accumulates a large staff of eager attorneys out to earn their stripes (and enhance their prospects for future employment). Instead of prosecuting crimes, the independent counsels begin prosecuting, and persecuting, people. Unlimited budgets, hidden (or sometimes not so hidden) political agendas, and media hype place individuals who thought they were just doing their jobs in danger of jail time. Criminalizing politics is no way to deal with political opponents.

On another front, oddly enough, the Clinton Justice Department has seemed half-hearted in the pursuit of something that really is its duty: narcotics trafficking. Astonishingly, the Clinton Office of Drug Control Strategy has focused its efforts on such important matters as the labeling on Royal Crown Cola and the packaging of Big League Chew bubble gum. The feds contend that R.C. Cola's new "draft" label looks like beer and that Big League's bubble gum pouches resemble those for chewing tobacco and thus ultimately will lead children into drug usage. This, in part, is what counts for the Clinton administration's war on drugs.

Nor is the federal judiciary exempt from some of the blame for our current predicament. Here are the people who, at the end of the day, stand between society and the criminal. Federal judges bear as great a trust as a government confers. The Constitution gives them unlimited terms. Federal judges are accountable to no one, answering only to their consciences and the laws they are charged with applying.

To put it bluntly, a number have proved unworthy of that trust. They have wandered far afield from their real responsibilities. Here a judge might order prisoners released because of crowding, there another might order huge expenditures to improve the prison library. And then there was the federal judge who found that one inmate's religious rights would be violated unless authorities provided him with the accoutrements to practice Satanism in his cell.

Another root of our crime problem is the way some members of the federal judiciary have reinterpreted how we apply the Constitution. Before the 1930s, the federal judiciary decided constitutional issues through a review of the original intent of the nation's founders who drafted the Constitution. This might involve study of such sources as the records of the Constitutional Convention or *The Federalist Papers*. The judicial branch understood that it was responsible for interpreting and applying the Constitution and the laws rather than legislating from the bench.

But this limited view of judicial power changed radically, beginning during the Great Depression, when the White House and Congress argued that the country's economic woes were caused by government inaction. The Supreme Court itself became more activist. The doctrine of original intent gave way to the stated goal of making the Constitution a living and breathing document. Under such a view the Constitution is a work in progress, to be shaped and molded by judges and academics.

As the Court remolded the Constitution, the "rights" of those convicted of crimes multiplied. Tragically, new "rights" theories have made a mockery of one of the ancient concepts of jurisprudence, that of habeas corpus.

Habeas corpus originally meant that the authorities had to show that they had the right to hold somebody in confinement. It was a safeguard against arbitrary imprisonment. Today, as it is interpreted, it means that convicted felons may file an unlimited number of petitions for habeas corpus to the federal courts. Indeed the prisoner convicted in state court may repeatedly petition a federal court for habeas corpus, claiming that he is being held in violation of the Constitution. The Supreme Court has ruled that the prisoner is entitled to have the federal court make its own determination without being bound by the state determination. This encourages piecemeal litigation of issues that should have been settled in the state court.

Amid this moral chaos, Republican leaders must speak with a clear and unequivocal voice. Our sympathies lie with the victims. Our responsibilities lie also with them and not with the predators among us. Yes, we want a society that offers hope and a second chance to all, but often we must recognize that government is wrongly miscast as the Great Rehabilitator.

If a government fails in its duty to protect its citizens, nothing else it does in the end will matter. A primary trust will have been broken. A government that tolerates or excuses crime does not deserve our faith. We assert that it is time to restore the link between crime and punishment.

We offer some proposals:

THREE–STRIKES–YOU'RE–OUT

Republicans believe in second chances, but not at the expense of public safety and common sense. There is nothing more infuriating to a victim of crime than to learn that the perpetrator of the crime has a long "rap sheet" revealing multiple prior crimes. How many times, ask such victims, must the criminal justice system determine that a person is a danger to the community before the public will be protected? For the relatively small percentage of all criminals who habitually prey upon communities in the most violent manner, life imprisonment is the only way to protect society. Several states have in recent years enacted "three-strikes-you're-out" laws or repeat offender statutes, following the lead of Washington state in 1993. In those states, many chronic predators are off the streets for good—saving hundreds of lives in the future.

ABOLITION OF PAROLE

If there is one thing citizens want from their government, it is honesty. For decades, however, liberal parole policies have returned incarcerated dangerous criminals to the streets long before they have served their actual sentences. The average prison sentence for murder, for example, is eighteen years (a shocking statistic in itself) while the average time served is less than *half* of that sentence. Overall, violent offenders spend only 38 percent of their sentences behind bars. As a result, tens of thousands of violent crimes are committed each year by criminals who should still be in prison under a previous sentence.

"Truth-in-sentencing" is a simple, yet vital reform—it requires criminals to serve at least 85 percent of the sentences they receive. A growing number of states, led by Virginia in 1994 under the governorship of George Allen, are now abolishing or curtailing parole to make criminals serve their full sentences. Congress should continue to encourage states in this crime prevention effort by assisting them financially to maintain sufficient prison space to keep criminals off the streets.

ALTERNATIVE SENTENCING

One of the great liberal myths is that there are too many criminals behind bars. They argue that many nonviolent offenders would be better off in alternative sentences, thereby freeing bed space for the truly violent criminals. The truth is that 93 percent of state prison inmates are either convicted violent offenders or repeat offenders. Releasing these offenders into alternative programs jeopardizes the legitimacy of our criminal justice system and the safety of the public. It is important to note that most offenders are already receiving a form of alternative sentencing: of the 5.1 million offenders in the criminal justice system, almost 75 percent are on probation or parole. Forty percent of all convicted *violent* offenders receive little or no time behind bars.

Many alternatives to incarceration have failed miserably in deterring nonviolent offenders from future criminal activity and from holding them accountable. For example, boot camps have been effective with certain types of offenders but they are not a panacea. Nevertheless, meaningful sanctions must exist for nonviolent offenders when prison sentences may not be a smart or efficient use of resources. But alternative correctional programs must be sensible.

THE ROLE OF THE FEDERAL GOVERNMENT

Over 95 percent of all violent crime in this country is handled by state and local law enforcement. While the unacceptably high rate of violent crime may argue for a more expanded federal role, it is preferable to consider how federal law enforcement authorities can best assist their state and local counterparts without "federalizing" the fight against crime. Indeed, the federal government has provided invaluable technical, financial, and tactical support to state and local law enforcement for many years. With regard to financial assistance, precious federal resources should be spent where they can have maximum impact, such as block grants for local governments to fight crime and grants to help states to acquire adequate prison space.

In addition, federal law enforcement should ensure the vigorous and effective enforcement of federal laws, while serving as a model for state-based reform. When tough federal laws are used against hard-core violent offenders, local law enforcement benefits. In addition to these forms of assistance, the federal government can be particularly helpful in eliminating federal interference with state and local criminal justice systems. Rather than expanding the federal role, federal intrusion in state and local law enforcement should be eliminated. These reforms begin with getting federal judges out of the business of running state and local jails and into the business of reforming current federal laws that needlessly delay the imposition of the death penalty at the state level.

GUN CONTROL

There are few issues that better illustrate the difference between Republicans and liberal Democrats on the issue of crime than gun control. At the heart of the matter is a debate about personal responsibility. Gun control proponents insist that the easy availability of firearms causes crime. The American people know better. They understand that crime is the result of criminals making wrong moral choices, and that gun control does not work. They know that even if the federal government set out to disarm every American, it could never prevent criminals from getting guns. After all, criminals, by definition, are those who operate outside the law. One landmark study on this point found that five out of six incarcerated felons who were armed during the commission of their crimes acquired their weapons from sources other than legitimate gun dealers.

The most effective way to stop gun crimes is to stop gun criminals. That is accomplished by enacting laws carrying tough sentences for crimes committed with firearms and enforcing such laws aggressively.

Despite the limited usefulness of controls directed at guns rather than those who unlawfully use guns, most Americans support screening firearms purchasers at the retail level to ensure that convicted felons do not acquire guns in this manner. Because such efforts affect relatively few felons, the best screening method is an "instant check" or "point-of-sale" system rather than the imposition of an unnecessary waiting period on law-abiding citizens. Technological advances have made it increasingly possible to determine at the time of purchase whether the buyer is disqualified from possessing a gun.

With regard to the ban on so-called assault weapons, opinions clearly differ. Here again, however, the futility and ill-advised nature of gun control is revealed. The term *assault weapon* has traditionally referred to an automatic firearm (one capable of firing repeatedly with a single pull of the trigger). This type of firearm has been tightly controlled in the United States since the 1920s, and new acquisitions have been outlawed since 1986.

But in the context of domestic gun control, "assault weapon" has come to mean a semiautomatic firearm (one capable of firing only one shot with each pull of the trigger) with a military-style appearance. Yet, less than 5 percent of all violent crimes are committed with such firearms. Moreover, since all semiautomatic firearms, and there are hundreds of different models, function in the same manner and since they have long been popular with law-abiding citizens for everything from self-protection to deer hunting, banning the manufacture, sale, and possession of some semiautomatic guns at best does not effectively reduce the availability of semiautomatics and, at worst, is an inevitable march toward banning more firearms.

9

Education

A popular government, without popular information, or the means of acquiring it, is but a prologue to a farce or a tragedy; or perhaps both. Knowledge will forever govern ignorance; and a people who mean to be their own governors must arm themselves with the power that knowledge gives.
—James Madison

★

AMERICA'S PUBLIC EDUCATION SYSTEM is at a crossroads. Too many of our citizens are not educated. Illiteracy has become a national epidemic. American students are scoring significantly lower than their international counterparts on international exams, and our Scholastic Aptitude Test (SAT) scores have fallen dramatically—down nearly eighty points in the past three decades.[1]

A number of alarming ironies have also emerged in our public education crisis:

- Many of the cities with the highest per-capita expenditure on students—New York, Chicago, and the District of Columbia, for example—have the worst schools.
- America has the best-paid educators and the least-educated teenagers in the developed world.
- America has the best-organized teacher unions and the most chaotic schools in the developed world.

All too often America's education activists offer only one solution to the crisis in public education: Throw more money at our problems. But in a country that already spends in excess of $502.5 billion annually on education and where the New York City school system alone has more bureaucrats on the payroll than the entire educational system of France, can more money really be the answer?[2]

Anyone willing to think about the condition of American education without bias will be immediately struck by the negative and far-reaching effects of centralization. The centralization of our education bureaucracies in Washington, D.C., has coincided remarkably with the decline of order and test scores. Schools used to be relatively free to respond to community priorities, parental demands, and the needs of students. But now an ever-growing agglomeration of federal regulations governs the way schools are run.

A web of government regulations affects almost everything that goes on in an individual school—its funding, administrative structure, teacher training, textbook selection, curriculum, teaching methodology, admissions, discipline, expulsion, parent-school relationships, standards, testing, and extracurricular activities. In any of these matters, a decision made in Washington, D.C., is one that has been taken out of the hands of those closest to the individual child—his or her own parents, his or her teachers, or the school administrators.

And the federal usurpation of state and local authority in the field of education continues. In 1994, for example, with the passage of a measure called "Goals 2000: Education for America Act," the Clinton administration came close to nationalizing American education. The proposed goals, which the Clinton administration insisted were voluntary, specify levels of "inputs" or resources local schools and school districts must meet in order to receive additional federal funding. In reality, of course, these goals are far from voluntary—if a state refuses to submit to the standards, it can lose federal dollars.

While Goals 2000 may have a high-sounding name redolent of academic excellence, it could in certain circumstances actually prevent a school from giving certain kinds of tough, scholastically oriented tests.

Another 1994 measure, the reauthorization of the Elementary and

Secondary Education Act (ESEA), takes Goals 2000 a step further down the road of federal control of education. Under ESEA, a state must submit a plan to the National Education Standards and Improvement Council established in Goals 2000 in order to qualify for its share of the billions the federal government spends annually on elementary and secondary education. This federal interference is ludicrous and takes more time away from what schools should be doing: educating children.

Of course, a major factor in the encroachment of the federal government into what had been state and local decisions was the creation in 1979 of the Department of Education, a $32 billion-a-year behemoth. The U.S. Constitution is silent on the issue of education, leaving it up to the various states. It is the state constitutions or statutes that declare that the states must educate their children.

Yet sadly for America's children, the Department of Education has increased the cost of education without bringing about any corresponding improvement in its quality. Indeed, student performance has declined significantly. The price tag for both programs and bureaucracy is enormous. According to a May 1995 Alexis de Tocqueville Institution study, taxpayers could save $15.7 billion over a five-year period if the department were abolished.[3] Similarly, a House of Representatives Budget Resolution, which passed in 1995 and endorses a plan to eliminate the Department of Education, estimates that administrative costs for programs that could be handled elsewhere would be cut by at least 30 percent if the department ceased to exist. One reason for the savings is that the mere existence of the department leads to increased pressure from interest groups that advocate more federal spending on education.

Dedicated teachers who really want to teach, meanwhile, are impeded not only by our massive system of federal regulations but also by the very union that claims to represent their best interests. The National Education Association (NEA) is the largest union in North America, and perhaps the largest in the world. The NEA puts its 1995–96 projected total membership at 2.2 million. That number includes 1.6 million active teachers. In some states, teachers who refuse to join the NEA must pay very high agency shop fees as a condition of employment.

A second union, the American Federation of Teachers (AFT), claims a smaller membership: a projected 875,000 for 1995–96. Unions often represent nonmembers as well as members in bargaining. Consequently, about 60 percent of the nation's 2.9 million public schoolteachers are employed on the basis of collective bargaining agreements.

Decades ago, the NEA distinguished itself as a professional organization. Today, however, it is an outfit with schoolmarm rhetoric and strong-arm tactics. The NEA/AFT of today has distinguished itself in the fight against competency tests for teachers—a reform desired, according to polls, by many American parents.

Not surprisingly, the goal of the NEA is more and more money for teachers and administrators. Truly, ignorance is bliss for the NEA/AFT: the worse things get in education, the more money they demand to solve the crisis. Of course, there is a downside. Voters, less inclined to approve a bond issue for school improvement, have begun to ask, "Why should I vote to increase funding to a school system more interested in money and propaganda than in reading, writing, and arithmetic?"

Tragically, it's reading, writing, and arithmetic that have been neglected in America's schools. In part this is because liberal education activists have encouraged schools to get away from their core mission of teaching children fundamental learning. What sorts of education programs have the NEA and AFT come up with to replace the basics? In recent years, the rallying cry has been "diversity."

A resolution adopted by the NEA in 1994 self importantly enlightens us on this subject:[4]

> The National Education Association believes that multicultural, global education is a way of helping students perceive the cultural diversity of the U.S. citizenry so they may develop pride in their own cultural legacy, awaken to the ideals embodied in the cultures of their neighbors, and develop an appreciation of the common humanity shared by all peoples of the earth.

One would think that teachers could say "Love thy neighbor" in fewer than fifty-eight words! But then writing skills aren't as important as they once were. Many public schools have all but jettisoned solid subjects such as math and science and English. Not surprisingly, the diversity craze has resulted in mediocrity as schools reject real studies in favor of lessons in such subjects as "self-esteem."

Of course, real self-esteem comes from a good, solid education.

If Americans are serious about saving our educational system, a number of suggestions are worthy of their consideration. Just as there is no single problem afflicting public education, there is no single solution.

But there are many proposals that offer hope:

ABOLISH THE DEPARTMENT OF EDUCATION

Schools should be free to respond to community priorities, parental demands, and student needs. The few valuable activities run by the federal government (such as information gathering and research, drawing attention to education, ensuring access to education, and guaranteeing student loans) do not require a separate cabinet-level department. They were running smoothly well before the department was established by President Jimmy Carter.

SCHOOL CHOICE

Our job is not just the obvious one of improving public schools. We need to empower parents to make choices and seize opportunities for their children's education. This is why Republicans are pushing ideas like school choice through vouchers or tax credits to assist the American family in paying for the educational services of their choice. Vouchers and tax credits will be available to people of any tax bracket and will open up unlimited possibilities of market forces applied to education.

The idea behind school vouchers or tuition tax credits is simple: Parents know best how to spend educational dollars on their children. This is related to another simple idea: Parents know best how to choose a school that is appropriate for the needs and abilities of their children. Parents also know how to judge the quality of a school without having to rely on stacks of reports and conferences in Washington.

Another benefit of school choice is that it forces schools and teachers to compete for students. Competition will force them to keep improving their product, much the way businesses improve their products to compete for customers.

Most public school districts make enrollment assignments without regard to student or parent preference. Students are assigned to the school nearest their home. While occasionally students can be assigned elsewhere for administrative reasons such as racial balance, the administrators who determine enrollment generally do not even consider the unique aptitudes and interests of individual students and the learning environment that would best foster their growth.

School choice remedies this inflexibility. The term school choice is used to describe three separate kinds of programs. The first and narrowest is the type of program that permits parents or students to choose any school within a given government school district. While intradistrict choice provides some parents with increased options, limiting the choice to government schools in a given district is like saying you can buy any car as long as it's a Buick. Being allowed to choose from among a Roadmaster, Park Avenue, or LeSabre is not much of a choice if what you had in mind was a Honda or a Ford Mustang. Intradistrict choice is a step in the right direction, but it leaves relatively few options open in areas where a parent is unhappy with all of the public schools in a district, as is the case in many of our cities.

The second kind of program, called *interdistrict choice* or *open enrollment*, allows a parent to choose any government school in the state. This is a further step in the right direction, but again it stops short of full choice. It is like saying you can buy any car as long as it's built by General Motors. While this allows a choice among many makes and models, it is not much of a choice if your prefer a vehicle from a competing manufacturer.

The third and most comprehensive kind of school choice allows parents to choose from among not only government schools but independent schools as well. While there are several ways to create this choice, the most common is through tax credits or state-financed and state-issued vouchers, worth up to a specified dollar amount when redeemed at participating schools for tuition.

School choice lets parents determine what schools best meet the needs of their children. Parents may choose any qualifying school with space available, public or private, either within or outside the district. The dollar then follows the scholar. Students choosing public schools continue to receive full state funding. Students opting for private schools may receive state scholarships worth, under most school choice proposals, half the per-pupil cost of public schooling. If a state's system of public education costs the taxpayers $6,000 per student per year—near the national average—a student attending an independent school could receive a scholarship of $3,000. That is more than enough to cover tuition at most independent schools (a fact that in and of itself speaks volumes about the state of our public schools).

Every student who switches from public to private school, moreover, saves tax dollars: in the example above, the taxpayers pay $3,000 instead of $6,000. More importantly, school choice enables all students to receive a better education. No other reform so dramatically increases equality of opportunity. Under school choice, schools will be funded only to the extent that parents voluntarily decide to enroll their children in that particular school. Like private enterprises, the schools will need to compete to satisfy their customers. No customer will be forced to accept unsatisfactory performance.

Survey data show that parents like this idea. Not surprisingly, the education bureaucrats and union bosses do not. Their vehement and amply-funded opposition to school choice reveals their fear that as soon as parents are free to send their children outside the government school system, they will do so. But that argues for parental choice in education, not against it. If the parents are so eager to take their children elsewhere, what does that say about the quality of the government schools? Why should we compel children to stay in mediocre schools?

CHARTER SCHOOLS

Like school choice, charter schools encourage innovation and decentralization. By definition, charter schools are "public" or government-funded schools that are created and operated by a group of teachers, parents, or other qualified individuals. These individuals enter into a contractual arrangement with the state or school system and, as long as they prove that they are meeting their contractual agreement with the state or local district, they operate largely free from state and district supervision.

Charter schools thus provide children and their parents with yet another educational option to choose from. Charter schools are often established to meet the special needs of individual classes of students.

The educator credited with the invention of the charter school idea is Ray Budde, a retired University of Massachusetts professor of school administration. Budde has termed charter schools "a wake-up call for the Establishment: the old organization doesn't fit the times. It's like the Berlin Wall—it's got to come down. But it's going to take ten or twenty years for something new to emerge."[5]

Legislation was introduced and, in June of 1991, Minnesota became the first state to authorize charter schools, with an initial limitation of eight for the entire state, a number that has more recently been increased to forty.[6] The impact of charter schools has been greater than even the increased number of chartered schools would indicate. The very suggestion of a charter school by parents and teachers can change the behavior of otherwise stodgy educational bureaucracies. In one district, for example, a request was made for a Montessori elementary school. The district denied the request, claiming it would be too difficult to alter an existing school for this purpose. But when it became evident the Montessori supporters might apply for a charter school, the district's administration had a change of heart, the administrative difficulties quickly disappeared, and a public Montessori school became a reality.[7]

The first Minnesota charter school, the Academy of St. Paul, opened in 1992 and has been successful in its stated goal of attracting dropouts. It has not only seen these dropouts work to obtain a regular high school diploma but it has also prepared many to go on to college as well. As of July 1995, nineteen states had charter school laws. More are undoubtedly on the way. Michigan has perhaps the strongest law in the nation, with no limits on the number of schools that can be established, and a very broad option of granting agencies. Any nonreligious, nonprofit corporation may apply for a charter, and grants may be made by school districts, community colleges, and public universities.

While the provisions of the individual laws vary, the average charter school is much smaller than the typical public school, and the exceptions, such as the twelve hundred–pupil Vaughn School in Los Angeles, tend to be former standard public schools that were granted a new status. Charter schools are quite commonly instituted by teachers even where, as in California, they do not require certified teachers in order to operate. (This is one more indication that teachers are frequently more receptive to changes than are their organizations.) At the same time, there is much more variety in charter schools than has ever been found, or is ever likely to be found, in the traditional public school environment.

Even the fact that two of the early charter schools have already closed has been termed a success because that is what should happen when a school malfunctions. But some defenders of the status quo have used the closing in midyear of a Milwaukee noncharter school that participated in the state-funded choice program as a point of attack by saying, "What happens to students when a school fails and closes?" The answer is simple, and obvious: While that may cause some inconvenience, they transfer to another school. A more important question is, What happens to students when a school fails and does not close?

COMPETITIVE CONTRACTING

There are additional ways to break the stranglehold of the education status quo, among them, competitive contracting. Simply stated, competitive contracting means purchasing school services from a private firm rather than producing them in-house. In a competitive process, a variety of providers vie with one another for the job. This allows schools to choose the company that best suits their particular needs. Competitive contracting creates incentives for accountability, allows schools to reap the benefits of specialization, and helps schools refocus on their primary mission: Helping children learn.

Competitive contracting in public education is nothing new. Many schools contract for services such as pupil transportation and food service: Nearly 40 percent of public schools contract with private companies for pupil transportation; between 5 and 10 percent contract for food service. Payroll processing, campus security, testing and evaluation, and legal and architectural work are all frequently contracted out. Cost savings from competitive contracting have been well documented and can range up to 50 percent. Says Mark Tennant, a trustee of the Pinckney Board of Education in

Michigan, "Contracting allows our school district to focus on what we're really supposed to do, which is to educate children. It means more resources in the classroom and less money spent on noninstructional services."[8]

Services once considered the sole domain of public employees are now being provided by private companies. From school management to classroom instruction, public schools are hiring private contractors. Districts in at least seven states now have contracts with private, for-profit companies to manage or operate entire schools.

One such company entered the public school sector in 1990 when it assumed management of the South Pointe Elementary School in Dade County, Florida. By the end of the five-year contract period, student test scores had increased and the students were performing at higher levels than at the district average and at a comparison school. The same company won a contract in 1994 to provide services to the entire district of the Hartford, Connecticut, public schools.

While full-scale private management has received the most media attention, public schools more often contract for services one piece at a time. Public schools find that contracting for services often results in cost savings and quality improvements. In addition, it can provide the schools with greater flexibility, accountability, and expertise. This is especially the case with contracting for instruction. Changes in enrollment, time schedules, and the academic needs of students can easily be met through contract service. A school that contracts for Japanese-language instruction, for example, can purchase—and pay for—only the services it needs. Should the school decide to switch to another language or discontinue the program, it can easily do so without encountering the problems of teacher layoffs.

Franchise learning centers—private, for-profit educational services—have been operating successfully on a fee-for-service basis all over the country. One that expanded into the public school market in 1993 began providing remedial reading and math programs to students in five Baltimore public schools. Results on state-administered standardized tests have been impressive. After one year, math scores of Baltimore students rose 14 points and reading scores increased by 1.5 points on a 100-point scale.[9] On the strength of this performance, the district added twenty-one additional schools to the existing contract, and by 1995, the company had contracts in over forty-three public schools in five states, including the District of Columbia.[10]

Another provider of specialized education programs for public schools is Project SEED, founded in 1963 by a math teacher concerned that too many students were failing at math. The private, nonprofit Project SEED uses mathematicians, specially trained in interactive teaching methods, to teach elementary school students. Project SEED targets disadvantaged and remedial-education students, although the program is also used in general classrooms. Roughly fifteen thousand students attending public schools in California, Texas, Pennsylvania, Indiana, and Michigan receive instruction from Project SEED each year.[11] Long-term evaluations of the program show that students who experience Project SEED consistently outperform control classes in mathematics and are more likely to enroll in higher-level math courses in middle and high school.

EDUCATION FOR SPECIAL POPULATIONS

Students who require special services or different learning environments are often better served by the private sector. Private sector education programs exist for dropouts, recovering alcoholics, teen mothers, and youths who have been through the juvenile justice system. Roughly one-hundred thousand students with disabilities, such as autism, emotional disturbance, or hearing impairments, attend private schools under contract with the public schools.[12] Rather than forcing these students to attend schools that don't meet their needs, the public schools contract with private schools that have developed an expertise serving a particular student population.

At Sobriety High in Minnesota, students in recovery from drug and alcohol abuse find a safe campus away from destructive influences. Sobriety High is a tightly controlled environment with just forty students, who receive the support and attention they need to complete high school drug free. The school is just one of many private alternative schools contracting with the public schools under the state's high school incentives program.

The Devereux Foundation in Santa Barbara, California, has specialized in educating and caring for people with autism since 1912. With a national reputation for excellence, its school is sought after by parents of afflicted children. Illinois-based Ombudsman Educational Services, for its part, specializes in keeping potential dropouts on track with their studies. Ombudsman schools boast an 85 percent retention rate with this at-risk population and operate for about half the cost of the public schools.[13]

Schools such as Sobriety High School, Devereux, and Ombudsman succeed because they are able to specialize in educating just one kind of student. Public schools must deal with a wide variety of students, from the gifted to the neurologically impaired and delinquents. By contracting with a private school, public schools can offer students the specialized instruction they need.

For all the benefits of contracting, there are powerful forces trying to block the way. Public employee unions are vehemently opposed to any form of competition from the private sector. A resource book published by the NEA directs members to "alert Association leaders and members to the dangerous convergence of organizations with political, religious, or economic agendas now striving to... substitute market competition and market-driven values for public service."[14] In several instances, union leaders have filed lawsuits to prohibit the public schools from contracting with private providers.[15]

OFFER MORE OPPORTUNITIES FOR TEACHERS

Just as a one-size-fits-all approach does not work for students, it does not work very well for teachers either. Unlike other professions that offer a multitude of different jobs and career options, graduates of teacher colleges face a lifetime of public employment. The public-education monopoly frustrates teachers whose creativity and ambition are often blocked by the bureaucracy.

Teachers who want independence and the professional rewards that go with it are turning to private-practice teaching to take charge of their careers. Private-practice teachers are educators who have gone into business for themselves or work for a private company, contracting their services to public or private schools.[16]

CHANGE THE ROLE OF SCHOOL BOARDS

Ambiguous state laws don't always make it clear whether school boards have the authority to contract for management and teaching. At the local level, collective bargaining agreements, negotiated by unions, often prohibit the use of contract providers. Teacher certification rules also throw up unnecessary roadblocks to contracting. With few exceptions, anyone teaching in the public schools must be licensed by the state in which they are providing instruction. While certification does not guarantee that an individual is fit to teach, it does bar entry to many talented adults interested in teaching, including private-practice educators.

Central to the success of schools in the future will be a changed role for school boards. The primary focus of school boards should be to determine the services students want and how they should be delivered—not how to produce them. Once that happens, public schools, like their private and charter school counterparts, will be prepared to compete in a market-driven system of education.

END UNION MONOPOLY

School choice and the abolition of the Department of Education would be two important steps toward ending the monopoly of the NEA and AFT. Still another is to reform our labor laws by prohibiting the NEA and AFT from their current practice of extracting fees from unwilling nonunion members, and requiring them to report any and all political expenditures.

State and federal laws regarding teacher certification laws should be rewritten. New laws should require primarily that teachers themselves be educated and demonstrate good moral character. Current laws requiring degrees in "Education Methodologies" and the like are one way the unions have assumed their chokehold on the profession.

Eliminate Taxpayer Subsidies to Teacher Unions

A crucial way to reduce the power of the teacher unions is to cut off the taxpayer subsidies that enrich the NEA/AFT coffers. These subsidies come in various forms, but the three largest are school district contributions to the teacher retirement system, which pay teachers on leave to work as NEA and

AFT officers and staff; time off with pay for teachers while conducting union business; and payroll deductions for union dues and political action committees (NEA–PAC and AFT/COPE), at no cost to the unions.

When teachers accept full-time union employment, they don't resign from their teaching positions entirely—they take a leave of absence from the school district to preserve their pension rights. These contributions add up; for example, the New York City Board of Education pays the retirement contribution for about thirty teachers on leave as full-time union staff. In some cases, these contributions are $15,000 annually per teacher.[17] In many cases, union staff receive a generous pension from the teacher retirement systems, even though those involved have actually taught only a few years. This practice could and should be stopped, by requiring the union to absorb the retirement contribution and by enacting a two-year limit on leaves of absence.

Another taxpayer subsidy is time off with pay for teachers to conduct union business. This subsidy comes in many forms: days off, or so many periods a day off, or a specified number of days to be taken upon notice by the teacher-union member. School districts also often provide generous amounts of released time with pay for the union bargaining team. In these situations, the district often pays the salary and fringe benefits for the teachers and the cost of the substitutes needed as well.

Perhaps the most critical subsidy is the automatic deduction of union dues from payroll checks and the transmittal of those payments at no cost to the union. Unquestionably, union revenues would plummet without payroll deductions, which are not costless to the school district even if they are to the union.

Empower Rank–and–File Union Members

The third category of changes would empower the silent majority in the union ranks with information about NEA/AFT internal operations. NEA and AFT state and local affiliates should be required to meet the reporting and disclosure requirements applicable to private sector unions under the Landrum-Griffin Act. Section 201 of the act provides that unions file an annual financial report with the secretary of labor that extensively lists the labor groups' assets and liabilities, their receipts, the salary and allowances given to each union officer, and any loans made to union officers or employees. The report should be made available to all members of the union; ideally, the more union members know about how their dues are being spent, the more control they will exert to keep their officers in line. Full disclosure would hold the NEA and AFT accountable to their members and make the public at large aware of their activities.

BILINGUAL EDUCATION

The Bilingual Education Act (Title VII) of 1968 was intended to improve the education of non–English-speaking children. The goal of this legislation was to allow these students an equal education by removing language barriers. The legislation did not advocate any particular method of instruction. Starting as a modest effort, it has now ballooned into a $13 billion-a-year industry.[18] The bilingual system, however, has not only failed the very students it should be helping, but it has also failed every taxpaying citizen who wants to help these students learn English and thus encourage them to become productive, educated, and contributing members of American society.

Although a variety of approaches are effective in teaching English to limited-English proficient (LEP) students, the bilingual education establishment has focused almost all federal funding, 96 percent, on the "bilingual" method—teaching school subjects in the native language for a number of years, a misguided method that has failed across the country. Even though decades of research show no advantage in native language teaching over programs using intensive English, an entrenched bureaucracy continues to insist on "bilingual" programs.

School districts need to have the flexibility to develop programs that best serve their own LEP students; and parents of these students need to be able to choose whether or not to enroll their child in bilingual programs. Options showing far better results than bilingual regimens are English as a Second Language (ESL), and English immersion programs. In a typical ESL classroom, a trained teacher can teach the English language and school subjects to students from a variety of backgrounds, using a curriculum specially designed to meet their needs.

The original intent of the Bilingual Education Act needs to be reaffirmed by incorporating the productive components of the original act while providing local school districts with greater discretion to design their own special programs for English-language learners. Block grants, and the decision-making authority to spend the money, should be given directly to the local school districts. Even if we are unable to do away with the entire Department of Education, at least we should be able to close the department's Office of Bilingual Education and Minority Language Affairs.

Official English unites Americans, who are speakers of more than three hundred different languages, by providing a common means of communication. "E pluribus unum"—out of many, one—is a guiding principle of this nation. The inability of neighbors to communicate with each other contributes to rising cultural tension and misunderstanding, as demonstrated by Quebec's desire for sovereignty from Canada. The designation of English as the official language will celebrate what unites Americans, rather than sharpening their differences.

It is imperative for all students to learn English. It is the key to increased economic opportunity and the ability to become a more productive member of society, which benefits all.

HIGHER EDUCATION REFORM

American higher education now faces new challenges that require a reexamination of the federal role in it. The budget deficit and the high cost of federal higher education programs suggest that even the most successful programs should be reviewed in order to lower their cost and increase their effectiveness.

The biggest challenges include keeping higher education affordable to all Americans, regardless of background. The cost of going to college continues to increase at a pace faster than the cost of living. Financing a post-secondary education is becoming more, not less, difficult. College costs appear to be rising faster than necessary, suggesting that federal programs and aid may have inadvertently encouraged increases in college costs—for example, that they would not have occurred in the absence of generous amounts of federal student assistance.

Similarly, easy federal funds may cause schools to admit students who are unprepared for post-secondary education. To the extent that this leads to increases in student loan default rates, students as well as taxpayers are the losers. There should be a requirement that student loan recipients maintain a certain grade point average (GPA) to remain eligible. Some of the schools with the highest default rates are vocational schools, various of which are poorly accredited and may be more interested in getting the federally guaranteed tuition checks than in seeing that students graduate, get jobs, and pay back their loans.

The Republican agenda for higher education should address these problems by rewriting the Higher Education Act and related statutes so as to base the federal Pell Grant Program on merit; make student loans more available for all eligible students; and cut down on the number of student loan defaults.

While federally guaranteed student loans have worked well, the private sector needs to assume greater responsibility for the risk in order for the loan program to work better and continue. What is not beneficial is a government-run program in the form of direct lending that takes the private sector out of the picture.

While the current administration claims that direct lending saves billions of dollars, the fact is that it costs taxpayers money. According to the Congressional Budget Office calculations, proposals to eliminate the direct student loan program save the taxpayers more than $1.5 billion over seven years. Further, under these proposals, even while balancing the budget, the annual student loan volume would increase from $24.5 billion in 1995 to $36.0 billion in 2002—a 47 percent increase.

Clearly, the guaranteed student loan program, in a true public/private partnership, can continue to assist millions of students as they obtain a higher education.

Several policy recommendations to help improve the education system include the following:

- Abolish the federal Department of Education, repeal Goals 2000, and rewrite the 1994 reauthorization of the Elementary and Secondary

Schools Act to return control of education to parents and local communities.

- Encourage states and localities to develop and implement school choice and charter school programs. ·
- Grant the local schools the legal authority to contract for services.
- Prohibit contracting from being a subject of collective bargaining in local labor negotiations.
- Amend all state and federal laws regarding teacher certification, requiring only that teachers be themselves educated in their field and that they demonstrate good moral character.
- Rewrite the Federal Bilingual Education Act (Title VII) and give school districts the flexibility to develop programs that best serve their own limited-English proficient (LEP) students, and give parents of LEP students the right to choose whether to enroll their child in bilingual programs. Teach English to all students, and urge states to establish English proficiency as a prerequisite to receiving a diploma.
- Eliminate taxpayer subsidies to teacher unions.
- Reform the labor laws to bar teachers' unions from extracting fees from nonunion teachers against their will, and require unions to report any political expenditures.
- Create a higher education block grant as the conduit for funding for all federal higher education programs except student aid. As noted above, funding would depend on development of a disciplined federal budget.
- Maintain the federal Pell Grant and College Work-Study Programs, but alter institutional eligibility to exclude questionable schools and base Pell Grants on merit. While vocational schools should remain eligible, such eligibility should exclude schools that do not produce acceptable educational outcomes.
- Repeal the federal Direct Student Loan Program and the federal Family Education Loan Program, and replace them with a program incorporating private-sector funding, market-rate lender yields, and minimum federal regulation. With the segregation of vocational school students into a separate program, lenders should be asked to assume greater risk of default in the student loan program. There should be better collection efforts, and the schools should assist in this responsibility. Borrowers of

student loans would pay a market-based interest rate. Subsidies to borrowers would be available only if the overall federal budget allows.

The lack of discipline in our schools is a major problem. Clearly, removing from the classroom chronically disruptive children such as drug abusers and those carrying weapons would go a long way to providing an atmosphere for the rest of the children to learn the basics. No child can learn in an atmosphere of fear and disorder.

The president of the American Federation of Teachers, Albert Shanker, in advocating alternative settings for disruptive students, refers to "First Things First," a report that found an overwhelming agreement among parents to remove disruptive students from the classroom. Likewise, a recent Gallup poll found that 77 percent of all Americans favor educating these youngsters in alternative settings. Academic arguments that these children are victims and should remain in the class forget that by having a chaotic and fear-filled atmosphere, no one is educated. As Mr. Shanker notes, by refusing to put disruptive students in alternative settings, they are being denied the special attention that may help them. And at the same time, well-behaved children whose life circumstances may be as horrific as those of the disruptive ones, are being left to suffer.

In the past thirty years, we have proved that more money, more bureaucracy, and more regulation are not the solutions to the problems in education. Original thinking is needed. As Albert Einstein observed, "We cannot solve the problem with the same thinking we used to create it."

10

Individual Rights and Responsibilities

INTOLERANCE IS INTOLERABLE IN OUR COUNTRY. The vast majority of Americans believe that discrimination is wrong, that the American way of life truly should offer equal opportunity for all and eliminate discrimination in all its forms. A strong commitment to individual and civil rights for all must be the goal of any party that wishes to lead our nation into the next century.

Unfortunately, when the term *civil rights* is used today, it is often a not-too-subtle code word for *special preference*—a development that would have horrified those who supported the Civil Rights Act of 1964. The Civil Rights Act was intended to ensure a color-blind society and a nation in which only individual character and merit mattered.

Affirmative action has come to mean just the opposite. It now means a system of quotas, preferences, set-asides, and government harassment. In many ways, policies that now pass under the name of civil rights have made us a more race-conscious society than ever before.

When did *civil rights* turn into *reverse discrimination,* and *affirmative action* into *special preferences*? Many would argue that the wrong turn was made shortly after the triumph of the 1964 Civil Rights Act and the Voting Rights Act of the following year, two pieces of legislation aimed at eliminating the political disadvantages under which black Americans suffered.

The acts succeeded. But within the next few years, the emphasis shifted from a quest for equality of opportunity and a color-blind country to one of racial balances and equality of results. The idea, we were assured, was to provide remedies for past discrimination. But this led to quotas and special preferences, with a reliance on government intrusion and mandates instead of individual effort.

A long-running court case in New Jersey illustrates how far we have come from the original goals of civil rights legislation. The case of the *United States v. Board of Education of Piscataway* involved a school that, in order to meet its racial quota, fired a white teacher instead of a black teacher with equal seniority during a required staff reduction. In other days, the school district decided such matters with a flip of the coin. Here, it made the decision explicitly on the basis of race.

During the Bush administration, the U.S. Department of Justice sued the school for violating the civil rights of Sharon Taxman, the fired teacher. A court agreed, ruling that dismissing the teacher merely because she was white was an obvious violation of her civil rights.

But the case didn't end there. The Clinton administration switched courses. It sided with the school in an appeal of the lower court decision. The school, it argued, was justified. This was deemed acceptable discrimination, serving as it did the goal of "diversity."

Although quotas are increasingly unpopular with the populace—one poll indicates that 77 percent of blacks and 73 percent of whites oppose quotas[1]—the Clinton administration continues to cherish them. A number of truly ludicrous personnel directives have grown out of the Clinton administration's love affair with quotas. For example, the 1994 Department of Housing and Urban Development (HUD) performance standards for evaluating managers and supervisors included such criteria as "speak[ing] favorably about minorities, women, persons with disabilities, and others of diverse backgrounds," "participating as an active member of minority, feminist, or other cultural organizations," and "participating in EEO and Cultural Diversity activities outside of HUD." Even at the Department of Defense, where one might assume there were more pressing concerns, President Clinton's secretary of defense, William Perry, has called for "vigorous action" to increase the number of "women, minorities, and persons with disabilities" at the department. An undersecretary at the Department of Defense sent out the following memorandum to the department's civilian managers: "I need to be consulted whenever you are confronting the possibility that any excepted position, or any career position at GS-15 level and higher, is likely to be filled by a candidate who will not enhance... diversity."

Over at the National Park Service, meanwhile, there was this memorandum from its director:

> Surely, we must be able to find a use for a Swahili-speaking person who has Peace Corps experience, is a cum laude in English from Harvard, and has a biological background in data manipulation.... Unfortunately, Mr. Trevor is white, which is too bad.

Unfortunately, the administration's pursuit of quotas has resulted in more than internal memoranda. Clinton appointees at the Federal Communications Commission (FCC) have issued stiff fines to broadcasters for failing to meet explicit quotas for hiring minorities. The FCC has also voted to set aside approximately half of two thousand licenses for wireless "personal communications services" (portable phones, pagers, etc.) to firms owned by minorities. These licenses are to be granted to such companies at discounts of up to 60 percent of their market value—a windfall indeed for these favored companies.

While some companies are favored, others are forced. Chevy Chase Bank in Chevy Chase, Maryland, is just one of the U.S. corporations that has been pressured by the Justice Department to open more branches in minority neighborhoods. Apparently fearing a costly Justice Department suit and a barrage of media coverage, this bank promised to adopt hiring quotas, approve below-market loans for minorities, provide grants to cover down payments for minority applicants, and advertise in minority-owned media.

Municipalities also face hiring quotas. For example, Fullerton, California, was forced to accept not only racial quotas in hiring for its police and fire departments but also to agree to preferential treatment for minority members who had applied and been turned down or felt discouraged from applying since 1985—with back pay and benefits! The alternative was to fight a Justice Department lawsuit, as the nearby town of Torrance had done, at a cost to the taxpayers of more than $1 million in legal fees.

In making the case against quotas, we should not overlook the most important practical fact of all: Quotas have not worked. They have hurt rather than helped the very people they are designed to help.

Quotas accomplish little or nothing, engender ill will all around, and are destructive and insulting to minorities—as Ward Connerly, a regent at the University of California and a staunch foe of affirmative action, noted in *Newsweek* magazine. Connerly, a contractor, said that white contractors were often eager to go into business with him in order to take advantage of his minority business breaks. He doesn't bite. "Look," Connerly told *Newsweek*'s Joe Klein, "I was born in Louisiana. I remember drinking from 'colored only' water fountains. That was degrading. But this is almost as bad. I won't be defined as an 'affirmative action' businessman. I want to be judged by the quality of my work."

In addition to being demeaning, harder statistics indicate that affirmative action not only fails to help but may even hinder minorities from rising on the economic scale. A Rand Corporation study, which traced the progress of black Americans from 1940 to 1980, concluded that, while blacks had made great strides during that period, 80 percent of that progress occurred *before* the era of quotas, racial preferences, and busing. The incomes of black Americans relative to white Americans actually declined from 1967 to 1977, as did the incomes of Hispanic Americans. During the Carter administration, a heyday of racial preferences and quotas, real incomes of black men *declined* by 5 percent.

Information from another study, by University of Chicago sociologist William Julius Wilson, should also dishearten advocates of quotas. Wilson found that, while about half of blacks had climbed into or near the middle class by the late 1980s, the other half seemed to have fallen farther behind. "The past three decades," Wilson noted, "have been a time of regression, not progress."

Evidence notwithstanding, Republicans who question the value of so-called affirmative action are met with stern rebukes from media commentators—usually with hints that they are racist. Sometimes these terrible accusations have been too much, and leaders have bowed to liberal opinion, even knowing that Americans in general reject preferential treatment.

Liberals have come to regard minorities and women as their partisan constituency. Many people even believe Democrats prefer to keep their constituency dependent rather than to liberate it through sound economic and social policy. And, of course, many of the ills besetting African Americans result from this very dependency. Given the choice, however, people of color might actually prefer, say, more cops on the beat to an elaborate and failed system of quotas.

The time has come for responsible leaders in and outside the Republican party to take a more effective lead on the issues of civil rights and racial equality. In place of quotas and institutional poverty, Americans should be guided by the genuine idealism of the 1964 Civil Rights Act: All are equal before the law. So many bitter quarrels over affirmative action and funding for this or that poverty program result from the agenda of a political establishment rather than the good of minorities and, as such, distract from the real issue, which is *opportunity for all*. In the end, most Americans want the same things—freedom, a good job, safe neighborhoods, self-sufficiency, and the respect of their fellow citizens.

Fortunately, there are signs that the times are changing—in the right direction. Already, reform is in the air. A proposed initiative for California's 1996 ballot will read:

> Neither the State of California nor any of its political subdivisions or agents shall use race, color, ethnicity, national origin, sex, or religion as a criterion for either discriminating against, or granting preferential treatment to, any individual or group in the operation of the state's system of public employment, public education, or public contracting.

That policy should be the policy everywhere, not just in California. Other reforms should also be adopted.

The Creation of Enterprise Zones

Enterprise zones, a policy that's been kicking around for years—and applied here and there in timid, grudging half-measures—should be put into effect throughout our inner cities. Distracted by the ideological mirages of quotas, a higher minimum wage, and federal make-work programs, Washington has forgotten what our poor neighborhoods most need—honest jobs.

Enterprise zones are not based on theories but on a simple truth: No company wants to locate in poor, dangerous, and ravaged neighborhoods. These same communities, moreover, are often beset by high taxes and regulatory intrusion. Government, local and federal, has managed to turn these areas into permanently dependent constituencies with almost no private economic activity.

The best way to entice private business into these stagnant areas is to remove those hindrances. Cut taxes, radically. Eliminate every needless regulation. And, wherever possible, get the politicians and bureaucrats out of the way of business.

Businesses, large and small, will move in, offering real work with real prospects. According to HUD such zones, even in their mild form, have yielded billions of dollars in new business investment and have created thousands of new jobs. Another HUD survey calculates that by the end of 1991 twenty-two states reported $40 billion in new capital investment and twenty-six states reported 663,885 new jobs within their zones. Indian reservations should be eligible for such enterprise zones, as well as inner cities and other impoverished areas.

An End to Forced Busing

Forced busing was one of government's grander experiments in social engineering, and perhaps the grandest of its failures. In many school districts, children are still being bused to meet the demands of federal judges. The real solution is to improve public schools within our cities, which means school choice and an end to teacher union monopoly-induced mediocrity, and worse.

The Rights of Individuals

Many of the freedoms and rights we possess just by being born Americans— those our parents, grandparents, and the Founding Fathers considered sacred—have been eroded over the past several decades. Government has come to think it knows better than parents how to raise and educate their children; courts treat criminals better than their victims; and private property, an original individual right guaranteed by our Constitution's Fifth Amendment, is all too often taken by the government without compensation. Concerned Americans are working on many fronts to recapture these rights, along with the corresponding responsibilities they convey.

Victims' rights. One true measure of a society is the concern and compassion that it accords those who have been victimized by crime. From the standpoint of crime victims, the criminal justice system today is often perceived to be a complex game in which the "rules" have more significance than the guilt or innocence of the defendant, and the impact on the victims themselves is ignored. Innocent victims, having experienced the trauma of crime, must be protected from further pain and suffering. Victims deserve to be assisted in every possible way, including restitution. They should receive special attention and protection throughout the criminal process, and procedures should ensure that the impact of the harm on the victim is made clear to the offender.

In a growing number of states, proposals for a "Victims' Bill of Rights" have been adopted. Some of the prominent elements of a victims' rights agenda would include the following:

- Notifying the victim of the arrest, bail, and release of criminal defendants.
- Notifying the victim of the conviction, appeals, reversal of an appeal, and confinement and release of the defendant.
- Being free from harassment or intimidation by the defendant.
- Receiving restitution.
- A speedy trial.
- Making a statement at the sentencing and parole hearing concerning the physical, financial, and psychological effects of the crime on the victim.

Parents' and children's rights. Child-rearing in America has increasingly come to be viewed as a public matter. Today, many take for granted that government should have great authority over the upbringing of children, since it is best able to ensure the well-being of children. Yet, as the authority of the government over children has increased, so has the number of children experiencing serious developmental problems. Over the past three decades, children have become more and more likely to experience emotional and behavioral problems, underachieve at school, become pregnant as teenagers, and develop alcohol and drug abuse problems.

Clearly, with our nation's children doing so poorly, something is terribly wrong. Some see the decline as reason for further government intervention in family life. But the evidence points in the other direction. The deterioration of youngsters in America is the direct result of the government's takeover of our children. Public policy must again ensure that parents have maximum authority when it comes to raising their families.

This does not mean that all parents will always put the interests of their children above their own. Indeed, some parents, especially those under the influence of drugs or alcohol, will even abuse their children. Certainly the government must intervene in such cases. But that some parents do not act in the best interests of their children doesn't mean the government should not act as though all parents don't. Rather, the assumption of government must be that, until proven otherwise, parents, not bureaucrats or politicians, are those best able to care for their children.

Congress and some states are now considering legislation to protect the fundamental right of parents to direct the upbringing of their own children. This legislation would ensure that government maintain a proper respect for parental authority and decision making, while allowing government to intervene in instances where parents abuse or neglect their children.

Additionally, since 1982, thirty-one states have specifically enacted laws to protect the constitutional rights of parents to teach their own children at home. All fifty states now recognize the right to home school by either statute or statewide case law. Over nine state departments of education and a number of independent surveys have found that, on the average, home-schooled children score thirty points above the national average on standardized achievement tests. With home schooling, parents personally supervise the education of their children and the good results contrast starkly with the steady academic and moral decline in many public schools today.

Private property rights. As discussed in chapters 5 and 6, private property rights must be respected. If the government takes private property, the owner is entitled by the Constitution's Fifth Amendment to "just compensation." John Adams declared in the early days of our nation, "Property is surely a right of mankind as real as liberty.... The moment the idea is admitted into society that property is not as sacred as the laws of God, and that there is not force of law and public justice to protect it, anarchy and tyranny commence."

Congressional term limits. Many Americans feel one of the biggest threats to their individual rights is a permanent government in Washington, one independent of the citizenry and thus politically unaccountable. The American people understand that term limits for members of Congress, which used to be adhered to voluntarily, is much needed. In former days, elected members didn't come to Washington to stay a lifetime. In June 1995, a comprehensive national poll of American voters conducted by the Tarrance Group for the Term Limits Legal Institute in Washington, D.C., showed that 74 percent of the American people *favor* term limits. Frustration with the institution of government would be greatly reduced by a return to the citizen legislature, accountable to the people, through a constitutional amendment that limits the number of terms members of the Senate and House of Representatives can serve.

FREEDOM AND FAITH

America has always been the home of religious liberty, a beacon for all who desire to worship as they choose or not to worship at all. For generations, people have come to America to escape religious intolerance, whether in the form of government interference or persecution. We regard this freedom as a cornerstone of our heritage.

We do not believe a person without religious faith is not a good citizen. Many great figures in history have not been religious. We simply believe it is important to recognize that religion provides one of the strongest possible groundings in the respect for others that is the basis for good citizenship. We have always valued people of whatever faith, knowing that religion fosters restraint and other qualities important for good citizenship.

All of the great religious traditions come back to one basic truth: No human being is a means or even an end in himself or herself. Rather all human beings are reflections of a higher being or a higher purpose and as such they are especially deserving of love and respect. Great religions impress upon us that every human being, no matter how broken, impoverished, or downtrodden, is a reflection of God and of mankind's higher purpose. It is because of such values that Americans are among the most generous people in the world.

Despite all of this, America has witnessed a strange and disheartening phenomenon during the past thirty-five years: an attempt to wrench us away from the religious faith that was the foundation of our culture. Why various elements in our society have tried to do this is a subject for another book. Suffice it to say here that because of these "reformers" many of our most important institutions have been declared *faith-free zones*.

Many private colleges and hospitals, established by churches as a testament to their charity and to the strength of their faith, are now either completely secularized or openly hostile to the religious values that created them. It is as though an unwritten rule of our society dictates that it's okay to have religious faith in private, but not okay to express it publicly. Sometimes it goes so far that this unwritten rule becomes written. When this happens, the full force of the law is brought to bear against those who would practice or express their faith in public. There have been far too many cases of people being thrown out of schools or other public places, or even arrested, for expressing their faith. Merely wearing or displaying a religious symbol is often enough to provoke such hostile actions. All too often in late twentieth-century America, freedom of religion has been enforced as freedom *from* religion.

It was not supposed to be this way in America.

As Speaker Newt Gingrich put it in his 1984 book, *Window of Opportunity: A Blueprint for the Future,* our nation was founded on different principles:

> Despite attempts by today's anti-deists to abolish God and religion in public life, it is impossible to study the leaders of the American Revolution without being profoundly impressed by their commitment to God and to divining His will. Even our most radical founding father, Thomas Jefferson, wrote in the Declaration of Independence that all men are "endowed by their Creator with certain unalienable rights." Thus the very document by which we proclaimed our freedom from British hegemony asserted that this freedom was granted to us by God and not man.

The compact of which Gingrich wrote clearly assumed that the state would never tell us *not* to believe.

History, however, has been rewritten by those who would airbrush God out of our nation's past. Many insist that the church must be relegated to the edge of our community life. One of the most astute critics of the diminution of religious values is the Rev. Richard John Neuhaus, an intellectual leader in both the Lutheran and Catholic traditions.

In his 1984 book, *The Naked Public Square,* Neuhaus visualized the colonial and early American public square—which housed the institutions so important to society—as government, church, commerce, and school. The public square gave support to individuals and the community. But today, Neuhaus asserts, the church is no longer present or even represented in the metaphorical public square. The church is kept away from the center and away from public view. Thus, Neuhaus writes, the public square, stripped of its foundation in morality and virtue, is now "naked."

A sign of the relegation of religion to a fringe role in society—its belittlement—is the way it is covered in the media, which never depict religion as important to people's lives. News about religion is generally sidelined into one or two articles in the Saturday paper, even though fully 94 percent say they believe in God. Many moreover make worship an integral part of their week.

Antireligious zealots have not merely torn the church loose from the center of our communities. They have also torn Americans loose from many of the moral underpinnings of a functional society. William Bennett addressed this problem in his immensely popular 1993 best-seller, *The Book of Virtues.* "A human being without faith, without *reverence* for anything," Bennett wrote, "is a human being morally adrift. The world's major religions provide time-tested anchors for drifters; they furnish ties to a larger reality for people on the loose. Faith can contribute important elements to the social stability and moral development of individuals and groups."

Our nature does not ensure that we will always behave in the best way, and as the past three decades make clear, without the kind of moral compass provided by religious faith, we as a society are, as Bill Bennett put it, adrift. Society's interest in this moral drift is more than passing. Think of the major cultural indicators: rising crime, teen pregnancy, millions of abortions, and low levels of achievement in schools across the nation. And it is quickly noticeable that many of these problems are five times worse than they were just a generation ago. As alarming as this is, it's easy to forget that every single statistic represents an American life that has been lost or hurt.

Taken in total, those statistics threaten us all. As Speaker Gingrich noted in a December 5, 1994, speech on Capitol Hill:

> No society can survive, no civilization can survive with twelve-year-olds having babies, with fifteen-year-olds killing each other, with seventeen-year-olds dying of AIDS, and with eighteen-year-olds getting diplomas they can't read.

Many have noted that the decline of morality in our society has occurred since 1960, during the most aggressively antireligion activity by "reformers." It is troubling enough that all these indicators are so much worse than they were thirty-five years ago. What is even more troubling for those who love America is that society now is not different just in degree but almost in kind from the America of 1960.

Of course, throughout human history, terrible crimes have been committed by those professing faith. But eliminating religion or banishing it from public view does not make us more enlightened. With a decline in faith and the accompanying lessening of respect for the lives of other humans have come

- skyrocketing murder rates in our cities, where homicide now claims more young black Americans than any other cause of death;
- an alarming trend toward leaving elderly people—those who built the America we enjoy—to die uncared for; and
- the staggering loss of one-and-a-half million lives a year to abortion.

Americans who think this loss of life is somehow different from what has occurred in other societies are missing the frightening parallel with other cultures that have forced religion out of public life: They lost their respect for human beings, and this ultimately destroyed their societies. We like to believe America is different. Or better. But there is nothing in our history that proves we are different. Or better.

Tragically, loss of the kind of respect for human life that is grounded in religious belief has many other negative side effects. When we lose our moorings, we sometimes begin to believe that people exist to be used for our own personal pleasure. We can see this in the phenomenon of runaway teenage pregnancy, the spread of sexually transmitted diseases, and the proliferation of pornography. Loss of respect for human life is also increasingly evident in the movies and television programs that infest the nation.

Fortunately, this isn't the whole picture. There is a more optimistic side to this story. In recent years, there has been a revival of interest in religion as a force in life. Most Americans have retained or returned to their belief in religion and in the values that came to us from the great religions. They understand better than the "reformers" that the great faiths of the world are repositories of the wisdom of the ages. They know that no single generation can possess the wisdom to redefine right and wrong, and that any culture attempting to do so is in great peril for its very existence.

If religion is once again allowed to take its place in our public life—not to dictate dogma or law, but to lend its wisdom in making society better and safer for us and our children—we will once again be using all of our nation's resources. We ask only that America regain her historic role as the home of religious freedom. We must recognize that—as Ralph Reed, executive director of the Christian Coalition, said in his book, *Politically Incorrect*—people of faith do not seek to write their church's doctrine into law.

Reed explained this explicitly: "It is time to set the record straight. If religious conservatives took their proper, proportionate place as leaders in the political and cultural life of the country, we would work to create the kind of society in which presumably all of us would like to live: safe neighborhoods, strong families, schools that work, a smaller government, lower taxes.... Families would function again; marriages would work; children would be considered a blessing rather than a burden; neighbors would be neighbors again.... In short, we desire a good society based on the shared values of work, family, neighborhood, and faith."

Hardly radical ideas. Most require only simple commonsense legislation, such as school vouchers and greater protection of children and the unborn. And majorities in polls support all these goals.

On the issue of school prayer—or more accurately, voluntary prayer in public schools—most Americans want something done to restore religious expression and moral awareness to our schools. While the state or school must not dictate or prescribe any prayer, the right to voluntary prayer in schools should be protected, whether through a constitutional amendment or through legislation, or a combination of both. Indeed, Congressman

Gingrich, in a speech just prior to becoming Speaker, endorsed both approaches: constitutional change and legislative trimming of the Court's jurisdiction over voluntary prayer in schools.

The idea that most religious people are "radical," as they are all too often portrayed in the media, is wrong. The overwhelming majority are mainstream, not extreme. They should not be treated as second-class citizens who may practice their faith in private but never in the public square. People of faith—of all faiths—have played important roles in the progress of the country and the development of our culture. Indeed, our culture is based on traditional American values, derived from our Judeo-Christian heritage, handed down to us, generation after generation.

POLICIES OF RESPECT FOR OTHERS

One of the abiding strengths of our people has been the value we place on human life and the respect we have for the rights of the individual. It is what leads us as a people to personalize and feel threatened by crimes that result from a fundamental lack of respect for the lives and rights of other individuals. What is done to one of us affects all of us.

When we hear stories on the evening news of children thrown to their death from high-rise windows and elderly women accosted on the street as others watch in silence or scurry away, we worry that we as a society may have lost a measure of respect for our neighbors, a respect that must begin, but surely does not end, with a deep value for individual lives.

Thomas Jefferson told us nearly two hundred years ago that "the care of human life and happiness, and not their destruction, is the first and only legitimate object of good government." If we take Jefferson's admonition seriously, government policies can and must protect and respect human life. Granted, government alone cannot correct a lack of respect, but it can ensure that its policies reflect society's needs to respect the sanctity of life.

At the very least, government cannot be in the business of encouraging or fostering indifference. It was perhaps this perceived indifference to the sanctity of life as expressed in our laws governing abortion that led Mother Teresa to ask our president and political leaders at a National

Prayer Breakfast in Washington in 1994: "How can you be surprised that your teenagers kill each other with guns when you teach your daughters to murder their babies?"

Many on the left advocate a policy of abortion on demand, for any reason or no reason, at any time during the pregnancy, with no state regulation or limitation allowed, and paid for by the taxpayers. This extreme position is unacceptable to the vast majority of Americans. It means a government policy of allowing abortion as a means of birth control and sex selection. Most people know this is simply wrong. (Even Hillary Rodham Clinton spoke out against abortion for sex selection in China.)

States should have the right to regulate and limit abortions. At the very least, parental consent or notification should be required before abortions are performed on minors; states should be allowed to impose waiting periods; and late-term abortions should be prohibited except to save the life of the mother.

Furthermore, we as a caring society must loosen government's stranglehold on adoption regulations. Reforming laws that keep children from the homes of people who would give them a family and the love they deserve would result in adoption being a positive alternative to abortion. Government policy should encourage adoption, not make it more difficult.

The founders of our country were aware of the necessity of personal "self-government" among a democratic people. Individual freedom and personal responsibility go hand-in-hand. Though government policies play a part in guiding public morals and behavior, the best guarantor of a healthy society has always been individual citizens and their community organizations: churches, families, and local clubs and charities. Through the realization that we are indeed part of a greater community and through a reinvigoration of our moral sense within that community, we can revitalize and renew the values we share as a society.

Freedom is not free: it requires as much to maintain as it did to establish. As citizens, we bear responsibility for our actions; and as we move into the next century, we must respect that responsibility for ourselves, our communities, and our country.

III

A SECURE AND STRONG AMERICA

11

Peace Through Strength in the Coming Decade

THROUGHOUT MOST OF THIS CENTURY, the United States has willingly provided leadership for the free world. During the Cold War, the United States and its allies confronted the Soviet empire and the threat of global communism, maintained world stability, and encouraged free trade among democratic nations. *For the past three years, however, American leadership has eroded, and drift and uncertainty have increasingly characterized world affairs. The challenge for Republicans is to reestablish constructive leadership in the world. The Clinton administration has failed to implement the first priority of American foreign and defense policy—the protection of American values and interests.*

The Clinton administration strategy simply does not reflect the centrality of U.S. leadership in winning the Cold War. During the years that Presidents Reagan and Bush were displaying strength and leadership around the world, those now serving in the Clinton administration were apologizing for, and often opposing, the very principles and policies that led to the free world's victory over the Soviet empire.

President Clinton has deliberately ignored foreign policy, except when driven there by domestic political pressures. We believe the dichotomy assumed by this administration between foreign policy and domestic policy is a false one. The United States must have a foreign policy based on clear objectives flowing from principles shared by the American people. Otherwise, American foreign policy will continue to lurch from crisis to crisis, with no coherent plan. The Clinton administration has neither stated the principles of a coherent foreign policy nor the way to carry one out. Republicans believe the vacuum created by the administration must be filled by restoring American political, economic, and military leadership. Republicans have a clear vision: *to ensure freedom and security for this generation of Americans and those to come.*

THE PRINCIPLES

United States foreign policy must rest on three principles of peace through strength:

1. *Political leadership.* The United States must once again be prepared to exercise leadership across the full spectrum of international relations. It can do so through bilateral or multilateral cooperation with other democracies or organizations, where appropriate. But if that is not possible, the United States must be prepared to act on its own when our national interests so require. If we exercise this leadership we are far more likely to attract support from others, as we did in the Gulf War.

2. *Economic strength.* The United States has the world's most free, most prosperous, and most technologically advanced economy. That preeminence must be maintained notwithstanding intense foreign competition, often government subsidized, in every world market. We must continue to lead the world in reducing barriers to trade. We must reduce the size and intrusiveness of the federal government through decreased regulation and lower taxes to stimulate growth, employment, and individual opportunity. Therefore, the United States must continue to improve its own competitiveness; we must work aggressively to build an international system of rules promoting free trade; and we must enforce those rules on trading partners who erect roadblocks when we attempt to do business with them.

3. *Military power.* The United States must provide the resources necessary to protect its territory and interests, and those of its allies. Our fundamental requirement is a strong, competent, and effective military, not only to prevail militarily when in our country's interest, but more fundamentally to dissuade potential adversaries from challenging the United States militarily and undertaking hostilities against U.S. interests. Our increasingly hollow military force can no longer be tol-

erated. The United States must apply the resources required to rejuvenate our military capability and to ensure its effectiveness in a still-dangerous world. Military life should not be made more difficult or more dangerous because of personnel policies that detract from unit strength, readiness, and morale.

THE OBJECTIVES

The underlying principles for United States foreign policy must be translated into action through clear-cut objectives:

1. *The United States will take all necessary measures to prevent the proliferation and threat or use of weapons of mass destruction around the world. We welcome the cooperation of others to these ends.*

With the end of the Cold War, the proliferation of nuclear, chemical, biological, and conventional weapons and their means of delivery are the most serious and pressing foreign policy challenges facing the United States and all democratic nations. The United States must demonstrate active and forceful leadership to deal with this problem and prevent it from becoming even more serious than it already is. Countries such as North Korea, Iran, Iraq, and Libya are rogue regimes with the financial means to buy and develop the technology of mass destruction. That, coupled with their demonstrated support of international terrorism, makes them a direct threat to the United States and its allies.

The United States must pursue active and aggressive diplomacy in dealing with the proliferation of weapons of mass destruction, as the Bush administration did against Iraq in the aftermath of the Gulf War. Together with our allies if possible, but unilaterally if necessary, we must deny rogue countries, ethnic, political or religious fanatics, or other aggressors access to weapons of mass destruction. Moreover, the United States must develop a military capability to protect it and its allies against this threat. It must be clear to both the United States and potential adversaries that the U.S. military can and will prevail even under the threat or use of weapons of mass destruction against our forces.

2. *The United States will adequately fund its defense budget and stop the erosion of our military capability brought about by the Clinton administration. This will include adequate resources for training and readiness, as well as needed hardware. Moreover, the American defense industrial base will be strengthened to prevent further deterioration of its capacity to respond to national needs.*

The "hollow military" of the 1970s is increasingly evident in our current force structure. After the enormous efforts by the Reagan and Bush administrations to rectify the neglect of a previous antimilitary Democrat administration, we once more observe a downward spiral in the capabilities of our forces. What is even more disturbing is the Clinton administration's willingness to short-change our men and women in uniform, while it commits American forces around the globe with little strategic forethought. The result is an American military that is underequipped, undertrained, and stretched to the breaking point. The United States must meet its national security commitments and do so with a force that is ready, well equipped, and well trained.

A strong military requires a strong industrial base. The United States cannot jeopardize its capability to produce the highly complex information-based technological and weapons systems that gave us and our allies the decisive edge in the Gulf War. Key industries and critical technologies like nuclear submarines, conventional shipbuilding, advanced aircraft production, and stealth technology are in jeopardy, as are the jobs and skills associated with those industries. We must not let this happen.

3. *The United States will not risk the lives of the men and women in the armed services unless (1) it is absolutely and unequivocally in the American national security interest to do so; and (2) those servicemen and -women are under U.S. or North Atlantic Treaty Organization (NATO) military command, and not under UN command.*

There is no greater trust invested in the commander-in-chief than his authority to commit American men and women—our sons and daughters—to military action. To waste even one life in the pursuit of an unnecessary, ill-considered foreign policy adventure betrays the trust invested in the president. The current administration has demonstrated the same tragic propensity for committing U.S. forces with no clear military objective, no end-game strategy, and no intention of winning that we demonstrated when we asked five-hundred thousand troops to risk their lives in Vietnam for a cause that we did not intend to win. The fiasco of the Clinton administration's effort at "assertive multilateralism" in Somalia is the most striking, but by no means the only, example of this tragedy. The administration completely transformed the original humanitarian mission into an ill-conceived, UN-controlled exercise in "nation building," and then failed to provide American forces on the ground with the military support they needed. The U.S. army rangers who died in the dusty streets of that country might be alive today if they had been provided the support that the Clinton administration thought would have been "too provocative."

When our armed forces are committed, they should be commanded by the officers with whom they have undergone their training and in whom they have the greatest faith—their American or NATO commanders. In NATO, common training, common operations, common maneuvers, and common doctrine provide the confidence needed for its various members to work together under flexible command structures. By contrast, there is no basis for such assurance in current UN commands. In short, we should not place American forces under UN command.

4. *The United States continues to support NATO as the most effective mechanism for collective security in the world. The United States will support the admission to NATO of qualified, independent, democratic countries, and it will not permit non–NATO countries to veto such admissions.*

NATO is the most successful alliance the world has ever seen. Under the leadership of Presidents Reagan and Bush, it brought about the downfall of the Soviet Union and the Warsaw Pact without firing a shot. Even after its Cold War victory, NATO remains crucial to American interests and to the execution of U.S. policy in Europe. NATO is the strongest institutional link between the United States, Canada, and Europe, and it must be preserved and appropriately expanded as a political and military alliance to defend American values and interests in Europe.

NATO should redefine its role to help create a post–Cold War Europe that is whole, free, and secure. Accordingly, the United States must adopt a clear stance concerning future membership in NATO. The Clinton administration's "Partnership for Peace" cannot effect this adequately. In a typical maneuver, in order to appease Russia, Clinton offered the Eastern European countries an empty framework instead of the NATO membership they wanted and should have. In a misguided attempt to give Russian leaders a role in U.S. and NATO decision making, the "Partnership for Peace" has become little more than a public relations ploy for the Clinton administration. The United States should support NATO membership for the newly democratic nations in Eastern Europe that meet the established criteria. While doing so, we can take steps through effective diplomacy to allay possible Russian security concerns, but we should not let Russia veto admission of four new countries that are ready for NATO and whose friendship we need.

5. *The United States will make clear, in the appropriate forums, that its membership in multinational organizations such as NATO or the United Nations will not prevent it from taking necessary and appropriate political and/or military action when to do so is either (1) in the national security interest of the United States or (2) in support of commitments made to allies.*

The current administration has lost sight of the fundamental truth that the United States is the world's leader. As a result, Clinton's foreign policy is bounded by the lowest-common-denominator consensus it is able to forge with other nations. The administration's policy toward the former Yugoslavia serves as the most poignant example. Aggressive one day, compliant the next, assertive and then retiring, the administration has lurched from policy to policy in almost random fashion. American leadership has been abandoned and its ability to influence squandered in the Clinton administration's reckless pursuit of United Nations approval of its actions. Russia can and does veto effective UN action. We should not let Russia veto our actions.

The United States must act on its own when it is in our national security interest to do so. Such action requires leadership and talent, but only an administration with courage, conviction, and capability can meet these challenges.

6. *The United States will promote increased economic opportunities for Americans to do business in Central and Eastern Europe, the former Soviet Union, and Asian nations moving toward more open, market-oriented economies.*

The United States must pursue innovative mechanisms to encourage American trade and investment in Central and Eastern Europe and the former Soviet Union. U.S. government aid alone cannot solve the problems of the newly independent states. These problems can be solved only by market-driven reforms in those nations themselves, and by increased political stability derived from stable democratic processes. The United States government should promote sound, open, market-oriented policies and programs in the newly emerging markets of Central and Eastern Europe, the former Soviet Union, and developing Asian markets. The Clinton administration's policies of expending American taxpayer dollars on failed foreign aid programs is no more likely to succeed there than in any other region where they have been tried.

7. *The United States will continue to seek cooperative trading partners throughout the world, but we will no longer accept uneven trading relationships with countries that do not grant American businesses the opportunity to compete in their markets.*

The Clinton administration has attempted to "talk tough" on trade policy, but its actions have sent mixed signals to the world. Inevitably, the results have been lackluster, apart from completing the Reagan-Bush achievements on the North American Free Trade Agreement (NAFTA) and the Uruguay Round. The United States is a world leader in technology industries, financial services, agriculture, capital goods, and many other areas, and it must find ways to open world markets to these competitive businesses in a consistent and effective way. Where trading partners continue to build barriers to open trade, the United States must use the World Trade Organization, NAFTA, and domestic laws to insist on the rights of our exporters and domestic interests. American trade policy must not be encumbered by the inconsistent and inappropriate application of noneconomic standards or rules as a price for trade liberalization. Free trade means less government regulation and more individual empowerment, and thus is consistent with traditional American support for democracy. Our people will only embrace an open U.S. market for the products of others if they are convinced we have ready access to those markets for American goods and services.

8. *The United States will provide economic and political support for emerging democracies whenever it is in our national interest. We will help friendly peoples to help themselves, both economically and politically.*

The United States must remain the friend and ally of people who struggle to emerge from the shadow of oppressive totalitarian regimes. The historic revolutions in Central and Eastern Europe from 1989 to 1991, which liberated millions of people from communist domination, are a testament to the courage and faith of their citizens, and to the vision and strength of the United States and its allies. By their own actions, the people of these countries acted unequivocally to reject oppressive communist rule. As one, they turned to the West, as did many Latin American countries that chose the democratic path.

But the peoples of the Baltic Republics, Central and Eastern Europe, and the former Soviet Union are now in a difficult period of transition. The United States must demonstrate leadership to help them—as well as those in all countries who yearn to be free—to become fully integrated into the family of free nations.

9. *The United States will establish clear and forceful regional policies based on its own national security interests.*

The Clinton administration has no real foreign policy, only a series of ad hoc, reactive policies that are without focus; these merely try to play "catch-up" with events and outcomes determined by others. When the administration does act, it is too often ineffectively, and guided by what is best for the administration's domestic political agenda, not America's larger interests.

Nowhere is this trend more evident than in the administration's current policy toward the Russian Federation. The future of Russia will be determined by the Russians themselves. Therefore, we favor a sober, practical view of Russia's possible future—and a U.S. military capability to match that more realistic view. But instead of this realism, the Clinton administration holds a romanticized view of the Russian Federation and its leadership, largely driven by the theoreticians at the Department of State. Even as Russian troops crashed the cities of Chechnya, President Clinton traveled to Moscow to stand arm-in-arm with President Yeltsin. Such displays are contrary to the interests of spreading democracy and ties to the West within the former Soviet Union and in Central and Eastern Europe. We favor a policy that leaves no doubt in the mind of any Russian leader that a return of Russia's imperial activity against its neighbors, or a resumption of military competition with the United States, would be a tragic mistake.

In Europe, the Clinton administration has weakened the ties that bind our Atlantic partnership, has nearly squandered our historic relationship with the United Kingdom, and has been generally destructive of long-term American interests. America welcomes the spread of free-trading opportunities, but opposes any political or military tendencies that undercut the primacy of NATO. We strongly believe that exclusionary policies benefit neither the United States nor Europe.

In Asia, the world's fastest-growing economic region, the administration's policies have failed to serve our best interests. Our policy toward China has been inconsistent; our policy toward Japan marked by careless rhetoric; our policy toward India neglectful; our policy toward the two Koreas marked by uncertainty on the one hand and appeasement on the other; and our policy toward the Republic of China on Taiwan marred by ignoring its long years of support for the United States. At the same time, our military presence in the region, long the bulwark of stability for our friends and allies, is dangerously eroding. The enduring American interest is in securing open markets in Asia while denying to nondemocratic nations the ability to threaten the stability and security of the region. The United States must maintain a central security role in the Asia Pacific region, including the protection of our nuclear umbrella.

In Latin America, we see perhaps the greatest opportunity for closer relations and increased trade. Economic growth in this region is the key to the consolidation of democracy and offers a major opportunity for U.S. business. Instead of promoting American economic interests and integration, however, the Clinton administration seeks to dictate its own environmental, labor, and employment standards to our Latin American friends and trading partners. Indeed, this administration's most aggressive foreign policy initiative in the region is the belated, clumsy, and costly reactive scramble to respond to the Mexican debt crisis. Concerning Cuba, President Clinton has dodged a historic opportunity to bring an end to that repressive regime. Ignoring thirty-six years of aggression against U.S. interests, Clinton agreed with Castro to detain Cuban refugees indefinitely at our expense, while easing economic sanctions.

In the Middle East, we must maintain our long-standing support for Israel, the region's only democratic state. We must also foster the peace process between Israel and its Arab neighbors that promises a true peace, and not simply a continuing cycle of violence. At the same time, we must ensure our own access to the region's oil reserves at reasonable prices. We must continue to provide unwavering support for our friends and allies and make every effort to contain aggressors in the region who threaten the peace and stability of their neighbors. With the exception of its support for the peace process, begun under President Bush, the Clinton administration has been little more than a spectator to events in the region as they have unfolded over the past two years.

In Africa, the interests of the United States are best served by establishing closer relations with countries that support and expand democracy, peace, open trade relations, and regional stability. The Clinton administration has essentially abandoned the region in the wake of the tragic collapse of its failed policy in Somalia. The United States, as one of the leading nations in the world, has a moral obligation to assist the millions of people on this continent who are leading lives filled with suffering and disease. Ultimately, however, Africa's problems are its own and their solutions must be provided by the Africans themselves. The movement in South Africa to develop democratic and pluralistic institutions while retaining the market-oriented economic system of the previous regime is an important example of an indigenous African approach to reform and modernization. Within this context, the United States should provide all economic, philosophical, and humanitarian assistance necessary for the task at hand. In this regard, the end of military dictatorships in Africa should be a main concern of American interests in the area.

Leadership in Washington should offer a world view that does not apologize for the United States. We believe our country can and should play a constructive and inspirational role in world affairs. Sound, well-conceived policies designed to serve long-term American interests are needed, not just responses to the latest domestic political pressure. Under the next administration, the United States will mean what it says and act directly, forthrightly, and consistently.

12

International Trade

The conduct of the United States in leading the cause of liberalized trade is going to have more to do with the process of peace than all the diplomats put together.

—William E. Brock, May 10, 1995,
National Policy Forum Megaconference on Trade and Economy

★

WHEN THE EXPERTS TALK about international trade, they speak in a bewildering language of daunting acronyms. Naturally, most of us want to cut through the jargon and find out how this enormously complex array of treaties and organizations will affect our jobs and futures. Will NAFTA bring prosperity to American families? Has GATT increased the number of jobs available for Americans?

Although Americans are distrustful of platitudes about the "global community" and don't want to see American jobs or sovereignty bartered away, most are sanguine about the prospect of prosperity from international trade. The fact is reliance on free trade instead of protectionism ultimately means a better economy at home and more jobs for Americans. We are not among those who would retreat into a protectionist shell. People who advocate such policies have forgotten that this is precisely what was done in the 1920s and 1930s, resulting in profound economic, political, and social calamity.

There is a different and better choice. We remember Ronald Reagan's belief in the twin policies of deregulation and free market trade that reinvigorated the American economy in the 1980s. Under President Reagan's leadership, we initiated a series of measures to ensure increased opportunities to sell American-made goods and services overseas, believing that exports equal jobs for Americans.

It was Reagan who first articulated a goal of free trade in the Western Hemisphere. America's first free trade agreement with Israel, implemented in the fall of 1985, was a Reagan achievement. A U.S.-Canada agreement followed. In 1986, Reagan launched the Uruguay Round, a series of talks aimed at the reduction of trade barriers among more than sixty nations. The North American Free Trade Agreement (NAFTA), providing substantial trade benefits to U.S. firms seeking to conduct business in Mexico and Canada—our best customers—was another initiative of the Reagan-Bush years.

Reagan's faith in free trade principles was vindicated abroad by the crumbling of state-controlled, centrally directed communist economies. At home, the economy responded vigorously to Reagan's faith in free trade and deregulation. We have in real terms more than doubled our exports since the mid-1980s and the total proportion of our gross domestic product (GDP) sold abroad has risen from 6 percent to almost 12 percent.[1]

U.S. exporters are the leaders in high technology products, services, and agriculture and are highly competitive in transportation and financial services. We control over 80 percent of the world's software market and are dominant in computer technology, advanced telecommunications equipment, and medical technology. Our businesses are the most creative and productive in the world. In short, we are still the world's premiere innovators.

Americans enjoy the highest standard of living in the world, a standard that has been helped, not hurt, by open markets. Open trade means giving consumers the broadest possible product choices and the best prices. When import barriers are low, our producers must compete with the best in the world to stay ahead. Once our economy was self-contained; now it is increasingly more reliant on the world economy as a source of economic growth, job creation, and rising national income.

Free trade has become an engine of growth for our economy. Any effort to withdraw from world trade would choke the economy, putting countless

Americans out of work. And even if we wanted to take that risk, modern communications technology and the information revolution make any long-term attempt to protect domestic markets or to regulate international markets futile. Globalized production makes it more difficult for bureaucrats to protect domestic industries.

What is needed to accomplish an economic rejuvenation similar to the Reagan era is strong, decisive leadership through the end of this century and beyond. Americans welcome the challenge of inventing new products and offering competitive new services to the world; and we have the confidence, built on experience, necessary to meet this challenge.

The most important goal of American trade policy is to preserve and expand the open, free international trading system created after the Second World War. As the world's number one importer and exporter, that system has mightily benefited the United States and has stimulated global economic growth from which we have directly and indirectly reaped rewards.

Aside from completing the Uruguay Round and NAFTA—two Reagan-Bush initiatives—the current administration has had little success in promoting free trade around the globe. It is our pledge to restore America's credibility as a leader in international free trade into the next century.

GOVERNMENT'S ROLE

A new perspective on government's role in international commerce is necessary. During the past decade, we have seen the governmental role in protecting our trading interests evolve in an ad hoc and often confused fashion. Several agencies/departments have sought to seize a greater role, and each year new government-funded programs appear. There is much duplication.

Government's role should be limited. Government must sometimes step in to protect national security or to perform a task that private business cannot do. The appropriate trade-related role of government should be to

- negotiate and enforce treaties that provide a competitive environment for the United States in the global marketplace;
- facilitate free and secure movement of capital by and among the United States and foreign countries;

- counter those trade practices of other sovereign states that harm U.S. economic welfare while preserving the principle of free trade;
- establish as a high priority the intent to expand U.S. business opportunities, when sufficient private sector financial involvement is not present or feasible in a particular market;
- enforce U.S. laws and international agreements and seek effective enforcement by other nations of a global consensus of standards of commercial and/or government conduct;
- provide a coordinated, efficient, short-term adjustment mechanism as a transition for workers adversely affected by changes in U.S. trade and investment laws or the unforeseeable negative consequences of international trade agreements; and
- increase coordination and effectiveness among federal and state government agencies to achieve these objectives.

BREAKING BARRIERS TO FREE TRADE

The cornerstone of American trade policy must be the expansion of the international system of free trade. We have made much progress in the years since the General Agreement on Tariffs and Trade, or GATT, was accepted in 1947. GATT has been the most significant international agreement contributing to the elimination of trade barriers. Average world tariffs have been reduced from roughly 40 percent to under 5 percent. Just as important, the world's trading nations have agreed to a set of rules covering important trade practices, including government procurement policies, subsidies, and dumping. A trade dispute mechanism has also been in place—an aid in avoiding destructive trade wars.

While GATT worked to reduce tariffs internationally, many nations independently increased their reliance on other forms of protection, or invented new ways to shield favored domestic industries from competition. The use of nontariff barriers—such as quotas, voluntary restraint agreements (VRAs), and a variety of thinly disguised licensing, procedural, and regulatory requirements—have grown. These nontariff barriers have largely escaped the disciplines of the agreement.

To deal both with these barriers and to cut tariffs further, the Reagan administration in 1986 launched the Uruguay Round of trade negotiations among 117 countries. Final agreement was reached in December 1993, and the act was signed on April 15, 1994, at a conference in Marrakesh, Morocco. With the conclusion of the Uruguay Round and the creation of the World Trade Organization (WTO), we have gone into a new phase of cooperative efforts toward an international system.

Among the achievements of the Uruguay Round was the further reduction of tariffs, which were pushed down by a third to an average of 5 percent.[2] Tariff rates in many sectors critical to the United States, such as semiconductors, computer parts, and chemicals, were cut even more sharply. The Uruguay Round eliminated tariffs on such important products as steel, agricultural and construction equipment, paper and pulp, beer, furniture, pharmaceuticals, and medical equipment.

The Uruguay Round eliminated exemptions that previously kept several sectors of the U.S. economy outside of GATT rules—textiles, apparel, and agriculture. Textiles and apparel have been brought under the discipline of the World Trade Organization (WTO), and quotas will be eliminated over ten years.

In agriculture, the United States succeeded in obtaining explicit commitments to reduce foreign agricultural subsidies. Nations agreed to replace their non-tariff barriers with explicit tariffs, while agreeing to reduce those tariffs gradually over time. These changes should increase our access to many previously closed foreign markets for agricultural goods.

Equally important to the United States, the rules were extended to cover trade in services. The United States is the largest exporter of services ($200 billion annually), which include telecommunications, financial services, construction, computer services, accounting, transportation, and tourism.[3]

Likewise, the WTO rules will cover intellectual property. Intellectual property rights such as patents, copyrights, and trademarks are vitally important to the United States in a different way. The United States is a leader in providing goods and services that rely on intellectual property—everything from computers and computer software to music videos to pharmaceuticals. At the same time, goods and services that rely on intellectual property have become more critical and more valuable in our economic life. The intellectual property itself has become easier to steal and duplicate. U.S.

firms have estimated that intellectual property thefts cost them over $60 billion a year.[4] The intellectual property protections accorded in the Uruguay Round, though far from comprehensive, are an important first step.

Foreign investment has become as important as trade in today's global economy, and restrictions on foreign investment can be as difficult to overcome as barriers to trade in goods and services. The Uruguay Round eliminated many barriers to foreign direct investment including local content rules and export performance requirements. American businesses should now be able to expand and sell abroad with greater ease and efficiency.

Some suggest that with the conclusion of the Uruguay Round and the creation of the WTO, new multilateral agreements may be unlikely in the future. But there are still areas of trade not fully covered under the Uruguay agreements. There is tremendous room for new agreements that break down even more barriers, reduce more tariffs, and open more markets.

Extending Multilateral Initiatives

The United States must focus its attention on making the WTO work for American interests. The WTO is charged with enforcing the numerous new market-opening provisions won in the Uruguay Round. We must push the WTO to fulfill its mission. Where countries have not opened their markets in compliance with WTO requirements, the United States should call them to account and, where necessary, utilize the WTO's new dispute resolution procedures. The WTO dispute settlement regime must become a platform for promoting market access for American business, and we should make aggressive use of it to eliminate foreign practices that violate the WTO's rules.

Although the Uruguay Round broke considerable new ground, the United States was unable to reach agreement in a number of areas important to American business. These are ripe topics for future trade agreements. For example, the Uruguay Round required compromises on the timing of tariff reductions over the next ten years. There is support for an acceleration of tariff reduction beyond the levels achieved in the Uruguay Round for a number of key products, such as agricultural goods. We support stronger investment commitments that provide access for American business to foreign markets on a nondiscriminatory basis.

In a number of sectors United States trade objectives were not fully achieved. Additional work to promote full liberalization is needed in telecommunications, aviation, financial services, broadcasting, and agriculture.

REGIONAL AND BILATERAL INITIATIVES

We must continue working toward the fulfillment of the Reagan-Bush goal of free trade from Alaska to Tierra del Fuego to create American jobs.

An important step in our efforts to open markets for American businesses came to fruition in the North American Free Trade Agreement. NAFTA is the most comprehensive regional trade agreement ever negotiated by the United States. It created the world's largest market, consisting of 380 million people producing nearly $8 trillion worth of goods and services.[5]

NAFTA progressively eliminates tariffs among the United States, Mexico, and Canada, providing substantial benefits to U.S. firms seeking to do business in Mexico, since their tariffs were over two-and-a-half times higher than our own. The agreement also eliminated Mexican export performance requirements, import licensing, and many forms of bureaucratic red tape that added delays and expense to U.S. costs of doing business. These barriers were hard on small U.S. businesses, particularly those less well-equipped to wade through needlessly complex and expensive export and import procedures.

Under the agreement, American firms are protected from discriminatory treatment and are given specific protection on imports, exports, production operations, and investment. NAFTA provides the strongest protection for patents, copyrights, trade secrets, and other intellectual property of any international agreement now in force. This protection fosters increased trade, while cutting losses for U.S. manufacturers of computer software/hardware, video/audio, chemicals, and pharmaceutical products.

NAFTA produced strong growth in American exports to Mexico in its first year. While the economic crisis in Mexico brought on by the December 1994 devaluation of the peso has cut that growth sharply, NAFTA continues to provide U.S. companies a competitive edge over their non-North American competitors and will position them for even stronger growth in the medium-to-long term as the Mexican economy recovers.

TRADE INSTEAD OF AID

In fostering a robust trade policy to benefit Americans, we must focus on international trade instead of foreign aid (discussed more fully in chapter 14). Ultimately trade is more important to the global economy than aid has ever been. Open markets encourage development of the private sector; foreign aid tends to foster government programs that thwart free enterprise.

Our free trade policies have helped increase the economic self-sufficiency of the world's developing nations. In this way, trade—not aid—is a unique underpinning of our approach to international economic development. Developing countries will benefit more by having access to open international markets and by being able to export than they would by simply being recipients of aid. The United States can be most effective in helping countries grow by working harder to keep international markets open, including our own.

It is time to reevaluate our aid policy to serve the interests of the United States in the twenty-first century. We are rethinking government spending at all levels, domestically and internationally, and trade is no exception. U.S. economic aid should be conditioned upon support for free market policies and openness to foreign trade and investment.

A new era of economic and political cooperation already has ushered in a period of growth and democratization in this hemisphere. To the north, the United States and Canada signed a free trade agreement in 1987. To the south, the Reagan and Bush teams encouraged a wave of economic reforms that entailed the opening of trade and investment regimes across Latin America, the privatization of state-run enterprises, the restructuring of external debt, and the deregulation of domestic economies. The Bush administration laid the groundwork for the current movement toward free trade in the Western Hemisphere through the Enterprise for the Americas Initiative (EAI). Partly as a result of these new policies, U.S. exporters of manufactured goods, services, and agricultural products enjoyed a dominant position in Latin America markets during the Reagan-Bush years. Total American exports to the region tripled between 1985 and 1993.[6]

TRADING PARTNERS

The United States should undertake concerted negotiations with individual trading partners throughout the world to reduce trade barriers blocking American suppliers. In many instances, the bilateral negotiating process can achieve gains for American producers and consumers that could not be won in a multilateral context. (U.S. foreign policy with respect to these countries is more fully discussed in chapter 15.)

Recognizing that the United States and the European Union (EU) share deep historical, cultural, and economic ties, as well as strategic interests, we must promote cooperation to advance a multilateral trade and investment system. The effectiveness of the WTO depends upon a common, constructive course. The United States and EU must share the burden of integrating the Eastern and Central European countries into a free market system.

The current administration has damaged the working relationship between the United States and EU. It is our challenge to repair this damage and foster an effective working relationship among these countries.

As an economic partner and strategic ally, Japan represents a special challenge to the United States. This nation has not torn down many of its market barriers to foreign suppliers. Many such barriers—tolerated or encouraged by the Japanese government—constitute significant discrimination against American products and to American investment in that country. These barriers thwart the international system's promise of full and mutual access to major markets.

Our relationship of trust and cooperation, weakened under the current administration, must be renewed. We must pursue a policy of clear, well-defined trade and investment objectives to dismantle the structural impediments to American access which now exist. The United States and Japan should be able to strengthen their economic and strategic relationship simultaneously and restore the mutual trust that is so essential to a bilateral relationship.

Russia's progress toward democracy and a market economy is essential for global stability. While our ability to influence Russia's domestic situation is limited, we support helping Russia move more rapidly toward economic reform, private sector development, and an open and stable trade and investment regime. In our bilateral relationship, we should encourage trade, not massive aid. If we are successful, we will reinforce both the international economic system and democratic forces in Russia.

The United States and the rest of the world have a historic opportunity to integrate China into the free trade community. China is largely a Marxist system that does not fit into a liberal international economic order. We favor Chinese accession into the WTO, but only on conditions that require Chinese adherence to international standards of behavior and a commitment to permanently and expeditiously dismantle trade and investment barriers to foreign products. We must also be vigilant to assure that China respects the obligations it has already stated to open its markets and to protect intellectual property rights.

The ill-fated attempt by the Clinton administration to tie Most Favored Nation (MFN) status for China to human rights resulted in a humiliating retreat and undercut both American political and commercial interests. We must pursue trade policies with China that are clear, realistic, and achievable and will oppose the dilution of these objectives by the injection of inappropriate criteria in trade relations.

DOMESTIC TRADE LAW

Working within the WTO agreements does not mean giving up domestic laws that can help keep trade free and open. Domestic trade law provides additional avenues to achieve market access objectives where foreign practices are deemed unjustifiable, unreasonable, or discriminatory. We believe the United States should preserve domestic trade remedies that are consistent with WTO rules and make use of these remedies when WTO rules are inadequate.

For example, Section 301 of the Trade Act of 1974 has allowed us to respond to trade practices, in particular those not covered by WTO rules or other international agreements, if we determine the practices are harming U.S. interests.

With the substantially broader scope of the new WTO and the greater organizational discipline that will result from new dispute resolution procedures, the United States may have less need to use its Section 301 authority. In the meantime, Section 301 continues to offer an effective tool to seek greater protection for American intellectual property, to reduce discrimination against our companies in foreign government procurements, and to open telecommunications markets and other markets that are currently closed to U.S. providers. Because of its unilateral nature and the recent potential availability of alternatives, future use of Section 301 could be very limited and selective as a mechanism against trading partners who are reluctant or unwilling to accept free and open competition.

EMERGING MARKETS

The world's emerging markets offer unparalleled opportunities to American businesses that are prepared to compete internationally.

Central and Eastern Europe. Central and Eastern Europe have emerged from communism and state-controlled economies to enter the community of free market nations. By some estimates the American taxpayer spent more than $12.3 trillion on the Cold War.[7] Although millions of Americans trace their heritage to this region of the world, little commercial activity took place between the United States and the Communist bloc during that time.

Under the communist system, normal elements of a free economy, including consumer choice and free enterprise, did not exist. Government fiat and control, rather than individual preference and choice, largely dictated which products and jobs were available. As a result, shortages and rationing were common; consumer and industrial products were of poor quality, and local currencies had no value beyond the confines of the system.

American leadership, particularly under President Reagan, culminated in communism's collapse. Five years later, the process of rebuilding that region's economic and political systems continues. This is a difficult task, but public sentiment favors democracy and reforms that will sustain economic freedom and self-government in the region. Entrepreneurship is flourishing, and food and consumer products abound as market mechanisms largely are permitted to determine supply. The free market is providing new choices and incentives.

The United States and other industrialized countries are helping the new democracies there help themselves. As of January 1995, U.S.-obligated resources to the eleven-country region totaled approximately $1.8 billion,[8] with Poland, Hungary, Bulgaria, and the Czech Republic (countries with strong market opportunities) receiving the majority of assistance. This sends a clear message that the United States will not turn its back on countries that ultimately choose to adopt the democratic, free enterprise system.

Poland, Hungary, the Czech Republic, and Slovakia are aligned as signatories of the Central European Free Trade Agreement (CEFTA) and are currently the leading trading partners in the region. American products and technology currently enjoy an excellent reputation among CEFTA countries. Consumers often prefer goods "Made in America ," and strong ethnic ties with our country helps to cement these relationships. For example, Poland's imports of U.S. goods and services have more than doubled since 1990.[9]

American exports to the region should increase partly as a result of the U.S. position as the dominant investor in the CEFTA region. That foothold can serve as a base to expand American products, services, and related investment throughout Europe and east to Russia and the former Soviet Union.

The American taxpayer has much to gain from the successful political and economic transition of countries formerly in the Communist bloc. In addition to the immeasurable political benefits of a strong and free Central Europe, the region has the capacity to contribute significantly to U.S. trade and job growth goals.

To advance this goal of expanded trade, the United States should firmly condition its economic assistance to countries in the region on their performance in working to achieve the full economic, legal, and trade reforms necessary to become self-sufficient and productive members of the global market community.

In that process, the United States must also ensure that American companies are afforded open and fair opportunities to compete in these newly emerging markets.

Newly independent states. The newly independent states (NIS) of the former Soviet Union are home to over 450 million people in twenty-one of the newly independent states who are now seeking to participate in the world economy.[10]

Some of these countries are responding to the challenges of reform more vigorously than others. Russia, for example, has privatized 62 percent of its economy in barely three years. It boasts a new constitution, a new civil code, and appears to be succeeding in its battle against uncontrolled inflation. Others continue to struggle with the legacy of central planning and the attitudes of the former regimes. As is the case in most emerging markets, there is a strong connection between government authority and commerce, and the NIS is no exception.

For U.S. business, the NIS contain substantial mineral and energy reserves, other natural resources, and agricultural capacity. As these economies improve, consumer demand will grow as well, offering strong possibilities for American business.

The economic success of the NIS is a vital national interest of the United States. The most effective way to prevent a return to central planning, militarism, and autocratic leadership is through increased commercial ties with the West and its markets. As in Central Europe, American policy should focus on the expansion and consolidation of the free market system throughout the NIS region, and develop a viable and self-sustaining private sector that can stand as a bulwark for democracy and free enterprise.

We must promote decentralized policies and programs that recognize other NIS countries and their potential markets. More attention should be focused on the development of small- and medium-sized businesses that can be capitalized with U.S. investment and operated using our technology and know-how. Not only would such commercial activity promote democracy in the NIS, it would increase our business interests in these emerging markets, overshadowed by the proximity of their European neighbors.

China. The Chinese economy is at a crossroads. Economic reforms are continuing in many sectors and market forces are assuming greater influence in their economy. But China is still a socialist economy burdened by an ailing state sector, a rapidly growing budget deficit, an aging infrastructure, and an uncertain political future.

Despite China's stated goal of reforming and liberalizing trade, and despite the recent agreement on intellectual property, import restrictions remain. Legal disputes with foreign investors and other trade issues have dampened the fervor with which companies move into China. Tension between the mainland and Taiwan fragment the country and is in the interest of neither the United States or regional stability.

China's absorption of Hong Kong in 1997 raises other issues. Some fear that Hong Kong's laws will be undermined by Chinese authorities, creating an uncertain future for Hong Kong. The United States has an interest in seeing Hong Kong not only remain open to American businesses, but become the model for future economic policy for the People's Republic of China.

The pace of further trade and investment reforms will be influenced by negotiations within the multilateral trading system. Membership in the WTO will speed China's integration into the global market system, reinforce economic reform, and open new opportunities for U.S. exports. China should not be admitted under special terms that delay these objectives. Vigilance is also essential to assure that trade agreements previously reached with China are fully implemented—particularly with respect to intellectual property.

Asia and newly industrialized economies. Several of the countries of East and Southeast Asia are the most dynamic and promising of all the emerging markets. Some of these nations—Hong Kong, Indonesia, Singapore, South Korea, Taiwan, and Thailand—are rapidly becoming global exporters and significant import markets. With growth, there is a surging demand for capital equipment, infrastructure, and consumer goods. Rising incomes and increased disposable income throughout the region are creating vast new markets for American goods and services. Even Vietnam, which like China still maintains a communist political system, has adopted economic reforms and is moving into the ranks of market economies.

These nations welcome U.S. investment and a strong U.S. economic presence. We believe it is vital to the long-term competitiveness of U.S. industry for our country to play an active commercial role in the fastest growing and most populous region of the world.

Special attention in our trade relations must be given to services, where business opportunity is growing but many countries continue to maintain formidable barriers. In order for the region to achieve its full economic potential, the U.S. must exercise leadership to assure that practical barriers to trade and investment are reduced.

Taiwan, Hong Kong, Singapore, and South Korea remain among the world's most dynamic economies, making them attractive to U.S. business interests. Taiwan and South Korea have recorded significant rates of economic growth in the past two decades, and trade and foreign direct investment have played a key role. These are important markets for U.S. goods and sources of U.S. imports. In the case of Korea, the United States is its most important export market. In Taiwan, the United States has accounted for a larger percent of its total exports in the early 1990s than has Japan, a reversal of the role played by the two some thirty years ago. Efforts should be made with both countries, through the WTO and the Asia Pacific Economic Cooperation (APEC) group (embracing nearly all nations of the Pacific), to accelerate market opening, particularly in financial services and agriculture.

Although Taiwan has made progress in opening its economy to the world market, barriers to imports do still remain. Agriculture and some manufacturing industries are still highly protected. Tariffs, an import licensing system, restrictive standards and lack of intellectual property protection still hinder imports. Recent developments indicate, however, that Taiwan is likely to pursue trade and investment liberalization as part of its overall strategy for continued development and growth. (A further discussion of our relations with these countries is contained in chapter 15).

Latin America. Latin America is the second-fastest growing region of the world (after Southeast Asia). Overall trade between the Latin American/Caribbean (LAC) region and the United States has grown from approximately $44 billion in 1988 to almost $100 billion in 1994. U.S. exports to Latin America, mostly of manufactured goods, more than doubled between 1985 and 1993, from $31 billion to $73 billion.[11]

Latin America has led the developing world in the pace and progress of economic integration and trade liberalization. Latin nations have cut tariffs unilaterally by an average of 80 percent over the last decade and fostered subregional groupings that are facilitating rapid growth and investment with partners both inside and outside the region.[12]

The growth of intraregional trade has been spurred by free trade agreements among the nations of Latin America and the Caribbean. For example, MERCOSUR is composed of Argentina, Brazil, Paraguay and Uruguay with an internal market of over 198 million people.[13] The Andean Act, composed of Bolivia, Colombia, Ecuador, Peru, and Venezuela, has an internal market of 96 million people.[14]

LAC nations are no longer the debt-ridden, protectionist regimes so prevalent in the past. They are experiencing sustained economic growth and generally declining inflation as a direct result of aggressive implementation of macroeconomic reforms, market opening initiatives and restructuring.

While efforts toward trade liberalization continue throughout the region, a number of bilateral issues remain relating to import policies, standards setting, export subsidies, intellectual property rights, investment barriers, and others.

The current administration has lost much of the initiative in catalyzing trade liberalization and economic integration in the Western Hemisphere. Without U.S. leadership, regional integration may develop in a way that places U.S. companies on the outside rather than the inside of a new regional framework. The United States must lead the process of Western Hemispheric economic integration in a way that expands NAFTA and opens the region's markets to U.S. business.

Together with Asia, the LAC region remains perhaps the best future area for growth in U.S. exports and investment. It is projected that by 2010, the United States will be exporting more to Latin America than to Japan and the EU combined. However, projections are not reality and current adminitsration policies, unless reversed, could impede this progress.

Middle East and Africa. Few regions of the world better demonstrate the close relationship between trade and foreign policy than the Middle East. Indeed, the idea that foreign policy is an extension of trade policy was promoted by President Reagan. The United States has important strategic interests in this region, linked on the one hand to the huge oil reserves of several Moslem countries and, on the other, to traditional support for the state of Israel. The United States/Israel Free Trade Agreement illustrates this relationship.

The Middle East enjoys stable currencies, excellent financial institutions and a strong desire to do business with Americans. The future economic progress of the Middle East is governed by the need for continued efforts at peace among the countries of the region. A complicated maze of barriers and uncertainties exist that affects U.S. domestic and economic interests and supports the need for a U.S. military and foreign aid presence in the region.

Oil constitutes the primary source of foreign exchange earnings for most of the Gulf Cooperation Council (GCC) countries. The United States is able to pay for its oil imports with the export of our goods and services. A significant portion of that merchandise is defense equipment and other high technology products. Obviously the Middle East is of great economic importance to our country, and the United States has worked for the free flow of oil from the region to the rest of the world during this century and will continue this course in the future. (Further discussed in chapter 15.)

In the case of Saudi Arabia, the United States is the largest supplier of goods and largest investor. In the case of Iran and Iraq, our trade relationship is entirely subordinated to foreign policy concerns.

Continued political and economic stability in the area hinges on the simmering social challenges. Issues surrounding the pariah states of Iran and Iraq must be resolved, as those countries pose a threat to the region and to the continuing flow of oil to the world. The ultimate effect of any serious turmoil in that region, given our dependence on foreign oil, would be directly felt in the pocket book of American citizens.

Africa. African countries constitute a significant source of new growth in U.S. merchandise trade flows. South Africa shows special promise as a major emerging market. It is already the largest market for U.S. goods in sub-Saharan Africa, and is poised to become a potent engine for growth throughout the region. South Africa will develop greater market opportunities as its new multiracial society develops and it assumes a larger role in the global economy.

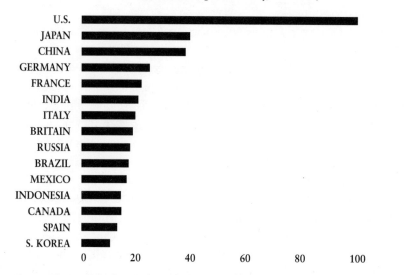

15 Largest Economies, 1992

(GDPs at Purchasing Power Parity, U.S. = 100)

(*Source:* The World Bank and *The Economist*, "The Global Survey," 1 October 1994)

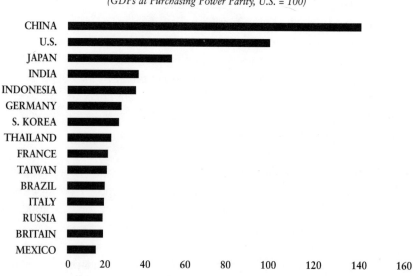

15 Largest Economies, 2020

(GDPs at Purchasing Power Parity, U.S. = 100)

(*Source:* The World Bank and *The Economist*, "The Global Survey," 1 October 1994)

India. India is in the midst of a market revolution of its own. After decades of heavy-handed government intervention, a large state-owned sector, and onerous tariffs and quotas that stunted trade, reforms are occurring. Much of India's industrial licensing has been abolished; many areas once closed to the private sector have been opened; and tariffs and exchange controls dropped. Foreign investment, once allowed only grudgingly, is now welcomed. As a result, business is booming, presenting major new opportunities for American business in a democracy with a huge middle class.

We must continue to recognize the importance of global markets—both developed and emerging—to American prosperity and employment, and to our own industrial competitiveness. It is necessary for the United States to work aggressively and consistently through multilateral trade organizations, regional trade negotiations, and bilateral fora to expand the international free trade system, reduce barriers to American exports and investment, and to support the efforts of American business to develop their full potential as participants in the global marketplace.

U.S. COMPETITION AND HIGH TECHNOLOGY
Telecommunications

Perhaps no sector of the economy has experienced technological change as rapidly as the telecommunications and increasingly interrelated computer field—the "Information Economy."[15] Virtually all of the changes in this sector are a direct consequence of pro-competition, pro-investment, and deregulatory policies put in place and vigorously pursued by the Reagan and Bush administrations.

A generation of unparalleled innovation. Scarcely a generation ago, "innovation" in telephones consisted of the answering machine. Fiber optics, digital switching, facsimile, cellular phones, worldwide messaging, cable television, videocassette recorders (VCRs), satellite television, personal computers, the worldwide Internet, and other advances that Americans today take for granted were almost unknown.[16] The telecommunications sector was dominated by a handful of firms—and intrusive federal and state regulatory bureaucracies. Heavy-handed regulation slowed progress. It limited choice, inflated prices, and hobbled innovation.

Many of the changes in telecommunications were fueled by the unregulated and fiercely competitive computer hardware, software, and microelectronics business. There, prices and costs dropped precipitously under the pressures of marketplace competition—and no government regulators intervened.[17] Computer technology has created a commercial and competitive renaissance in telecommunications. Republican administrations throughout the 1980s demobilized regulation and allowed the forces of competition fully to engage.

A beacon on the American economic scene. Today, the U.S. "Information Economy" constitutes better than 8 percent of our $6 trillion national economy. It employs more than 2 percent of the workforce directly. Competitive, deregulated communications markets have proven a prime source of new investment and employment opportunities. Forecasts call for the global "Information Economy" to top $2.3 trillion by the early years of the next century. Importantly, the "Information Economy" is one high technology sector where American business, industry, and research clearly leads.[18]

Public policy challenges. Public policy challenges affecting the "Information Economy" are very much the same as Americans face in other fields. Competition and opportunity are being curtailed by costly, regulatory regimes. The solution lies in pursuing key national policy goals.

Reliance on competition and free enterprise. Competitive free markets will demonstrably work better than regulation ever could. Since competition policy initiatives in the early 1980s, American telecommunications has been literally revolutionized. Everything from cellular and other pocket phones to communicating laptop computers has materialized in abundance. The rate of overall sector growth has approximately doubled—from scarcely 5 percent to about 10 percent or higher each year.[19] This electronic abundance has been accompanied by drastically lower prices coupled with broader choices. Competition, deregulation, and reliance on private initiative have paid impressive national dividends.

Devolution. Where competitive markets are unable to achieve a clearly defined public policy purpose, the least regulation necessary should be undertaken and, wherever possible, undertaken at the state, not federal level. An attic-to-basement review of current government regulations such as Federal Communications Commission regulations should be commenced.

Curtailment of waste, duplication, and overlap. Duplicative regulations across many government agencies should be combined and streamlined.

Privatization when functions can be better performed by the private sector. Private sector coordination and negotiations have worked throughout the deregulated transportation sector, as an example. That approach can work here.

Honing America's technology edge. Legislation and trade negotiations aimed at removing barriers to communications investments are a priority. The U.S. "Information Economy" is heavily dependent on international trade today. Free and open markets for American high technology products are especially important. Overseas sales not only account for substantial earnings, but help project the image of American political freedom abroad.

Limiting U.S. domestic investment by foreign-based firms imposes very real costs on American consumers. Any limits here are typically mirrored in restrictions placed on American competitors overseas. That limits growth of U.S. companies in world markets. Limiting the number of firms that can invest, employ, and compete in America, moreover, denies consumers greater opportunities and choice.

Through efforts including ongoing WTO negotiations, the United States should continue to press for expanded opportunities for American firms abroad. At the same time, attention needs to be paid to removing communications law, technology transfer, and other potential barriers to international activities within our country.

Computers
Facilitating computer industry competitiveness. The United States should continue to emphasize the importance of intellectual property

rights, particularly in computer software. Too many of our global trading partners wink at widespread piracy and illegal copying of American computer software programs. China and South Korea, as well as Taiwan, are notoriously weak in their defense of international intellectual property rights.

As international markets become more and more critical to the success of U.S.-based computer companies, it is critical that governments safeguard international property rights. This is the best means of ensuring an incentive to produce. If software firms' incentive to create and produce new and better products is eroded through international piracy, the U.S. economy and consumers will be net losers.

Computer network growth. The worldwide Internet computer network constitutes a prime example of how markets and technology can work if freed from regulatory intervention. Online services afford businesses quick and efficient access to computer databases and communications. They thus can be a powerful catalyst for rejuvenating and reinvigorating the American system as well as our economy.

Most important is the need for government not to impose traditional regulatory regimes on this evolving high technology "marketplace of ideas." Restrictions, rules, and philosophies that might once have been appropriate to yesterday's telephone network should not be carried over and applied to the Internet. Thus concepts, including government-guaranteed access to the Internet, periodically urged by the vice president and others wedded to yesterday's regulatory world, should be rejected.

Government should reject the notion that some online communications customers should be overcharged in order to finance cheap service to specially favored groups. The government needs to stay out of the way. The "Information Superhighway" cannot be allowed to become a government-run toll road.

AGRICULTURE AND TRADE

We must reaffirm that our farmers in the production of agriculture are a vital segment of our economy and of our international trade policy.

Agriculture creates jobs—employing more than 21 million people from shore to shore—and accounts for nearly 16 percent of our nation's gross domestic product.[20]

American agriculture policy today is the result of supply controls, income support, and other farm programs emanating from the 1930s' Depression "dust bowl" era. Today, these programs are, at best, antiquated, ensuring lower productivity and efficiency, while holding down exports and export earnings. For American farmers, ranchers, and other agricultural producers to compete around the world in the next century, they must be able to produce efficiently and profitably. Unburdening American farmers from excessive environmental regulations and government price-fixing will lower the cost of agricultural production. That means more affordable food at home, and more competitive farm products to sell abroad.

Washington, however, imposes rules and regulations that entangle farmers in paperwork and red tape, and forces them not to grow on large sections of their land.

Some parts of the nation's farm policy can be eliminated outright—for example, the Acreage Reduction Program, which keeps domestic prices high by limiting farm production. This program is one of the most injurious to American agriculture in world markets. Because the price of domestic farm products is inflated, it makes it harder to sell U.S. agricultural goods in the rest of the world. The big-government solution has been to reduce the price of export farm products by subsidizing their sale abroad. These export programs, in effect, require the American taxpayers and consumers to pay twice for the diseconomic effect of Washington's farm policy: first we pay at the grocery store, in the form of higher domestic food prices; and second, we pay on April 15, with our taxes going to support part of the cost of agriculture shipped abroad.

The simplest and most effective program for promoting our agriculture in world markets is the elimination of domestic regulations that make U.S. farmers less productive. We must unshackle U.S. producers and take a series of aggressive steps to remove existing barriers to world trade in bulk and processed agricultural products. If we are successful in meeting this challenge, it will pay rich rewards for the U.S. agricultural economy in the years to come.

The United States currently uses export programs from as early as the 1950s to compete in world trade of the 1990s. The Export Enhancement Program (EEP), providing humanitarian aid and sales to emerging democracies, and the General Sales Manager (GSM) credit guarantee programs should be phased out according to the timetables of the world trade accords, overhauled, or replaced with new, innovative programs better meeting current demands and worldwide challenges.

Getting rid of burdensome and counterproductive regulations and revising export support programs are just the first steps in improving the competitive posture of U.S. agriculture.

American farmers and growers can compete with anyone in the world if they have access to foreign markets and if the rules governing trade are fair. While GATT, NAFTA, and the WTO are slated to reduce barriers to free trade and increase opportunities for U.S. agriculture in world markets, the United States must not underestimate the strength of the sovereign self-interests of our competitors. When necessary, we should not shrink from defending our markets. American agribusiness has found itself competing for years against the treasuries of Europe.

Similarly, we must not single out agricultural products to bear the burden of foreign policy through unproductive embargoes such as President Carter instituted late in his administration.

Whether the products are computer chips or potato chips, American businesses have the strength, creativity, ingenuity, and perseverance to compete with firms from any nation in the world. The world economy is not a zero-sum game. As nations that used to be poor become rich, we do not become poor in turn. Instead, the people of those newly prosperous countries become valuable customers for valued American goods.

Open markets represent an opportunity for American businesses to create new, higher paying jobs for our citizens, fulfilling the world's demand for America's quality products and services.

13

Restoring America's Power

AMERICA HAS FOUGHT FIVE MAJOR WARS and a host of
smaller conflicts in the twentieth century. It was not prepared for four of
them. In the case of World Wars I and II, Korea, and Vietnam, the United
States was forced to undertake major military and industrial buildups under
severe time constraints, and achieved uneven results. In particular, an
unready America suffered major setbacks in the early days of World War II
and the Korean War. Both of those conflicts had been preceded by major
and sustained declines in defense expenditures that resulted in devastating
military losses in 1941–42 and 1950–51.

During the Bush administration, the United States, benefiting from a
Reagan-Bush buildup of the military, was truly prepared for effective operations during Desert Shield and Desert Storm. But now, once again, we are
losing our military edge. The Clinton administration has diverted resources
from military preparedness to social programs and put the efficacy of our
armed forces at risk. We must sustain our capabilities to deal with a full
range of threats, from terrorist and criminal organizations, as well as from
the traditional nation-states. In modernizing our armed forces, we should be
guided by three important principles.

1. *We must understand present threats.* Although the Soviet Union no
   longer exists and the threat of a major nuclear war has lessened, the
   world abounds in direct and indirect threats to American interests and
   the lives of its citizens. These include the spread of weapons of mass
   destruction (chemical, biological, and nuclear); regional conflicts in
   areas of strategic importance; actions of rogue states—for example,

such as Iraq, Iran, Libya, North Korea—against U.S. interests; terrorism; international organized crime; and political unrest that creates waves of refugees.

2. *We need a strategic doctrine to guide our efforts.* The United States must develop its force structure and equipment to deal with the full range of conflicts. Although the possibility of major conventional war in Europe has lessened, the potential for major regional conflict remains, particularly in Asia and the Middle East. The United States must maintain the capability to support its allies in case of need or to take unilateral action if necessary to defend its interests. The spread of nuclear weapons also makes it imperative to develop the response capabilities to deter aggression and to neutralize the threat of long- and medium-range missile attack. The United States must also enhance and sustain its ability to operate in conflicts short of major war, such as peacekeeping, counterterrorism, and counterinsurgency operations.

3. *We must focus on readiness, modernization, and technology.* In order to prepare our forces for future conflicts, the United States must sustain its readiness through appropriate recruitment, training, and development of sound doctrine. Readiness also requires sustained attention to strategic lift and combat support capabilities as well as the efficiency of combat units. The United States must continue to maintain its lead in technology and exploit emerging capabilities in order to continually modernize its military forces.

Throughout this century, Republican presidents have worked hard to preserve our national military preparedness. By contrast, during the Carter administration, America's power and prestige around the world fell to an all-time low. The Reagan years saw a revival in our military strength—and not a minute too soon. Reagan's commitment to military preparedness, often in the face of ridicule from the national press, was a major factor in the fall of communism.

THE HOLLOW MILITARY
Jimmy Carter came to office in 1977 promising to reduce the defense budget and particularly expenditures on new defense programs. It reflected his optimism about the Soviet leadership's commitment to "détente." His term was marked by the persistent underfunding of both the personnel and the operations and maintenance accounts. The military, seeking to recover from the Vietnam experience, suffered material and readiness shortages so serious that it came to be designated "the hollow force."

Recruiting was affected, and people left the military. Training suffered, as did proficiency in military skills. Not surprisingly, morale and discipline, still fragile after Vietnam, plummeted even further.

Shortfalls in modernization led to an overreliance on poorly maintained equipment left over from the Vietnam era. There were widespread shortages in spare parts, which led to increasing use of parts from otherwise operative equipment and drove up maintenance backlogs. By 1980, these shortages were devastating. In that year less than 40 percent of all divisions, air squadrons, and ships were rated by their commanders as fully mission-capable.[1]

The lack of military readiness was highlighted by the disaster at Desert One in 1980. The failed American hostage rescue mission in Iran made it clear that the nation could not tolerate a "hollow military" force. The Carter administration's defense catastrophe stimulated challenges to American interests throughout the world. These challenges were met only when the Reagan and Bush administrations implemented decisive policy changes.

THE REAGAN REVIVAL
Beginning in FY 1981 and continuing through the five ensuing years, our national defense capability benefited from increases in spending in real terms. The growth in defense spending led to a rapid and sustained improvement in recruitment, retention, training, and readiness. Increases in military pay and benefits, and new spending on quality of life, led to a significant improvement in the quality of recruits and the retention of prior enlistees. Within five years, from FY 1980 to FY 1985, the percentage of

high school graduates among new recruits rose from 68 percent to 93 percent, and the reenlistment rate rose from 55 percent to nearly 84 percent.[2]

Similarly, readiness rates showed sharp increases over the previous decade. Air Force mission-capable aircraft rose, as did training for air crews of Air Force tactical fighter and attack aircraft. The U.S. Navy's surface fleet's material readiness rate also rose. The overhaul backlog dropped to zero in FYs 1986 and 1987.[3] The opening of the National Training Center at Fort Irwin in 1982 led to highly effective training of an increasing number of battalions.

Along with readiness-related programs, we funded research and development (R&D) that produced the underpinnings for long-term force readiness. By the start of Operation Desert Storm, the United States had not only the most highly trained and highly motivated force in its history, but could also field, or begin to field, many of the advanced systems funded in the 1980s. These systems included the F-117, F-15, F-16, F-18 tactical aircraft, and the still in development but highly effective JSTARS ground surveillance aircraft, the conventional Tomahawk cruise missile, the M-1 tank, the Bradley Fighting Vehicle, the Patriot Air/Missile defense system, and the Apache and Blackhawk helicopters.

All these systems made major contributions to the smashing victory over Iraq. As four senior-level military officers reported in their recent review of American defense programs in the 1980s, "The return on this renewed and balanced investment in America's military came in 1991 when U.S.-led forces achieved a stunning one-hundred–hour ground war victory following a naval blockade and a thirty-nine–day air campaign against Iraqi forces in Operation Desert Storm."[4]

LAG TIME

There is always a lag between resource allocation and its impact on force, structure, and inventories. As a result, despite declining budgets imposed by the Democratic Congress beginning in the second half of the 1980s, there was virtually no draw-down in actual capability and force structure by the time Desert Storm was launched. There were two more active Army and reserve divisions in January 1991 than there were by the close of FY 1980.

There were also an additional Army special forces group and a new Ranger Battalion.[5]

The Navy had 16 aircraft carriers and Surface to Action (Battleship) Groups when Desert Storm was launched in 1991, in contrast to the 12 carriers in its FY 1980 force structure and no Surface to Action Groups. All told, there were over 530 deployable battle force ships in the fleet as the Iraq War began—60 more than in 1980.

The active duty Air Force fielded nearly one hundred more fighter and attack aircraft and one additional squadron in FY 1991 than it did in FY 1980. There were also six additional reserve fighter and attack squadrons, representing another one hundrend additional aircraft, at the outbreak of the war. The Marine Corps also had more aircraft in their inventory during Desert Storm: twenty additional active and about another twenty reserve fighter and attack aircraft. The United States had also expanded its long-range air- and sealift significantly during the decade between FY 1980 and the launching of Desert Storm.

RETURN TO THE HOLLOW MILITARY

These increases could not offset the impact of an accelerated decline in defense expenditures that was called for by the Clinton administration. The ability of the United States to field an effective military force has suffered dangerously. Defense spending has in fact entered a free fall. During his presidential campaign, Bill Clinton promised a further reduction in defense spending of $60 billion for the five FYs 1993–97. By mid-1995 he had cut defense by $113 billion, nearly twice his own target, to finance increased spending on domestic social welfare programs. Moreover, although the Clinton administration claimed that it was increasing the so-called readiness accounts, in fact most if not all of those Defense budget increases were devoted to nondefense activities, such as environmental cleanup, the Technology Reinvestment Program, and breast cancer and AIDS research. The Operations and Maintenance (O&M) accounts were further drained by a series of open-ended "peacekeeping" commitments in Somalia, Haiti, Rwanda, Liberia, and elsewhere. These operations used as many as three times the forces actually serving on the ground in these missions because of overall funding constraints, and deprived them of training that was critical to their primary war-fighting missions. By 1995, eighty-five thousand U.S. Army troops were deployed in detachments outside of regular units.

Once again, personnel readiness appears to be declining. Exercises are being routinely canceled at the end of each fiscal year. There are ominous signs of a new downturn in recruit quality, while retention of key personnel continue to diminish. Hollowness is back.

Long–Term Hollowness: The Acquisition Shortfall

The decline in military spending has resulted in ever-larger proportions of the defense budget being consumed by readiness accounts. And these themselves continue to be underfunded. Estimates of the magnitude of the overall shortfall vary. At one point the administration denied anything but the most minor funding shortages. Subsequently, when confronted by the reality of readiness problems, the administration acknowledged a shortfall of $40 billion, which it claimed it had somehow remedied with an increment of $25 billion that it announced in December 1994. The General Accounting Office estimates the shortfall to be $150 billion.

Moreover, the administration has been forced to backpedal since the Clinton announcement. It has reestimated its readiness shortfall for FY 1995, adding another $1 billion, due in large part to its underestimating the cost of the deployment to Haiti. It has acknowledged that its predicted savings from base closures have fallen short. And it has reversed its previous firm position against assuming savings from acquisition reform and instead postulated a level of savings that far exceeds anything justified by experience.

The current force not only suffers from shortfalls in the O&M accounts, however. It is also in the throes of a crisis in weapons acquisition. Our forces continue to age, while procurement levels drop. In FY 1995 dollars, procurement of new weapons has fallen by two-thirds from its level a decade earlier. The administration's FY 1996 request is the lowest since FY 1950.

Compare procurement levels the administration has proposed for FY 1996 with those put forward exactly a decade ago. In 1985, the administration requested funds for 840 main battle tanks; no tanks were being built ten years later. In 1985 the administration's program provided for the construction of 23 new ships and the conversion or life extension of 5 more. The current administration request is for only 3 ships. The Reagan administration's FY 1985 request for 84 F-18s for the U.S. Navy exceeded the entire fixed wing tactical aircraft request put forward by the Clinton team ten years later.[6] There can be little doubt that in savaging the acquisition accounts the administration is sacrificing the readiness of future troops to fight future wars.

Further planned procurement budget cuts will weaken an industrial base that is desperately trying to cope with an already shrunken defense market. Recovery will be much more difficult than in the 1980s, because it will take more than a few years to revive the industrial base and bring complex weapons on line. Initiatives such as the Technology Reinvestment Program effort divert funds needed for defense modernization and readiness to industrial "make work" projects of little commercial value.

The need to modernize the Department of Defense (DoD) inventory is underscored by examining the depreciation value of its inventory of equipment. With an average platform life for major systems of twenty-six years, the annual depreciation DoD must fund with new procurement is $100 billion, $60 billion more than the administration has asked for in FY 1996. Yet annual procurement has declined to approximately $40 billion. Because of the reduction in the defense force structure—Army divisions, Navy aircraft carrier battle groups, and U.S. Air Force air wings—only the most modern equipment in the inventory has been retained. While this practice has allowed the administration to claim deployment of the "most modern force in history," it has in fact produced a preparedness "time bomb." Because the administration has woefully underfunded both R&D and modernization, large portions of the armed forces will reach the end of their useful life nearly simultaneously in the first decade or so of the twenty-first century.

A future president will face, on a much larger scale than did President Reagan in 1981, a need for a costly crash program to rebuild America's defenses. We know, from bitter experience, that allowing American military power to hemorrhage through neglect will embolden nations and the growing numbers of nonstates to threaten our security in the future. Only by taking action, now, can we enable future presidents to protect American security.

MODERNIZATION AND RESOURCES

We must take advantage of the extraordinary advances in civil sector technologies, such as computation, telecommunications, microelectronics, signal processing, and materials, to modernize the defense establishment. Because the civil sector industrial capabilities are involved, this modernization can be accomplished at a much lower cost than when military modernization was forced to depend entirely on the defense industrial sector. Defense modernization must incorporate the technologies of the information age to permit the armed forces to respond to the full range of threats American interests may be exposed to in the next century.

Modern technology permits employment of a wide range of information-age technology for military applications. Targets can be struck with great precision no matter the range at which the operation takes place due to technologies that utilize the sophisticated interaction of survcillance (space- and air-based) and strike systems (land-, sea-, or air-launched). Technologies that exploit information age opportunities will permit U.S. military forces to be smaller in size and far more effective than in the past. The success of U.S. forces in Operation Desert Storm gave a glimpse of what can be accomplished.

But the modernization effort in the Reagan and Bush administrations has been all but stopped by the Clinton administration. Within the defense program, resources that would have otherwise been available for the DoD's investment accounts—modernization and R&D—have been siphoned off to support a score of operations under the aegis of the United Nations.

DEPARTMENT OF DEFENSE

The manner in which the Department of Defense is managed, its resources allocated, and its priorities established needs to be reformed and modernized.

A vigorous program to reform management throughout our national defense will enable us to modernize the defense establishment with, at most, modest increases in planned budgetary allocations. The largest increase in resources can be derived from reforming the defense management and focusing defense resources on defense-related missions rather than the present profligate use of U.S. forces for international peacekeeping efforts. Nondefense expenditure financed by the Department of Defense has been estimated by the Congressional Research Service of the Library of Congress as $11 billion in FY 1995 alone. Closing excess facilities, ending inappropriate DoD competition with private industry, increasing the use of commercial products and practices, and other reforms can substantially help to finance the modernization of the national defense establishment to meet American needs in the uncertain years ahead.

FIVE MODERNIZING PRIORITIES
The diversity of potential threats, both with respect to the kinds of military capabilities required and their geographic dispersion, requires a highly flexible and responsive defense modernization effort. For this we must focus on five areas.

1. *We must improve existing capabilities and develop new ones to cope with the potential failure of the existing policy to contain the proliferation of weapons of mass destruction and their means of delivery.*

This involves the deployment of effective theater ballistic and cruise missile defense (to protect forward deployed U.S. forces and our allies) and national missile defenses (to deter, and protect American citizens against, long-range missile attack), and is reviewed elsewhere. Related capabilities—including intelligence, surveillance, passive defense, such as gas masks and protective clothing, and counterforce, such as precision strike systems—are complementary requirements that must be addressed by the DoD.

2. *We must accelerate the modernization of U.S. aircraft, ships, submarines, missiles, logistical support, and intelligence platforms to leverage the information warfare opportunities created by American scientific and industrial leadership in the underlying technologies.*

A number of important programs, initiated during the Reagan and Bush administrations, have been deferred, delayed, or stretched out to accommodate the Clinton administration's emphasis on social welfare programs and United Nations support. A renewed emphasis on high-leverage modernization initiatives such as the F-22 program, F-15 upgrades, F-16 replacement, a naval variant of the F-117A, and precision surveillance/ strike and associated command and control systems will provide the basis for effective military operations in the coming decade and beyond.

3. *We must strengthen the ability of the United States to project power abroad from both the continental United States and from forward deployed bases either unilaterally or as part of an alliance coalition.*

As a maritime nation, the United States has benefited from the mobility of its military power. Sea-based military power, synergistically augmented by long-range air power, and the ability to deploy sophisticated ground forces make it possible for the United States to conduct highly effective expeditionary operations. The collapse of the former Soviet Union as an integrated military threat and the availability of high tech weaponry makes it likely that the United States will face an increasingly sophisticated range of regional military powers in the future. The ability to insert American military power wherever the need may arise allows us to defend American security interests at the point where our leverage is greatest—at the source of the threat.

4. *We must refocus and modernize the U.S. intelligence collection, processing, and command and control system to support our national security interests.*

We must exploit American leadership in information-driven technologies by collecting, processing, and disseminating information related to the disposition of American, allied, and adversary forces. We must be able to use this information to direct the precise application of military power as determined by the president and Congress. The Clinton administration's denigration and underfunding of the intelligence/command-and-control function has made it difficult to rebuild America's intelligence community to its former effectiveness.

5. *We must strengthen our special operations forces and training programs to cope with low intensity conflict.*

PEOPLE IN THE MILITARY

Weapons systems and high technology are extremely important to our national security, but hardware alone cannot guarantee a strong national defense. Because our armed forces depend on volunteers and their families, we must maintain sound, time-tested personnel policies that ensure readiness, cohesion, and unit strength, while avoiding politically inspired directives that detract from the deployability, morale, recruiting, and retention of quality people.

The success of the all-volunteer force is a great achievement. But it will survive only if we honor the commitments we have made to the men and women who serve: adequate pay, advancement, medical care and retirement benefits, technical skills and training, and provision for families and loved ones. In particular, we must avoid ill-advised social engineering initiatives that make military life, which is unlike any civilian occupation, more difficult or dangerous than it already is.

For example, the announcement that President Clinton was prepared to lift the ban on homosexuals in the military sparked an immediate and overwhelming response from thousands of Americans, both military and civilian, who demanded that Congress write the military's long-standing ban into law. Congress did just that, with overwhelming bipartisan majorities. That law should be properly enforced and defended by the Departments of Defense and Justice.

In addition, the interests of women in the military who proudly serve their country should not be undermined by double standards and recruiting and promotion quotas that cast doubt on qualifications or heighten risks for both men and women in physically demanding, hazardous jobs.

HEROES WHO SERVED

America should never forget her military veterans. These heroes know first-hand the personal sacrifice of time away from home, families, and careers in the service of their country. According to the 1994 Veterans Administration statistical data, there are 26.5 million veterans today in America.

They are a diverse group. All answered their country's call in extremely different and challenging times. World War II veterans, of whom approximately 8 million are still living (average age: seventy-three), answered a call to fight totalitarianism and returned home to become the backbone of this country. Veterans of the Korean War, of whom 6.8 million are living (average age: sixty-two), were the first to fight as part of a force that moved rapidly around the globe in response to communist aggression. With no clear capitulation or declaration of victory, these battle-hardened veterans came home quietly and got on with their lives. They have been called "the forgotten warriors."

In Vietnam we were never allowed to win yet we asked 58,196 Americans to sacrifice their lives in the war—a crime that should never be repeated! Nine million men and women served in uniform in Vietnam. Slightly fewer than 3 million served in the combat theater. Slightly more than 8 million Vietnam vets are still alive (average age: forty-eight).

Service in Vietnam took many forms: regular career service members, draftees, volunteers, reservists, Guardsmen, and civilian technicians. They joined forces under new rules of engagement using high technology and were subject to increased public scrutiny, instantaneous television news coverage, and a divisive public debate. Many returned home with no time to assimilate into normal civilian life. Although many still struggle with emotional and physical disabilities, most have fully returned to civilian life. Universal among them is a keen awareness that no commitment to battle should be made without full on-record political support from the American people.

Our veterans also include American men and women who were asked to stand ever ready during the Cold War, and the over seven hundred thousand active and reserve men and women who fought and won in Operation Desert Storm, one of the most decisive battles in American military history.

In view of the diversity among our veterans, we believe that several key principles must guide us as we move into the twenty-first century. We must honor our compact, in the words of Lincoln, "to care for him who shall have borne the battle, and for his widow and his orphans." We must stand by this principle, seeing to the current and future needs of today's veterans and future service members. We must recognize that different sets of veterans have different experiences but that the sacrifice of all must be honored by all.

Health care for veterans. The Veterans Administration health care system, currently the largest in the country, must be robust enough to handle combat casualties as well as a significant population of aging veterans. Fiscal realities of the twenty-first century will demand creative solutions to ensure excellent veterans health care, without losing our medical support in combat situations. Health care for veterans must be fully included in whatever national debate occurs in the future concerning health care in America. Efficiencies of the marketplace should be brought to bear on veteran health care without breaking the faith with America's commitment to veterans.

Veterans' employment. Veterans' preference programs are not an affirmative action item, but rather an important commitment and means of recognizing the sacrifices veterans have made and their role as protectors of our freedom. Service in any armed force, regardless of the conflict, has taught entire generations of Americans the values of discipline, individual responsibility, integrity, and leadership. These factors combine to demonstrate that hiring veterans is simply good public policy and smart enterprise.

Disability compensation and pensions. We owe veterans timely and adequate help when they are disabled while serving their country. We must respond to such needs in the same spirit as these vets met their country's call. Unfortunately, the claims process is currently slow, cumbersome, and inefficient. We must review the disability compensation program to increase its effectiveness. This review should include all economic and management tools, especially the impact of market-driven benefit payment systems. We should seriously consider increasing the efficiency of the benefit payment system through privatization, when appropriate.

Other benefits. In the past, because so many Americans were veterans, many veteran benefit programs had impacts, direct or indirect, on the daily lives of all Americans. With an all-volunteer force, fewer Americans are now in the military and participating in these programs, yet the impacts continue to reach well beyond the users.

Of the original six provisions of the "GI Bill of Rights," which was signed into law in 1944, the educational and training benefits and the home loan guaranty programs have been the most successful. The original GI Bill, and its subsequent extensions, educated and trained more than 20 million veterans and their dependents. These education benefits have had a significant impact on American society by allowing those who serve an opportunity to gain or upgrade skills and reclaim their place in society. This is a vital recruiting tool and a retention incentive. It is cost effective and should be maintained.

The Veterans Home Loan Program not only enables service members to buy their first home, it also results in many economic spin-offs in home building and construction trades and financial industries.

Regardless of what conflict and how called, every veteran set aside his or her personal life to serve America's interests, at great personal risk, including death. That selfless sacrifice and unquestioned courage cannot be ignored without tearing at the fabric of what is America.

Only if we recognize the sacrifices of patriots who served in the military will we be able to attain a level of military preparedness for the military challenges of the coming century.

14

Meeting a New
Generation of Threats

AMERICA'S BIGGEST CHALLENGE in the twenty-first century will come from the proliferation of weapons of mass destruction (WMD)—nuclear, chemical, biological, and conventional—and the missile technologies that deliver them. Over twenty nations have, are suspected of having, or are developing WMD and their means of delivery. The cost of acquiring these weapons is declining because of technological advances, liberalization of export controls since 1994, and the clandestine availability of both the expertise and the fissile material in the former Soviet Union.

We are menaced in a number of ways. First, there is the direct threat of such weapons in the hands of hostile regimes such as Iraq, Iran, Libya, and North Korea. This is a covert threat, potentially extensive and not subject to the traditional calculus of deterrence. Secondly, there is the threat to the regional stability and security of U.S. allies. Third, as indicated by the World Trade Center bombing and other acts of international terrorism, these weapons can be used for terrorism, state-sponsored or otherwise, directed at the United States. And, finally, the failure of the United States and the international community to deal effectively with proliferation may stimulate the creation of new proliferators.

The problem of proliferation is multidimensional. It requires solutions directed not just at rogue regimes but also at front organizations or companies controlled by these regimes.

The threat to our security from weapons proliferation has worsened because of policy decisions by President Clinton. As usual, the Clinton administration's rhetoric has been inversely proportional to the results achieved. Appropriate leadership must provide the vision and expertise to mobilize our resources to ensure that the U.S. government meets its most fundamental obligation—the protection and defense of American territory and American citizens.

The centerpiece of current U.S. nonproliferation policy has been a near-total reliance on UN and multilateral institutions to establish a set of global standards to control the spread of nuclear, biological, and chemical weapons. The heart of this effort has been the Nuclear Non-Proliferation Treaty (NPT) and a system of safeguards monitored by the International Atomic Energy Agency. But the era of reliance on such mechanisms is passing. The nonproliferation regime has had some important successes, but it has also served to protect the illegal nuclear activities of some of its signatories (Iran, Iraq, North Korea). It is time to recognize that the community of nuclear nations has grown, albeit quietly and covertly, and that a new approach focusing on the regions that encourage nations to acquire these weapons is long overdue. Reliance on the NPT to do this is no longer realistic. New bilateral agreements designed to reduce the risk of escalation and war in a crisis among nuclear rivals in places like South Asia and the Middle East should be pursued without delay.

As a start toward meeting this obligation, the United States as a top priority must demonstrate leadership to implement parallel initiatives to deal with all aspects of the threat caused by the proliferation of weapons of mass destruction and their means of delivery. Among the measures that the United States must take to combat the causes, and not merely the symptoms of proliferation, are:

- Use every appropriate means to ensure compliance with the NPT, including expanded export controls, intelligence cooperation, and effective enforcement operations. Through diplomacy, security assistance, arms transfers, and other means, deal with key regional states to reduce tensions and provide incentives for them to forego development or acquisition of weapons of mass destruction. Providing access to ballistic missile defense (BMD) to enable nations threatened by the proliferation of WMD should be a central component of America's counterproliferation strategy.
- Enhance American capabilities of verification and undertake diplomatic initiatives to allow robust monitoring, verification, and compliance programs.

- Obtain the agreement of the leading industrial nations committed to the counterproliferation struggle to create an effective consultative organization derived from the Coordinating Committee on Multinational Export Controls (COCOM) model. It would integrate the proliferation control of regimes of the NPT, the Chemical Weapons Convention (CWC), the Biological Weapons Convention (BWC), and the Missile Technology Control Regime (MTCR). Such an organization would also provide a vehicle to expand the declaration of stockpiles, provide transparent registers of facilities and equipment, permit on-site inspections, allow for independent verification, and authorize the imposition of sanctions and other active measures against noncooperators.
- Pursue measures to enhance verification mechanisms in the BWC and establish binding confidence-building measures among participants, including annual declarations of high-risk biological research facilities and improved methods for detecting and deterring prohibited activities.
- Develop effective U.S. export control policies that support counterproliferation initiatives, including strong multilateral institutions that can ensure equal enforcement of counterproliferation objectives.
- To combat the threat of leakage of nuclear materials and technology from Russia, condition future bilateral and multilateral assistance (including trade credits and political risk insurance) on its counterproliferation performance.
- To the same end, launch an urgent joint U.S.-Russian program to inventory and increase security for stockpiles of highly enriched uranium and plutonium in Russia.
- Restore and accelerate efforts to install an effective BMD system in the United States, and provide access to effective BMD to nations at risk from WMD.
- Working through the Department of Defense and other appropriate agencies, develop a credible chemical and biological warfare defense system.
- While pursuing unilateral counterproliferation measures, demonstrate strong leadership and consistent, unequivocal purpose in multilateral forums such as the Australia Group, Nuclear Suppliers Group, MTCR, and similar bodies.

- Increase the effectiveness of the intelligence community to enable it to combat both proliferation and terrorism through improved collection and processing capabilities and, where appropriate, conduct covert operations against proliferators.
- Develop and dedicate rapid response forces for both preemptive and retaliatory action to root out the sources of terrorism involving weapons of mass destruction and to put on notice those who would use such weapons that the cost will be direct, severe, and relentless.

DEFENSE AGAINST MISSILE ATTACK

We face an increased threat from ballistic missiles of all ranges, armed with conventional, chemical, biological, or nuclear warheads. (Ballistic missiles are the means of delivering some of these rapidly proliferating weapons.) This growing global threat to American security and that of its allies is the proximate consequence of the looming threat of the proliferation of WMD and their means of delivery.

This is one aspect of the picture that has changed drastically. Since the advent of the German V-2 rocket during World War II, ballistic missiles have been used primarily to threaten civilian population centers rather than military targets. Rogue regimes use ballistic missiles almost exclusively as "strategic" weapons—to intimidate, coerce, and blackmail adversaries, through threatened or actual use.

As rogue states such as North Korea, Iraq, Iran, Syria, and Libya build or purchase missiles, we become more and more uneasily aware of this reality. They already threaten overseas U.S. troops, friends, and allies with ballistic missiles potentially armed with WMD. Eventually, some or all of these rogue states will obtain missiles that can threaten the U.S. homeland.

The CIA recently acknowledged that North Korea's Taepo Dong II, which Clinton administration officials have acknowledged could attack American cities, could be deployed in less than three to five years.[1] Moreover, North Korea has a reputation for "selling to anyone with the money," according to testimony by former CIA Director Jim Woolsey. Furthermore, Representative Curt Weldon (R–Penn.) recently concluded from CIA briefings that any nation with the money could purchase a "space launch" version of the SS-25 Russian ICBM and modify it to threaten American cities in less than three years.

Russia and China are potentially unstable politically, but continue to modernize their long-standing capability to threaten U.S. territory—and other nations around the world—with nuclear-armed missiles. Former CIA Director Woolsey recently gave his personal judgment that there is a "two-in-three" chance of conflict between Russia and her neighbors— and a "one-in-three" chance that Russia will become a serious threat to the United States.[2] China recently tested a new solid propellant ICBM and a new nuclear warhead, heralding a new generation of long-range missile systems.

Effective defenses are urgently needed to counter the ballistic and cruise missiles' potential for blackmail, terror, disruption, and destruction. Without such a ready response to this threat, the United States and its allies and friends will be subject to coercion and attack by otherwise peripheral powers. Chinese and Russian missiles have long posed a potential threat to Americans and their interests worldwide. Deterrence, based only on the threat of retaliation, is an unreliable policy in the post–Cold War environment where leaders such as Muammar Qaddafi (Libya), Saddam Hussein (Iraq), Kim Jong II (North Korea), and Iran's clerical leadership are not likely to be deterred. Both America and its overseas troops, friends, and allies need effective defenses now.

Thanks to Reagan-Bush investments in the Strategic Defense Initiative, technology is ready and deployment can begin within the next three years. But the policies, plans, and programs of the Clinton administration are an obstacle to this objective and must be changed. In particular:

- The administration's efforts to sustain and add to the ABM Treaty will prevent our ever being able to deploy effective defenses for both ourselves and our allies. We must refocus on a security network that will include effective theater and national missile defenses.
- Plans and programs should be reinstated and funded to build effective global defenses—first with sea-based interceptors coupled to space-based sensors (Brilliant Eyes) and then with appropriate space-based elements.

A GLOBAL PROBLEM
The realities of WMD and missile technology proliferation compel a response to a global problem that diplomacy alone cannot handle. The Cold War doctrine of "Mutual Assured Destruction," a theory based of the destruction of civil populations, is unthinkable and, moreover, inadequate to cope with the WMD threat in the post–Cold War era. BMDs are an essential part of our security response. Missile defenses are needed on-station to counter the threat and use of ballistic missiles in crises and conflicts that can erupt at unpredictable places at unpredictable times.

- It is time-consuming, risky, and ineffective to depend entirely on the ability to move defenses into needed locations after a crisis develops—as we saw in moving the Patriot system to South Korea in 1994.
- It is prohibitively expensive to proliferate ground-based defenses to all the locations needed to deal with the full panoply of possible future WMD/missile proliferation crises.

DEFENSE IN DEPTH
Missile defenses must be very effective to provide the needed protection from even a limited number of missiles. An effective defense will provide multiple opportunities to intercept attacking missiles. Even a 90 percent effective defense would allow one in ten attacking missiles through. But two 90 percent layers would reduce this lethal leakage to one in a hundred, and three 90 percent layers would reduce the leakage to one in a thousand. (The largest salvo during the 1990 Gulf War involved several, but fewer than ten, SCUDS launched within a few minutes.) Furthermore, providing multiple layers is the best way to ensure that offensive countermeasures do not easily negate the defensive system. Countermeasures to one layer generally makes other layers more effective. On the other hand, a defensive architecture that emphasizes a single class of intercept capability increases the likelihood of effective offensive countermeasures.

For example, the earliest and most effective response to defenses (however based) that intercept missiles in space (such as those that are the primary focus of the Clinton administration's wide-area BMD programs) is to release multiple weapons and/or decoys early in the attacking missile's flight. Boost-phase intercept capability can effectively defeat such countermeasures. And efforts to defeat a boost-phase intercept capability improves the effectiveness of other defensive layers. Thus both are needed, and if they are developed simultaneously there are no cost-effective offensive countermeasures. But the Clinton administration's narrow approach almost certainly guarantees that offensive systems will be developed relatively quickly to defeat the defense systems now being developed, thus requiring that we employ the most costly approaches to missile defense.

The least costly and most effective defenses will include a defensive layer to intercept attacking missiles beginning early in their flight when they are most vulnerable. If attacking missiles are destroyed in their boost phase before they release their lethal weapons and decoys, then their toxic residuals fall on the heads of those launching the attack rather than their intended victims. Such a defensive capability, which is very hard to avoid, could deter attack from missiles armed with weapons of mass destruction. Although sea- and air-based defenses can provide some near-term boost-phase intercept capability, space-based defenses offer the best prospects for effective boost-phase intercept capability in the long term. Today's technology makes such effective layered defenses feasible and affordable. However, substantial political barriers severely curtail U.S. efforts to conduct research and development on the least costly and most effective systems.

Overcoming the ABM Treaty Obstacle
The 1972 ABM Treaty was designed to codify the Cold War–era reciprocal vulnerability theory of nuclear deterrence—for example, mutual destruction. All Americans, as a matter of U.S. policy, have been and are being held hostage to a bizarre proposition that they are most secure when most vulnerable. A very questionable policy under any circumstance, it makes no sense in today's post–Cold War, multipolar world of undeterrable rogue states led by isolated and mercurial figures.

Yet the Clinton administration's attachment to this policy continues to block the development of the most effective defenses and to make those that are being built less effective and more costly than necessary. In particular, the Clinton administration has reaffirmed its attachment to the ABM

Treaty, and has refused to deploy even the limited defense permitted by the treaty. Further, it has eliminated almost all research and development (R&D) on the most effective defenses, and is developing only the least widely useful, and most costly type, "theater missile defenses" for overseas American troops, friends, and allies.

The United States should declare its intent to terminate the ABM Treaty, if possible along with the Russians and others who could benefit from the needed global defense, but if not, then alone. The architect of the ABM Treaty, the late President Nixon, remarked on the twentieth anniversary of the treaty in 1992 that "the time has come to move beyond the treaty, and to treat it as 'overtaken by events.'" Failing Russian agreement, the United States should do so unilaterally by exercising its right under the terms of the treaty to withdraw. No nation, including Russia, should be permitted a veto over America's efforts to defend itself and its troops, friends, and allies. No effective defenses can be acquired or deployed until we abandon the ABM Treaty as we can and must do.

Americans will support this policy. As poll after poll has shown, and recent focus group sessions with average citizens confirm, Americans believe they are already defended and are appalled to learn the sad truth—their government has deliberately left them totally vulnerable to attack by even a single missile.[3] They support—indeed, demand—more responsible political leadership.

Effective Missile Defenses

The United States should move as quickly as technology and industrial processes will permit to deploy the most effective BMD that our defense resource base will support.

A blue ribbon team of former defense and national security officials, assembled by the Heritage Foundation, recently came up with recommendations for an appropriate missile defense deployment strategy and program.[4] They recommended supplementing the ongoing development of ground-based defenses by building the sea-based global defenses immediately, followed later by space-based defenses. This "Team B" operated independently of the Clinton administration, but within the constraints imposed by budget realities in which the Republican leadership is operating (as "cheap hawks"). The team's most important conclusions and recommendations are (1) build the Navy's Upper Tier and the Air Force's Brilliant Eyes as soon as possible; (2) reestablish space-based defense technology demonstration programs; and (3) direct related planning toward refining the final architecture to be deployed by 1997. Because of previous investments in the Navy's AEGIS air defense system (approaching $50 billion), inexpensive modifications can provide global, continuously on-station, wide-area BMD capability. It could do so from international waters, which cover nearly 70 percent of the earth's surface.

- The initial AEGIS cruisers can be operational in three years for slightly over $1 billion; for a total of $2–3 billion, 650 defensive interceptor missiles on twenty-two cruisers could be on-station worldwide by late 2001.
- If urgently developed, unobstructed by the ABM Treaty, this sea-based system could also provide the earliest possible limited defense of the U.S. homeland—as well as U.S. overseas troops, friends, and allies; improvements could come with follow-on modifications.

The Brilliant Eyes space-based sensor should be built as rapidly as possible to ensure that the Navy's Upper Tier system, as well as all other defensive systems, can defend the largest area possible and respond to likely offensive countermeasures. For $4–5 billion, the system can achieve initial capability as early as 2001, when the Navy's Upper Tier can be fully deployed. Deployment can begin as early as 1999.

For the long term, space-based defense programs should be revived and directed toward deployment. Space-Based Interceptors (SBIs) and Space-Based Lasers (SBLs) are the most affordable and effective long-term BMD systems to counter advanced ballistic missiles.

- The Brilliant Pebbles program, a fully approved Defense acquisition program before the Clinton administration canceled it in 1993, should be reinstated and directed toward achieving an initial capability by as early as the end of the decade.
- The SBL program should be directed toward a demonstration of a boost-phase intercept capability from space by as early as 1998—and toward deployment by the middle of the next decade.

- Between $250–300 million should be invested in each for the next two years, after which the precise architecture should be selected to begin deployment around the end of the decade. The cost of developing and deploying the combined Upper Tier/Brilliant Eyes/SBI/SBL system is expected to be less than about $25 billion.
- No other global system architecture can achieve comparable effectiveness for the same total cost.
- The program to develop and deploy a less effective four- to six-site ground-based defense of the U.S. homeland in response to the Missile Defense Act of 1991 was estimated to cost $35 billion in 1991 dollars—and nothing has since changed to reduce this estimate. This hit-to-kill, kinetic energy, ground-based interceptor system would have no boost-phase intercept capability—indeed it could intercept attacking missiles only after they had traveled over halfway to their targets. The SBI system alone would be far more effective in intercepting attacking missiles in all phases of their flight—and can be built for less than 20 percent of the cost of the ground-based system.
- Defending NATO and the Far East with an advanced ground-based system would cost another $20 billion, about the same cost as the combined SBI/SBL space system that would provide a robust defense of the entire globe.

A Complementary Diplomatic Strategy

Diplomatic efforts should focus on replacing, rather than reinforcing, the adversarial premises of the ABM Treaty. In today's world, defenses—and particularly U.S. defenses—will be a very important stabilizing influence. In particular, the Clinton administration should cease its efforts to "strengthen" the ABM Treaty and concentrate instead on eliminating the treaty that now blocks American freedom of action to meet our current and future defense needs.

As a matter of national policy, the United States should take the principled position that effective global defenses are essential to preserving the peace, and that all interested nations should cooperate in building and operating the most effective defenses possible, as early as is practical. However, the United States needs to make it clear to other nations, including Russia, that it intends, no matter what, to build the most effective defenses technically feasible at the earliest possible date. While such defenses might draw on Russian President Boris Yeltsin's 1992 proposal for a Joint Global Protection System, no nation, including Russia, has the right to veto U.S. efforts to defend America's people, friends, and allies against missile attack. If this means withdrawing from the ABM Treaty, so be it.

In conjunction with enabling diplomatic efforts, the secretary of defense should be directed to proceed, as fast as possible, to field a Global Protection System, first at sea and then in space. This program should proceed under the assumption that all restrictions of the ABM Treaty, perceived or explicit, will be removed either by agreement or by withdrawal from the treaty.

The Technology Revolution in Military Affairs

The revolutionary impact of advanced technology on our everyday lives is also having a profound, if poorly understood, impact on military affairs as well. The driving force behind these revolutionary changes are technologies associated directly or indirectly with the transmission, management, processing, and exploitation of information. The application of advanced information technologies to military purposes goes to the heart of long-term military power. We have seen the primitive precursor of application of information technology to military operations during Operation Desert Storm. By being in full command of the data necessary to understand not only the military weapons and disposition of Iraqi forces, but their decision processes as well, we were able to "get inside" the minds of the Iraqi military leadership and destroy their ability to manage their military forces effectively.

Doing so in the twenty-first century will be crucial to protecting the security interest of the United States and its allies. This will be necessary not merely to preserve the leadership in military technology so apparent from the Gulf War, but because the technology of information has become widely disseminated. Military application of advanced technology per se is usually not unique to military technology. Apart from a few specific applications (such as low-observable technology employed on such aircraft as the F-117A tactical aircraft and the B-2 strategic bomber), advanced military technology is derived from leading-edge civil sector technologies such as micro-electronics, advanced materials, signal processing, telecommunications, and computation. The United States needs to ensure its future leadership by modernizing its incorporation of advanced civil sector technology in its weapons, logistics, and command-control-communications-intelligence systems.

A central element of American military advantage that is at the nexus of civil and military technology is command of space-related technologies. Space-based technologies are key to future U.S. power projection and national and theater missile defense through their ability to support worldwide communications, intelligence, and targeting. The U.S. lead in space-related technologies is clear, but fragile. A focused effort to sustain the U.S. lead in the military applications of space must be an integral part of our defense modernization effort.

Accessing America's Commercial Technology Base

The core of America's technological advantage in military power resides with its vibrant civil sector. Defense procurement accounts for a smaller fraction of industrial production and gross national product than at any time since 1939. The ability of the U.S. armed forces to cope with well-equipped adversaries at points distant from either the United States or our forward deployed forces or their bases abroad has resulted from advances made to support such diverse civil sector requirements as commercial aviation and the personal computer industry.

Procurement regulations imposed by the 103rd Congress and its predecessors have hamstrung the ability of the Department of Defense to exploit the wide variety of advanced technologies to lower the cost of defense and accelerate its ability to respond to changes in the technical characteristics of the threat. Procurement reform is an essential part of a more affordable defense. The Clinton administration failed to propose legislation to modernize the Department of Defense acquisition system. The task of compressing the costly and potentially dangerous pattern of fifteen-year cycles between R&D and deployment of advanced systems has remained largely unchanged. The 103rd Congress produced a piece of legislation under the misnomer "acquisition streamlining." Change has been imperceptible, and the Clinton administration has done little to rewrite the underlying Federal Acquisition Regulations that are the proximate source of the department's inability to modernize at a pace comparable to advanced technology organizations in the civil sector. Defense procurement has declined by two-thirds in real dollars from 1985 to 1998. In the face of so drastic a reduction in resources, regulatory and administrative obstacles to the DoD's use of civil sector technology poses unconscionable risks to U.S. security.

Our most advanced tactical aircraft are run by military computers with skills that the civil market left behind a decade ago. Quality and financial controls processes that have revolutionized the American automotive industry, with its emphasis on sophisticated statistical quality control, are unattainable because of current Department of Defense acquisition regulations. Testing procedures mandated by previous Democratic Congresses are so protracted and costly that they deny deployed U.S. forces access to advanced technologies when they need them. The sophisticated U.S. Air Force aircraft-based ground surveillance system, JSTARS, was denied to U.S. forces in Operation Desert Storm for weeks because its emergency use in combat operations would "disrupt the test program." Only the insistence of President Bush was able to overcome the iron grip of the DoD's dangerously antiquated acquisition system. Clinton administration inaction has left the acquisition system largely as is, despite its reformist rhetoric. The DoD acquisition system must be modernized.

The Defense Industrial Base
Effective reform of the DoD acquisition system will also permit modernization of the defense industrial base. Defense investment—the sinews of long-term readiness—has been cut by two-thirds over the past decade, and military manpower by one-third. Yet the core DoD overhead structure remains largely intact. The DoD network of laboratories, maintenance depots, and industrial facilities is competing with the private sector to sustain the industrial base. In fact, our ability to sustain defense industrial readiness for future contingencies, and to respond to current needs, resides largely with the civil sector, not the government sector.

As it is unlikely that recent trends in DoD acquisition will change in the near future, it is important that, to the maximum practical extent, the private sector rather than the public sector perform maintenance and modification work. Many of the research, maintenance, and industrial facilities operated by the Department of Defense or the armed services can be readily privatized.

Defense Export Markets

The international market for U.S. defense equipment has become an important factor in sustaining our defense industrial base. Defense exports currently account for one-quarter to one-third of domestic procurement. But unlike many of our international competitors, U.S. law makes defense exports an instrument of foreign policy. As a consequence, only sales approved under the terms of the Arms Export Control Act can be made. Within this foreign policy constraint, there is considerable room for improvement. The Clinton administration's Conventional Arms Transfer policy promulgated in early 1995 after a two-year intra-administration policy dispute has failed to construct a policy able to meet U.S. post–Cold War needs. The administration refused to authorize the creation of a defense export credit facility comparable to those available to allied nations or what is already available to the U.S. civil sector. Constraining the ability of U.S. industry to meet the defense modernization needs of allied and friendly nations also constrains U.S. influence in parts of the world crucial to peace. An effective defense export policy will simultaneously strengthen the U.S. defense industrial base at no cost to the taxpayer and enhance the ability of the president to influence events in areas of the world important to American security.

International Defense Industrial Cooperation

With the collapse of the former Soviet Union, allied defense capacity must be rationalized and the global defense industry measured to meet the new market conditions. Improved opportunities for cross-border collaboration between American firms and industry in allied nations make it possible for the cost of defense to be reduced through well-thought-out cooperative development, production, and marketing activities. The performance of modern defense products is increasingly dependent on software and less so on unique hardware design. This is particularly true of electronic equipment—fast becoming the major cost and performance defining element in defense products.

By the administration's failure to modernize the DoD's acquisition system, long-standing barriers to effective international defense industrial collaboration remain. This regulatory edifice prevents the armed forces from gaining access to the fruits of advanced civil sector technology that would lower the cost of modernization and impedes innovative cost-reducing international collaborative projects as well.

RELATIONSHIPS, ARMS, AND INTELLIGENCE
Alliance Relationships in Post–Cold War America

During the Cold War years, the United States carried out its foreign and security policy with the assistance of many friends and allies, who generally shared our interests and values. With them, we established institutions, as well as ad hoc arrangements, for common goals. With our effective military establishment, economic strength, and stable, consistent political leadership, we typically led the institutions and partnerships in maintaining peace and protecting freedom. These same characteristics also enabled us to act unilaterally when required. The existence of a strong adversarial, imperialist power gave a clear priority to both our relationships and policies.

NATO has been the most successful alliance in history. Significantly, it achieved its main goal of deterring a Soviet/Warsaw Pact attack on Western Europe. NATO has also achieved several other important objectives. It has

- integrated a defeated Germany into the West;
- provided a framework for democracy and market economies in post–World War II Europe;
- provided an overall framework for peace in NATO's sphere, including among long-time adversaries such as France and Germany, and Greece and Turkey;
- placed national security policies within a broader framework, thus constraining the reemergence of shifting, and potentially destabilizing, power blocs and subregional alliances; and
- initiated openness and cooperation among the militaries of the member nations.

Nature of the Problem

Some of the current challenges are derived from historical trends. For example, our economic strength represents a reduced portion of the global economy. Other problems stem from shortsighted policy decisions. Today, American military power is diminished by significant reductions in our defense budget. Our political leadership has also been erratic and frequently purposeless. Threats to our interests and values appear in many different forms. The institutions and partnerships we have built up over the years need to be reformed and adapted to a changed world. In addition, America's attitude about alliances and our involvement therein must change.

Under the Clinton administration, NATO has fallen into a state of disrepair lacking as it does strong U.S. leadership and vision. The United States has vital security, political, economic, and cultural interests in Europe. The United States must have a European policy that realistically and accurately reflects these national interests.

Policy Recommendations

In an uncertain international environment, the United States must exert leadership. There is especially a need for U.S. leadership in multilateral forums. We must clearly define our policy goals while adhering to our principles.

We should avoid any further reduction in America's military capability and regain resources that have been diverted elsewhere. Our ability to act unilaterally to defend our vital interests has been eroded and, along with it, our leadership role in the security alliances and partnerships we have created over the years. Military power has never, in itself, persuaded our allies and friends that our policies were right; it has, however, been an essential element in persuading them that, when those policies were right, they were also likely to be successfully implemented. Successful alliances depend on our maintaining an effective military capability. We must also be able to project superior power rapidly anywhere in the world and protect our allies as well as our own interests.

We need consistency and credibility in our diplomacy. Again, neither allies nor friends can effectively support us if they do not know what objectives we seek because we do not know them ourselves. None can follow where we do not lead. Erratic, unprincipled policies from North Korea and

China to Bosnia and Haiti have undermined confidence in America's word, the essential element in all our alliances.

We need to recognize that regionally based alliances and partnerships have dealt effectively with security threats over the years and that the United States has been able to protect its interests by working with them. We should work to adapt these institutions, whose histories have shown them to be responsive to our diplomacy, to the post–Cold War world, not supplant them with untested ones. We should also continue to support those strategic alliances that are predicated upon common political values. In particular, the United Nations is no substitute for NATO in Europe, the Japanese and Korean alliances in the Western Pacific and Northeast Asia, or other regional alliances such as the Organization of American States in this hemisphere. In their own regions, the Association of Southeast Asian Nations, the Gulf Cooperation Council, or even, sometimes, the Organization of African Unity may prove as useful as the United Nations when it is necessary to respond to a security crisis. The United Nations membership, taken as a whole, after all, does not have the sort of serious stake in a particular region's stability that encourages responsible policy, nor are its structures or procedures as responsive to American leadership. The likely variety and local character of future crises underscore the advantages of regional institutions over global ones.

Although we may participate in, or support, UN-peacekeeping missions that are truly peacekeeping—for example, agreed to by all recipients and supported by all nations—we should never relinquish or subordinate U.S. military command or decision making to any international body. We must protect first and foremost America's own vital interests.

In support of our participation in both regional and global institutions, we need to revitalize our bilateral diplomacy in important capitals. Alliances and multilateral institutions are driven, in the end, by the positions of their member states. Our resources give us an enormous advantage over other governments in conducting multilateral diplomacy, but only if we recognize that international organizations supplement the countries that make them up rather than replace them. Multilateral forums cannot be used to by pass national governments, particularly friendly ones, without undermining their own effectiveness.

The end of the Cold War enables us to strengthen NATO's ability to preserve the security of Europe by bringing in new members who share our values and have a stake in the continent's peaceful future. Including Poland, Hungary, the Czech Republic, and other former Warsaw Pact states that want to join in the alliance at an early date will not only enhance their security, and Europe's, but encourage and reinforce their integration into other European institutions crucial to their political stability and economic prosperity.

We need to develop constructive bilateral ties across a wide spectrum with former adversaries, including Russia, outside the context of NATO as well as within it. Military cooperation should form an important part of this relationship. At the same time, we must convey to such former adversaries that such efforts will be jeopardized by behavior that contradicts international norms.

Additionally, we should maintain U.S. troops in Europe at the current level (100,000, down from 320,000 in 1990), with no further cuts, provided this level continues to reflect operational military needs and provides an effective deterrent in light of current and anticipated circumstances.

We must also encourage the work of the European Union, the Organization on Security and Cooperation in Europe, and the Western European Union, while making clear that none of them is a substitute for NATO and that none should expand its powers at the expense of NATO.

Arms Control

The collapse of the former Soviet Union has fundamentally altered the role of arms control in U.S. foreign policy. Arms control is no longer a preoccupation of American security policy. Its role is now primarily associated with multilateral initiatives directed at controlling the spread of technologies linked to the proliferation of WMD and their means of delivery. While these arms control regimes have utility, the United States cannot rely solely upon them as a vehicle for the control of WMD. Both Iraq and North Korea are, for example, signatories of the NPT, yet both managed successfully to evade its strictures. Indeed, the official preoccupation with arms control in the 1970s misled American officials and allowed the leadership of the former Soviet Union to sustain an organized policy of noncompliance that jeopardized U.S. security. The disinterest on the part of the Clinton administration in insisting on compliance is having predictable consequences; Russia, for example, is currently violating chemical, biological, theater and strategic nuclear, and conventional forces agreements.[5]

The most detailed and thoroughly managed arms control agreements are the Cold War–centered agreements made with the former Soviet Union, particularly the Strategic Arms Reduction Treaties (START), the Intermediate-Range Nuclear Forces, the Conventional Forces in Europe Treaty (CFE), and the ABM Treaty of 1972 as amended. The successor to the Soviet state, the Russian Federation, has refused to ratify the START II agreements (and has indicated it will not comply with its CFE obligations), although the United States has implemented its obligations under the agreement as if the treaty had already entered into force.

The ABM Treaty has proven to be more problematic. The Clinton administration continues its belief in the Cold War doctrine of the "assured vulnerability" of its citizens to nuclear attack in the belief that the reciprocal threat of WMD attack will deter it. Although the role of deterrence in the acquisition of WMD by such rogue states as Iraq, Iran, Libya, and North Korea appears limited, the administration continues to impose ABM Treaty–driven constraints on the American missile defense development program. Ironically, two of America's primary allies—Israel and Japan—will gain access to American missile defense technology that will enable them to protect their civilian population against hostile missile attack. The Clinton administration has, however, denied such an opportunity to American citizens. This form of "Alice in Wonderland" arms control serves no relevant security interest of the United States and should be abandoned at the earliest opportunity.

To cope with the threat of the proliferation of WMD, the United States will continue to have to deter the use of nuclear weapons by rogue states. This in turn will require continued deployment of nuclear weapons and their periodic testing. The Clinton administration's proposed Comprehensive Test Ban Treaty is inconsistent with U.S. security interests.

The effectiveness of multilateral arms control arrangements are heavily dependent on the success of multilateral export controls. Regrettably, the Clinton administration agreed to the disestablishment of the COCOM organization in 1994, and has been unprepared to assume a leadership role in constructing a meaningful successor regime that would undertake the coordination of the export control function. As a consequence, apart from ad hoc arrangements within the (London) Nuclear Suppliers Group, the Australia Group (chemical weapons), and the MTCR (ballistic missile components), there is so far no centralized and coordinated multilateral effort as a successor to COCOM able to address the full scope of arms control concerns.

Arms control as it is managed by the Clinton administration is a relic of the Cold War, has been both deceptive and dangerous to the American people, and should be discontinued as a diplomatic practice.

Intelligence

The ability to collect, process, and disseminate intelligence to elements of the U.S. government who need it in a timely fashion is one of the most profound strengths of our national security system. The intense threat posed by the former Soviet Union during the Cold War period has shaped our perception of what a modern intelligence organization should be. The nature of the Soviet threat, while posing a clear and present danger to American and allied security, also permitted a highly focused national effort. Collection of information against our highly secretive adversary caused the United States to undertake a long-term effort at the frontier of advanced technology to stay ahead of developments in the former Soviet Union. The resources in place, including such technical collection systems as satellite-based and other forms of monitoring systems combined with supporting collection activities ranging from newspaper searches through traditional human source intelligence, enabled the United States to prevail in the Cold War.

The challenges of the post–Cold War period are more diverse, but no less difficult and important. The secretive and threatening character of a single state—the former Soviet Union—has been replaced by a multitude of threats to American security. While no single threat can be compared to that of the Soviet Union, the cumulative effect of geographically dispersed proliferation of weapons of mass destruction, state-sponsored and subnational terrorist organizations, and widespread regional disorder is to create an equally demanding requirement for intelligence.

Regrettably the national undertaking to sustain an intelligence collection and processing infrastructure that was up to the demands of the Cold War has, to an alarming degree, been dismantled by the Clinton administration's failure to understand the vital importance of protecting sources and methods of American intelligence gathering capabilities, or dismantled outright by the administration as it reallocated funds from the national security sector to meet the demands of new government social welfare programs. A renewed commitment needs to be made to modernize and sustain the U.S. intelligence community so that its capabilities and performance will be able to cope with the compelling demands of the post–Cold War security environment.

Protection of sources and methods. Perhaps the best example of the Clinton administration's attitude toward protecting intelligence capabilities has been its establishment of an unprecedented intelligence-sharing program with the United Nations. This administration either fails to understand the United Nations's inherent limitations as an international organization or, even more troubling, is unconcerned about these limitations.

When the United States establishes intelligence-sharing arrangements with a friendly foreign government, we do so through an intelligence-sharing agreement that requires adequate protection for the sources and methods of intelligence sharing. No such intelligence-sharing agreement exists, however, with the United Nations, underscoring the fact that the UN is not a sovereign government and lacks even the most basic capabilities to protect sensitive information. The organization has no security background investigation procedures, has no security clearance system, and reserves the right to make available any information it receives to any of its member states—including countries that sponsor international acts of terrorism, such as Iran or Libya.

Previous administrations have, on a carefully-prescribed basis, provided U.S. intelligence information to the UN in circumstances that clearly advanced U.S. national security interests. These instances have ranged from revealing overhead imagery during the Cuban Missile Crisis to information that has identified dangerous activities by rogue states, such as the weapons of mass destruction programs of North Korea or Iraq. But the Clinton administration has broken this vital nexus. Administration officials have argued that the United States must provide intelligence information to the UN even in circumstances where it does nothing to advance American national security interests, to prove to the UN that our nation can be considered a regular and reliable source of intelligence information. This attitude dangerously treats the UN as just another "consumer" of the U.S. intelligence community, and the long-run erosion of the secrecy of our intelligence-gathering capabilities may be incalculable.

Intelligence community organization. The role of intelligence is increasingly important in enabling the United States to succeed in managing the now-pivotal role of information-related technologies in modern conflict, whether or not the conflict takes place in a militarized form. Doing so requires an intense national effort that will focus involved government agencies in employing the intelligence community for the purposes intended by Congress—to support the national security of the United States. The intelligence community should be organized around this central purpose and be freed from the dangerous distractions of using the community for commercial aims as is increasingly being done by the Clinton administration.

Technical collection programs. The ability to adapt highly sophisticated civil and military technology to facilitate the collection and processing of information concerning other nations, subnational organizations, and individuals abroad constitutes a great source of strength for the United States. The heart of this capability is America's network of sophisticated satellites, aircraft, and other platforms—technical collection systems—able to collect and process information concerning developments outside of the United States. Key modernization initiatives that have been terminated by the Clinton administration jeopardize our ability to adjust to the needs of American security in the post–Cold War period.

Clandestine intelligence/covert action. Clandestine intelligence is the secret gathering of information, primarily through human agents; covert action involves U.S. efforts secretly to influence the domestic or foreign policies of another nation. The needs of American security are dominated by the requirement to understand developments abroad. While traditional diplomatic interaction and exploitation of unclassified material provides many useful insights, clandestine intelligence remains a major tool for gaining insights into a foreign country's military and diplomatic plans and capabilities that it wishes to deny to others. Rebuilding our clandestine intelligence infrastructure from the devastating impact of traitors and resource cuts needs to be a key objective of our national leaders.

On a recurring basis, our national leadership needs to undertake actions to implement decisions to protect American interests. While this is normally done through overt means such as diplomacy, military presence or operations, and foreign assistance, it is sometimes necessary for the president to act in secret. The need for covert operations to counter the shadowy operations of nuclear proliferators, transnational terrorists, narcotics traffickers, clandestine arms dealers, and similar criminal elements did not expire with the Cold War. The decimation of the capacity of the American intelligence community to conduct effective covert action as a result of Clinton administration policies, supported until recently by a Democratically controlled Congress, must be reversed.

Intelligence community industrial base. The scientific and industrial base upon which the intelligence community depends for its success is the unique product of a process that adapts the most sophisticated civil and military technologies to national needs. While the underlying technology reflects the fundamental strength of American science and technology, the process of adapting this technology to intelligence community needs has been effected by a unique industrial establishment. The steep decline in funding for the intelligence community has placed the vital industrial base at risk. In many cases, key applications technologies are provided by a single firm with unique expertise. The failure to sustain the modernization of the technical collection and processing assets of the intelligence community places the ability of future presidents to understand and anticipate future threats in jeopardy. This cannot be tolerated. New approaches to sustaining the intelligence community's industrial base that will allow it to continue to apply the most sophisticated and appropriate technology for the nation's intelligence community must be introduced.

15

To Aid and Protect: Related Security Issues

WE MUST REFORM U.S. FOREIGN AID to reflect post–Cold War realities. Our present policies, stuck in the past, do not meet current conditions. Despite substantial reductions in other forms of domestic discretionary government spending, the Clinton administration proposes to raise funding of foreign aid programs to a level that is 10 percent above its level of only two years ago. The Republican-led Congress rejects this profligacy and has cut foreign aid almost 20 percent below President Clinton's request for 1996.

Most Americans are rightly skeptical about foreign economic aid. The tens of billions of dollars spent on economic aid in the past four decades have done little to encourage economic development. And while security assistance was an effective tool in protecting America's national security interests in the past and contributed to our Cold War victory, it must be retooled to meet the challenges of the twenty-first century.

Economic assistance has not only failed to contribute to meaningful economic growth in the developing world, it has also been counterproductive because it has inhibited policy reform. Private sector initiatives and reforms have, by contrast, proved to be the source of genuine economic growth in the developing world. All too often, a nation's dependence on government-sponsored aid programs serves temporarily to obscure failed state intervention in the economy. But even as the government-directed economies of many developing nations falter, U.S. foreign economic aid continues to be disbursed, using outdated tools and policies.

America's foreign economic aid program no longer reflects a clear purpose. Rather, it represents the grandfathered programs of special interests, often combined with a numbing bureaucratic myopia. This program is out of touch with present international realities and in desperate need of focus. The program itself, moreover, is a bureaucratic nightmare, whimsically spawning "new" programs that are simply layered on top of the failed "new" programs of the past. In addition, bilateral programs often include initiatives that should not be funded or carried out by the U.S. government. Added to these burgeoning bilateral economic aid programs are an increasing number of multilateral aid programs. Many of these programs simply proliferate expensive and redundant administrative structures, often with contradictory objectives and little or no differentiation.

We believe the United States' outmoded system of foreign aid must be revamped.

MODERNIZING FOREIGN AID

- U.S. strategic interests must be paramount in our new foreign aid policy. Resources should be used to benefit our nation. U.S. foreign aid should advance American trade, enhance the prosperity of all Americans, and improve our security in a still dangerous world.
- U.S. foreign aid must be conditioned upon meaningful economic and fiscal reform, privatization, support for a free and competitive marketplace, adherence to sound macroeconomic policies, and openness to foreign trade and investment.
- Foreign aid waste must be reduced by increased auditing and impact accountability in the program to include *both* foreign recipients and the administering U.S. agencies and private organizations.
- Reductions should be made in U.S. contributions to multilateral economic assistance organizations.
- Participation in multilateral economic assistance programs should be supervised by the secretary of state instead of the secretary of the treasury. This would ensure that positions taken in multilateral economic assistance organizations reflect American foreign policy interests.
- Changes must be made in the bureaucratic structures. U.S. aid to worthy recipients should be distributed by the secretary of state, as opposed to the administrator of one of the many agencies involved in foreign aid.

EXPORT CONTROLS AS AN INSTRUMENT
OF NATIONAL SECURITY POLICY

Our modern system of export controls had its genesis in the early 1940s when the United States first imposed restrictions on the export of commodities, such as aluminum, scrap steel, and munitions, that could directly assist the Axis powers in their war-making capability. The theory was simple: "Don't sell them what they can throw back at us."

From the onset of the Cold War in the 1940s, there was a logical transition from specific, war-time export controls to Cold War–based controls on similar types of exports to the Soviet bloc. Then, following the start of hostilities in the Korean War (1950), U.S. export controls began to be used for a wider variety of national security purposes than the initial objective of limiting an adversary's war-making capability. In certain cases, controls took the form of partial or total embargoes. The purposes behind these controls, apart from the immediate one of keeping war materiel out of our adversaries' hands, have been to retard the development of our adversaries' general military-industrial base, to influence our adversaries' behavior, to express our moral or political outrage, and so on. The accretion of these objectives has tended to obscure the underlying national security rationale for export controls. A return to basics is now in order.

The Clinton administration's approach to national security issues is lacking in coherence, and this has had a profound effect on the management of the export control function. In particular, an unreconciled tension between the Clinton administration's counterproliferation and competitiveness goals has adversely affected the management of the export control function. On the one hand, the administration has launched largely rhetorical and symbolic initiatives to control proliferation. On the other hand, the administration's deep unilateral cuts in the scope of export controls, in an evident desire to serve the broad policy goal of enhancing U.S. competitiveness, has inadvertently facilitated the proliferation of technologies crucial to the proliferation of weapons of mass destruction and their means of delivery. Clinton administration export control policy changes, such as raising the threshold for general license computer exports, changing the technical definition of "supercomputers," and lifting controls on virtually all telecommunications exports, will increase the weapons of mass destruction (WMD) capability, force-projection, and cryptographic security capability of would-be proliferators.

The administration's performance in the export control arena belies its commitment to counterproliferation—especially on the critical issue of achieving a successor regime to the Coordinating Committee on Multilateral Export Controls (COCOM). Established in 1949 as a complement to NATO, the Paris-based COCOM organization included all NATO countries (except Iceland), plus Japan and Australia. By putting into place an effective multilateral control regime over the export of critical nuclear, munitions, and dual-use technologies to the then-Soviet Union, Warsaw Pact, and the People's Republic of China, COCOM was instrumental in asserting the economic and technological pressure that helped accelerate the breakup of the Soviet empire. For its forty-five years of existence, COCOM operated on a veto ("consensus") basis under which (apart from low technology items) any single member could block the export of militarily significant exports to proscribed end-users.

But with the collapse of the Soviet Union and its allies, efforts have been made to structure a replacement organization for COCOM that would address post–Cold War security needs.

At the request of President Yeltsin at the 1992 Vancouver Summit, the Clinton administration developed a scheme to dismantle COCOM and replace it on March 31, 1994, with a new counterproliferation regime. Presidents Clinton and Yeltsin jointly blessed the plan at the 1994 Moscow Summit. The successor regime to COCOM was supposed to prevent "rogue states"—Iran, Iraq, Libya, and North Korea—from obtaining such things as technology and weapons. But it was predicated on the abolition of all multilateral controls on exports to the former COCOM target countries, thereby giving Russia in particular both technological help and political acceptance. Indeed, the COCOM successor regime was to include Russia, despite its current failure to implement an effective national export control program to carry out its counterproliferation obligations.

The failure of the administration to lead the European alliance has been reflected in its inability so far to put in place a meaningful successor regime to COCOM. The target date for a new regime has repeatedly slipped by. Although the administration has criticized COCOM as being "based on

Cold War principles" and has held talks toward developing the counter-proliferation regime blessed by Presidents Yeltsin and Clinton, there is a serious question (with existing U.S. leadership) whether any effective control regime will ever emerge. Indeed, Moscow's sale of nuclear reactors to Iran shows exactly how meaningless the new system is.

In the meantime, the allies have shifted to a pattern of unilateral export controls based on loose coordination that varies from country to country. The United States, for example, has lifted controls on high computer technology and telecommunications exports. While most observers would accept that some liberalization and streamlining was in order, the depth and breadth of the cuts inevitably increase the risk of the diversion of sensitive technologies to proliferators of WMD. In contrast to the United States, other countries have declared their intention of maintaining tight COCOM-era controls.

The tragedy of this policy is that, in two ways, it dissipates precious assets cultivated over forty-five years. First, COCOM had developed a mature mechanism and had a long record as an effective multilateral export control program. In particular, over the years COCOM had developed a multinational secretariat with a substantial and unique expertise. Indeed, it may have been the only multinational body with the competence to develop lists of controlled technologies. In addition, COCOM's secretariat had mechanisms for sharing intelligence related to its mission not replicated elsewhere.

These facts suggest that the former COCOM secretariat might have had an increasingly important role to play as both multilateral and unilateral efforts evolved toward more refined control of so-called choke point technologies, and as the states of the former Soviet Union developed their own export control regimes. Unfortunately, except for a skeletal caretaker staff left in place pending development of a new regime, COCOM's secretariat has been disbanded.

Second, the essence of COCOM's success for forty-five years was the single-member veto. The success of any follow-on regime, if it ever comes to fruition, could hinge on the reinstitution of this essential attribute. The single-member veto provided an approximation of a "seamless web" of multilateral controls that precluded any export from COCOM of an embargoed technology to a targeted country. It therefore was effective, at least insofar as the relevant technology came from COCOM (or associated) countries. Moreover, it precluded the exporters of any one country from being disadvantaged because all countries' exporters were equally disadvantaged. It thus established in theory, but also largely in practice, a level playing field.

But COCOM has been replaced by what one observer described as NOCOM. As a result, the proliferation of WMD and their means of delivery is a looming threat of an immensely more dangerous magnitude than was the case less than four years ago.

The next administration must stop this drift and take affirmative measures to strengthen national and international export controls. These measures are:

- Analyze and articulate with precision what the specific objectives of controls are and stick to them.
- Develop and implement export controls only as part of a comprehensive approach to these objectives.
- If multilateral controls are to be pursued, exercise U.S. leadership in establishing the objectives and devising the export controls.
- Demonstrate U.S. leadership by achieving allied agreement on a successor regime to COCOM and establishing and sustaining it as an effective institution.
- Make controls meaningful by sustaining the decision process employed by the COCOM organization.

DEMOCRATIZATION AND THE PROTECTION OF HUMAN RIGHTS

Among the more than 180 sovereign states in the world today, about 76 of them are political democracies. These include about 20 percent of the world's population. At the end of World War II, there was a bipartisan consensus that only by providing political assistance to help the people of defeated Germany, Italy, and Japan rebuild their institutions as democracies would these countries cease to pose security threats. It was clearly understood that economic reconstruction, while necessary, was not sufficient to transform the international conduct of Germany and Japan. This now applies to Russia and the postcommunist countries of Europe.

The U.S. National Interest

President Ronald Reagan summarized America's national interest in encouraging democracy abroad when he stated that in the modern era virtually all democracies have been peaceful—they have used force only defensively. Therefore, the consolidation of democratic institutions in more countries, especially in those that are heavily armed such as Russia, Ukraine, other post-Soviet republics, and Eastern Europe, will reduce the military threats faced by the United States and its allies.

Countries that are governed democratically, it should be further noted, have not cooperated with the former Soviet Union or other hostile regimes in activities that are threatening to the United States or its allies. Thus the extension of democracy contributes to reducing threats from indirect aggression, terrorism, and other forms of clandestine warfare.

The United States also has a humanitarian interest in the welfare of people abroad. The best guarantee for the protection of individual human rights is in the institutions of a functioning political democracy. And it is evident that at all stages of economic development, living conditions are better for people in political democracies because these permit market-oriented economic institutions to function.

U.S. POLICY

During the 1980s, the prodemocracy policy of President Reagan was successful in Latin America and in a number of other places. This resulted in a return to the broad consensus that the United States should act to encourage democracy abroad. The unraveling of communist rule, which began in Eastern Europe in 1989, was followed by the dissolution of the former Soviet Union in 1991. As a result, historic, new opportunities to assist the transition from communism to democratic and market-oriented institutions have emerged.

In a world marked by political change within countries and where more than one hundred countries are governed by authoritarian regimes, many prodemocratic groups attempt to build a democratic state or end an existing dictatorship. Yet, in most such situations there will not be the consensus for large-scale political involvement or economic assistance by the United States that exists with respect to Eastern Europe and the former Soviet Union. Rather, the problem for U.S. policy will be whether and how to provide assistance. One existing institution, the National Endowment for Democracy, can be useful in promoting democracy in a broader policy.

Several important principles should underlie our approach: (1) the United States should help the people of foreign countries help themselves establish the institutions of freedom; (2) the United States should consistently provide symbolic support in the international arena for the cause of political democracy and human rights; and (3) the United States should support the use of military force only in rare instances or when a repressive regime is inflicting genocidal levels of human suffering and could be quickly defeated by an international military coalition.

From a worldwide perspective, the following are prudent proposals for means that the United States might use to encourage democracy and human rights abroad:

Example. The United States can set an example by maintaining the vitality of U.S. democratic and market-oriented institutions, and communicating this internationally.

Encouragement. U.S. leaders and citizens' groups might express direct encouragement to courageous men and women who are seeking to challenge dictatorship and repression.

International symbolic support for genuinely pro-democratic and human rights groups. The United States must use every international organization and forum to encourage and promote democracy and economic freedom, with the understanding that democracies are fragile and require time to consolidate. While short-term reversals should be expected, the United States should set democracy as the standard for a special relationship with all nations.

Linking democracy and trade opportunities. "Free trade with free countries" should be the policy of the United States. This means that trade access to the countries that are democratic or making a transition to political democracy and free markets—where both labor and business have the political freedom to articulate and defend their interests—would receive Most Favored Nation trade status.

Direct political assistance. This concerns pro-democratic groups seeking to establish democratic and market-oriented institutions after the unraveling of dictatorships (for example, Eastern Europe, the former Soviet Union).

Assistance short of U.S. military force. Such assistance could help pro-democratic groups replace hostile dictatorships (for example, Cuba, Iran, Iraq, Libya, North Korea). In some countries this could be done through open means, while in others it could be both covert and overt.

Direct United States assistance, including support for the international use of sufficient military force to alleviate and end massive human suffering by neutralizing or replacing highly repressive regimes when this can be done at comparatively little military risk. In exceptional circumstances, the American tradition of quickly responding to humanitarian tragedies leads us to use military force in pursuit of highly time-limited, narrowly defined missions of aid (for example, Operation Provide Comfort for the Kurds in Iraq; Operation Sea Angel in Bangladesh; and Operation Provide Hope, the original Bush mission in Somalia). This does not mean open-ended exercises in multilateral "nation-building."

Timely and well-designed political assistance to encourage the establishment of democratic institutions abroad requires very few material resources compared to economic assistance programs and can achieve extraordinarily positive results. Nevertheless, the positive results already visible since President Reagan proposed an open program of democratic institution-building assistance in 1982 make it clear that it is possible for the United States to have a more farsighted and strategically oriented program of political assistance to encourage democracy and the protection of human rights abroad.

IMMIGRATION

We must reaffirm our traditional commitment to encourage lawful immigration and to reiterate unequivocally our right to deter those who would come here or remain here in violation of our laws. We must reserve the sovereign right to decide the rules by which people wishing to come to the United States may do so.

A high level of immigration will have a significant impact on a number of economic and social problems. Studies tend to confirm that legal immigration is an economic benefit in the long run but that the economic and social costs of illegal immigration are alarming.

We must approach our immigration policy on both an individual and group basis. The safety and well-being of our citizens is a primary concern. As the World Trade Center bombing made tragically clear, terrorism is a new immigration issue that must be taken into consideration. To prevent terrorists from entering the United States, there should be more sharing of intelligence information by the FBI, the CIA, and the INS. The FBI and other enforcement agencies should be authorized to do whatever is necessary to locate suspected terrorists. Our courts should have the right to deport those who appear to have come here to threaten our society without a lengthy appeals process.

Many people come to the United States illegally to partake of our publicly funded social services. The United States should deny such services to those here illegally, except for emergency care or medical services necessary to protect the community as a whole. We should also implement effective procedures to expedite removal of those who are in the United States unlawfully, with emphasis on those who have committed serious crimes.

Short-term assistance to offset the fiscal impact of unlawful migration should be provided to state and local governments. But this assistance should be contingent upon the cooperation of recipient governments with federal efforts to combat illegal immigration. Foreign policy initiatives designed to promote democratic capitalism, particularly through trade and investment, in developing countries that now produce large numbers of illegal immigrants should be developed.

Continue Generous Humanitarian
Admissions Policy for Those in Need

To maintain America's leadership in world affairs and preserve the moral authority upon which it is built, we must continue to extend our generosity to those who need shelter on political and humanitarian, but not economic, grounds. We cannot—and should not—accept responsibility for protecting all of the world's refugees or humanitarian migrants, but we must continue to do our share and to encourage others to join us in that effort. We must strengthen our ability to detect those whose claims to our protection are unfounded so that we can extend it to those truly in need because of political and humanitarian passions.

Adjust Legal Immigration Policy to Reflect Economic
Reality and Serve the National Interests

Legal immigration tied to family relationships has been a positive influence in building America. Studies indicate that immigrants from all over the world bring to this country a strong devotion to family and a determination to better their own lives as well as the lives of their children through hard work and education. This influence is desirable, and our legal immigration policy should reflect the importance America places on these virtues.

Dependents of American citizens must be given preference over others; the reunification of other families lawfully here should be encouraged as well when it is possible to do so without causing economic dislocation in our own communities. To meet this goal, the United States should continue to give preference to immediate family members of United States citizens in family admissions. There should be an upward adjustment to the numbers of immigrant visas available to immediate family members of lawful permanent residents to reduce current waiting periods. We should eliminate family categories based on extended relationships to ensure the availability of visas to immediate family members and to discourage expectations in cases where the current waiting period may be more than a decade.

Facilitate Trade and Promote
Competition in American Business

The United States should develop reliable, efficient administrative mechanisms to determine labor market shortages so that the legitimate needs of employers are met through temporary or permanent immigration when necessary. We should also establish a periodic consultation process to permit adjustment in the numbers of immigrant visas available in skills-based categories to reflect developing economic trends and, when possible, to offset reductions in extended family-based categories. This would provide alternative possibilities for immigration to low-skilled workers affected by those reductions—but only where such alternatives would not adversely reduce employment opportunities to American workers.

None of the benefits of even the most well-crafted immigration laws will actually result if these laws cannot be enforced. It is widely recognized that satisfactory prevention of illegal border entry is unlikely to be achieved solely by patrolling the very long U.S. border. And patrolling the border is, of course, inadequate when dealing with foreign nationals who enter the United States *legally*—for example, as tourists or students—and then choose to violate the terms of their visas by not leaving when their visas expire or by working at unauthorized jobs.

In short, we should enforce the law after we reform it.

16

The United States Around the World

THE UNITED STATES IS A WORLD POWER, and its broad economic and political interests demand that it remain so. Because Republicans historically have grasped the link between our domestic security and prosperity and international security and prosperity, Republican leaders have led the way in establishing and sustaining a national consensus on international affairs. The Clinton administration's legendary disinterest in international affairs—the president has admitted to spending only an hour per week on them—is a stark abdication of American alliance leadership. The results are undoing the efforts of every previous post–World War II president.

The failure of the Clinton administration to sustain a leadership role in the NATO alliance has led to an acute crisis of confidence that has stirred the centrifugal forces in Europe to a dangerous level of activity. The current crisis in the Balkans exerts an increasingly powerful attraction to the multitude of forces that have produced continental and worldwide tragedies.

The most acute failure of policy since the end of the Cold War has been our Bosnian policy. For three years, the Clinton administration refused to address the issues of American security interests around the world. Subcontracting American interests in Europe to the United Nations is an astonishing betrayal of America's long-term interests in the continent where we remain the dominant political and economic power.

The current congressional leadership's efforts to restructure the resources and institutions that sustain our national interest in Europe and elsewhere reflect the public's rejection of the status quo in the Clinton administration's mismanagement of foreign affairs. This was one of the lessons of the mid-term elections of 1994, which is now being implemented through congressional enactment of the Contract with America.

STRUCTURAL CHANGES IN EUROPE

The collapse of Soviet military power in Europe coincided with Europe's terminal inability to sustain its extravagant welfare state. In addition, the democratization of the nations of Central and Eastern Europe (including the Baltic states) has materially slowed the momentum toward European economic, monetary, and political integration. The vast shifts in the policy environment in Europe continue to produce effects the consequences of which have yet to be fully absorbed. As a consequence, American leadership, particularly in foreign affairs and security policy, will be particularly important to the future configuration of European politics.

The profound structural changes in Europe are only beginning to have their impact on Europe's political leadership. The outcome is uncertain, but American interests are clear. The abandonment of American interests in Europe by the Clinton administration constitutes a perverse form of isolationism; posturing without commitment, rhetoric without leadership.

It is likely that, over the next decade or so, every major industrial democracy will undergo significant political and economic restructuring parallel to the changes being wrought by the new majorities in Congress. These changes will bring an end to continuing deficits and to the corrosive cumulative impact on economic activity and innovation that come from the high taxes and excessive involvement of government in private decisions. But absent firm American alliance leadership during this important transition, this restructuring could undo decades of American involvement in European security affairs. The failure of the American government prior to World War I and World War II to recognize and act on American interests in European security affairs was a contributing factor to this country's two great wars of destruction. History need not repeat itself if American leadership is resolute.

Costs and Benefits of European Integration

The United States has long recognized that the centrifugal factors in

European politics, economics, and culture have stimulated conflict for years. For that reason, the policy of the United States has long supported the establishment of European institutions that would bring about a more cooperative and eventually integrated set of arrangements among the states of Europe. The end of the arbitrary division of Europe occasioned by the collapse of the former Soviet Union provides an opportunity to create the institutional base for an enduring regime of peace and prosperity in Europe.

While it is clearly in the American interest for effective Eurocentric political and economic institutions to be established, this should not eliminate the American link to Europe, or create European economic, political, or military institutions that, as a bloc, would constrict rather than expand trade and other relations. We do not automatically accept all European efforts at integration as beneficial to us or to the interests of the world.

Policy Recommendations

The United States should reaffirm its long-term interest in European security, and its determination to remain involved in European political and security institutions that have a significant impact on American interests.

- NATO is the only European security entity with the infrastructure, organization, and experience to act in European security contingencies. Moreover, it is the only European entity with a transatlantic security component that permits effective regional security integration. The United States is the only member able to provide centralized support including intelligence, airlift, command and control, and demanding military missions. The role of NATO should continue to be central to Europe's management of its security problems; no political or military efforts should exclude or limit the U.S. role. American policy should reflect this aim.
- The integration of the democracies of Central and Eastern Europe into the security arrangements of Europe should be a goal of American policy in Europe. The aim of such integration should be to provide for the collective defense of democratic nations in Europe against those who would use military force to impose undemocratic changes in Europe. Membership from Central and East European nations that have resolved

residual territorial claims and related sources of political discord should be encouraged.

- Security assistance should be provided to cooperating Central and Eastern European nations moving toward NATO membership to enable their military forces to operate with their NATO counterparts.
- Foreign assistance to the nations of Central and Eastern Europe should be limited to technical advice and to facilitating their transformation from centralized nondemocratic states to market-oriented nations with democratic institutions and practices.
- The United States should assume leadership once again in the movement toward alliance-wide integration of defense and defense-related activities, including such activities as NATO-wide ballistic missile defense, surveillance technologies and platforms, and counterproliferation measures including export controls.

Facilitating improved defense industrial and scientific cooperation between the United States and the alliance should be implemented by harmonizing reciprocal access to the defense markets of the alliance. Procurement reform now under way in both Congress and the executive branch provides the opportunity to establish the necessary regulatory and legal changes to permit increased intra-alliance cooperation.

THE FUTURE OF RUSSIA AND U.S. POLICY

The failure of the hard-line communist coup attempt in August 1991 was followed by the formal dissolution of the Soviet Union in December 1991. This opened the way for Boris Yeltsin, who had been elected president of Russia in June 1991, to take leadership of the movement for democratic and market-oriented reforms in Russia, a country of 160 million people. The years of the post-Soviet era have been marked by intense political struggle as communists and ultranationalists oppose the reform agenda and criticize the economic dislocations and deprivations that accompany the initial "shock therapy" program of Yeltsin.

The U.S. National Interest

Russia continues to be armed with nine thousand strategic nuclear weapons and therefore could inflict massive and sudden damage on the United States. A bipartisan consensus understands that the consolidation of democratic and market-oriented institutions would likely result in a peaceful Russia and that the future of Russia might well determine the future of the eleven other post-Soviet states (all of the former Soviet Union except the three Baltic republics).

Russia—The Uncertain Future

From the start, the reform efforts of Yeltsin were resisted by former members of the communist elite, the ultranationalists, most of the highly influential managers of the military-industrial complex, the large state industrial and agricultural entities, and significant proportions of both the military and the security apparatus leadership. This resistance grew as Yeltsin's failure to implement market reforms led to implosion of the Russian economy and created further misery for its citizens.

The December 1993 elections approved a new constitution that strengthened the formal authority of President Yeltsin, but the communists and ultranationalists opposed to reform received 43 percent of the votes, while those backing Yeltsin's new reform agenda received only 34 percent. This was a sharp setback for the hopes of the reformers and encouraged both the communists and ultranationalists to believe that they could use the political process to gain full control of the new national legislature, to be elected in December 1995, and to win the presidency in the scheduled June 1996 election.

If either or both the communists or ultranationalists succeed in assuming power in Russia, much the same would probably soon occur in most of the former Soviet republics. The Soviet Union (except for the Baltic states) might well be reconstituted and, as described by Secretary of Defense William Perry in 1994, the result could be an "authoritarian, militaristic, imperialistic nation hostile to the West." This unsavory result is possible but it can still be avoided.

U.S. Policy

During the past four years the United States allocated $4.6 billion in grants and credits to assist Russia and the other post-Soviet republics while an additional $120 billion have been committed by other major countries, the World Bank, the International Monetary Fund (IMF), and the European Union. Despite this huge outlay, the aid program has failed in its most crucial purpose: to help transform the former Soviet economies to market-oriented nations. Indeed, the aid has largely sustained the existing state institutions. In doing so, it has had the counterproductive effect of strengthening the most reactionary forces in the former Soviet Union while gravely weakening those that favor economic reform.

There are four elements to a comprehensive U.S. strategy toward Russia.

Political Assistance. There must be more vigorous and effective efforts to assist genuinely pro-democratic leaders in building citizen groups, including political parties, independent trade unions, and business and civic associations. Among the components of this assistance are

- establishing a democratic working group for Russia at the highest level of the U.S. government;
- identifying major genuinely pro-democratic groups;
- designing and implementing a program that uses appropriate and effective means to assist genuinely pro-democratic political, labor, business, and other civic organizations;
- linking the availability of economic assistance to the ability of pro-democratic groups to organize and function; and
- channeling some portion of international economic assistance through genuinely pro-democratic civic organizations.

Economic Assistance. The United States has mistakenly delegated most of the strategic decisions and management of the international economic assistance effort for Russia to the World Bank and IMF. The United States should take the lead in designing a new economic assistance strategy that accomplishes two purposes simultaneously: (1) it provides support for the political authority of pro-democratic leaders and institutions; and (2) it contributes to economic improvement through expanding a genuinely private and market-oriented sector, including a capital market, without causing massive reductions in the standard of living. Such assistance should emphasize technical advice and assistance rather than large-scale resource transfer.

Demilitarization. In 1992, Presidents Bush and Yeltsin signed agreements calling for U.S. assistance in the destruction of Russian strategic weapons and the conversion of the military industrial complex to civilian production. At the initiative of Senators Nunn and Lugar, an account of $1.2 billion has been established during the past four years to accomplish these purposes.

While some progress has recently been made, overall too little has been done because of inept management of the effort, and the U.S. failure to exert effective leadership. Using these available funds, the United States should move immediately to help Russia destroy additional offensive strategic weapons if Russian accedes to the pending START Treaty and if it abides by its obligations under the CFE Treaty.

Collective Security. The United States must provide adequate defense through its own forces and through alliances if Russia should become hostile or a Soviet Union should be reconstituted. This requires

- Maintaining adequate strategic and conventional military forces.
- Strengthening the NATO alliance.
- Developing and deploying a strategic defense system (perhaps with President Reagan's offer to give this defensive system to Russia also, thereby mutually reducing the threat of thermonuclear war).
- Providing leadership to Eastern Europe and the Baltics to help them develop their own collective security and defense cooperation. This is compatible with the Partnership for Peace and, until the expansion of NATO, would permit them to deter military threats with their own military force.
- Assisting Russia to succeed in establishing and consolidating democratic and market-oriented institutions. This would add immeasurably to the security and well-being of the citizens of the United States, its allies, and those in the former Soviet Union.

THE ASIA AND PACIFIC REGION

Three of the most destructive wars in this century have been fought in Asia. Asia has nonetheless emerged as our largest trading partner, accounting for $370 billion in trade in 1993—60 percent more than our trade with Western Europe. Fueled by East and Southeast Asia's high sustained rates of economic growth, the region is a magnet for American products and services. Our open market similarly serves as the Asia Pacific region's most important single market.

The Clinton administration has chosen to view America's interest in the Asia Pacific region almost exclusively in trade terms. Regional security matters, which have been simultaneously at the heart of both Asia's prosperity and America's security interest in the area, have been virtually ignored. The Clinton administration has severely damaged American relations with many of the major states of the region. The administration's failure to assert a clear long-term security interest in our Asian military presence convincingly has stimulated anxieties about America's intentions and its long-term role. The administration's truculent and threatening posture on specific bilateral trade issues, moreover, has done little to address the underlying economic issues. The reassertion of America's enduring interests in the Asia Pacific region is now an urgent policy matter.

Japan

America's relationship with Japan is, and must remain, the center of American interests in Asia. As the region's largest economy, buttressed by a vibrant democracy and a shared culture, and bound to the United States by a tested network of security relationships, Japan serves as the cornerstone of the evolution of American economic and security-related interests in the region.

The generational change in Japan's leadership structure makes it particularly important for the U.S. government to encourage effective alliance leadership. China and North Korea both represent significant regional security issues, and this has made the question of Japan's access to ballistic missile defenses especially important and timely. As a nonnuclear state allied with the United States, Japan faces three nuclear armed nations (Russia, China, and North Korea) that pose potential threats.

This administration's failure to address the regional nuclear threat swiftly creates the risk that other nations threatened in the future will avoid the nonnuclear path to security.

Korea

Korean unification may be an eventual consequence of the Republic of (South) Korea's economic vitality and political liberalism. It is precisely the lack of these two characteristics, democracy and a free market system, that makes North Korea such a dangerous adversary. North Korea's present conventional military strength is a wasting asset based on Chinese and Russian technology of 1960s and 1970s vintage. For this reason, and to sustain its grip on power, the North Korea leadership has turned to developing weapons of mass destruction (WMD) and their means of delivery. Its manipulation of its nuclear weapons program has been used to strengthen its hand in the Korean unification process. Regrettably, the Clinton administration has played into the hands of the North Koreans.

The North Koreans were rewarded by the Clinton administration with petroleum and perhaps the eventual transfer of a large light water nuclear power plant with a capacity for producing more plutonium (though more complex to extract) than the reactors North Korea claims it will sacrifice as part of the deal. But inspection by the international community of North Korean facilities has been deferred for a decade. In the interim, North Korea's "No Dong" missile system with a range sufficient to reach Japan has entered production. A new series of longer-range missiles able to carry out intercontinental missiles is under development.

The administration's slow-motion response to the emergence of a renewed military threat to U.S. forces in South Korea—more than a month was required to ship a Patriot missile battery to Korea by sea compared to forty-eight hours to Saudi Arabia and Israel during Desert Storm—underscores Asia's concerns about the Clinton administration.

The administration's policy in Korea, as elsewhere in Asia, requires fundamental change. Such change appears unlikely until there is a change in executive leadership in the United States.

China

The inability of the Clinton administration to manage American foreign policy interests abroad is painfully illustrated in its gross mismanagement of its policy toward China. Moving China from its communist past toward the political and economic reform that could mature into a democratic and market-oriented state has been America's policy for two decades. While substantial progress toward this goal has been made, powerful pressures within the communist leadership to suppress the desire for greater personal freedom that sparked the forces of economic development threaten to drag the country back to its most rigid totalitarian past. The brutal suppression of pro-democracy demonstrators at Tiananmen Square in Beijing in 1989 revealed how threatening the mix of economic and political reform is. The preoccupation of the Clinton administration with the question of trade coupling with empty rhetoric over human rights abuses has created a China policy that is now in total disarray.

China, in the throes of a succession struggle to replace its octogenarian leadership, continues its human rights abuses, fails to comply with its international trade commitments, has expanded its exports of nuclear and missile technology to known proliferators, has undertaken a menacing buildup of its defense establishment, and shows signs of threatening Taiwan militarily. To all of this, the administration's only response has been to extend China's Most Favored Nation trade status.

The incorporation of Hong Kong into the sovereign territory of the People's Republic of China in 1997 provides an important opportunity to nurture the cause of political and economic reform in China. Hong Kong has provided 60 percent of the direct foreign investment in the People's Republic of China (PRC)—a process that has stimulated both economic and political reform. The PRC's commitment to sustain Hong Kong's free economic and political institutions for fifty years after unification, if honored, would permit Hong Kong to continue to play a constructive role in the reform and modernization of China.

Meanwhile, China is increasing its territorial claims and military pressure against its regional neighbors. It is also upgrading its military capabilities through purchase and theft of advanced technologies and through modernization of its strategic forces, some of which are able to reach the United States, with new missiles, and warhead and submarine capabilities. China's record on proliferation of deadly weapons is poor, especially with regard to Iran, North Korea, and Pakistan. China has continued to threaten states in the region through missile flight tests in the proximity of other Asian states and to stress its capability to employ WMD through its current series of nuclear tests.

America has an extremely large long-term interest in China that requires a well-thought-out approach. We must encourage economic and political liberalization while firmly resisting initiatives that threaten American regional interests. The United States's relationship with the PRC can be greatly improved, even before desired reforms are finally accomplished on the mainland. From the days of "ping-pong" diplomacy, foresighted leaders have recognized the widsom of a continually improving the U.S.-PRC relationship, even while significant or sharp differences remain between the two countries. For ten consecutive administrations, the United States has observed a "One China" policy, as has the PRC and Taiwan. A free, democratic, and market-oriented unified China remains the goal of America's China policy.

Taiwan

The rapid pace of political and economic reform in Taiwan is further separating China and Taiwan. Taiwan's first direct election of a president in 1996 completes a process of democratization begun in the 1980s. Taiwan's democratization has enraged Beijing, which has stepped up its threats of military action against Taiwan. Yet despite statutory requirements that enable Taiwan to acquire the U.S. arms it needs for legitimate self-defense, the administration continues to deny Taiwan access to the equipment it needs to cope with the most likely threats—a naval blockade of its territory and a ballistic missile attack employing both conventional weapons and WMD. Instead, the administration has offered a visa to Taiwan's president to undertake a nonofficial visit to his former university in the United States.

Moreover, Taiwan's viable claims to participate in international forums, justified by its economic and its political reforms at home, continue to be resisted by the Clinton administration. In particular, Taiwan should be supported in its efforts to win formal UN representation. As long as 1971, the United States was prepared to support representation in the UN for both the

PRC and ROC consistent with long-standing U.S. support for universality of representation in the world organization. Just as the United States supported UN membership for the two Germanies (which later became one Germany), and even cosponsored the admission of the two Koreas, so too should we support Taiwan's desire for a UN role. Moreover, beyond any question, we should support ROC membership in the IMF and the World Bank. Its indefensible policy toward Taiwan reinforces the impression the Clinton administration has created elsewhere in Asia, further separating this crucial region from American interests.

Asean

The growing membership in the Association of Southeast Asian Nations regional association reflects its political and economic maturity. The region's economies are the fastest growing in the world. The ability of the region to sustain its economic growth and democratic reforms has depended on continued American engagement in the region in political, economic, and military terms. The administration's abandonment of a credible long-term American security interest in the area has, however, allowed China to assert its territorial claims in the region. Currently this claim is being asserted only in the South China Sea, but China's historic territorial claims extend throughout the Southeast Asia region. If there is any lesson to be learned from the military conflicts of the twentieth century in which the United States has been engaged, it is that American failure to assert its security interest clearly and forcefully in the early stages of a dispute is an invitation to future trouble.

The administration appears incapable of implementing a coherent foreign policy anywhere in Asia.

Indochina

Vietnam's substantial economic potential has been stifled by the communist regime. Absent liberalization, Vietnam is doomed to be a Southeast Asian backwater state in a region otherwise enjoying vibrant growth in its economic and, for the most part, democratic institutions as well. Like China, Vietnam's communist leadership seeks to obtain the benefits of economic growth without the political liberalization that has taken place elsewhere in the world. Continued pressure on the Vietnamese leadership to extend the process of economic reform to the political sphere should be a central element of U.S. policy in Vietnam.

Despite the Clinton administration's decision to extend formal diplomatic recognition to the Vietnamese regime, the communist leadership has failed to complete its accounting for American MIAs—reversing a position held by all previous presidents since 1975.

Laos and Cambodia are also beginning to emerge from their communist servitude as the "dominoes" of North Vietnam's conquest of South Vietnam in 1975. The United States and its allies should contest China's continued sponsorship and support of the infamous Pol Pot regime, which continues to conduct a guerrilla conflict against the current regime in Phnom Penh. The ongoing civil war in Cambodia and its lack of real progress toward democratization reflect poorly on the UN operation that has spent nearly $3 billion in its unsuccessful effort to promote peace and democracy. The transition of Laos to a stable and prosperous regime will depend on the degree to which it implements economic and political reforms. The United States should encourage it to do so.

American policy with regard to the Asia-Pacific region should do more than it currently does to reflect the Asian and Pacific Islander heritage of many of our citizens. Mutually beneficial interaction at the citizen level is much needed in the cultural, economic, and political spheres.

As the world moves toward the twenty-first century—which could be the Pacific Century—it is important that the United States have a clear sense of leadership in the Asia Pacific region. That vision should be based on a continuing and evolving U.S. security role, prosperity in a free enterprise environment, expanding trade, democratic institutions, and respect for human rights. American leaders need to have confidence that such a vision will prevail over the long term.

Latin America and the Caribbean

Latin America and the Caribbean are important neighbors of the United States. Under the Clinton administration, the region has been treated as a secondary interest by foreign policies that seem to be of greater concern to special interest groups than to the American people. Between the threats of uncontrolled and massive flows of immigration and narcotics, and the opportunities from beneficial free trade and a prosperous and secure neighborhood, the importance of Latin America to the United States is immense.

The policies of a future administration toward the nations of Latin America must be a blend of clearly defined U.S. interests and prioritization. The criteria for our general policies should at least include the following principles:

- The United States should continue to support democratic processes, including, but not limited to free elections, free markets, and basic human rights.
- The United States must give high priority to technical assistance that will enhance economic and institutional reform already under way in the region.
- The United States must cooperate with key countries to assist in the development of a broad antinarcotics production, smuggling, and use strategy.
- The United States should encourage the development of loyal democratic opposition parties, through the International Democrat Union, non-governmental organizations (NGOs), and the National Endowment for Democracy, particularly in democratic states whose political life is dominated by a single party.
- The United States must develop a consistent and enforceable immigration policy, based on self-interest. We need and welcome those who would contribute to our nation through work or capital. An element of our immigration policy and a basic requirement for U.S. citizenship should be a willingness to use the English language; assimilation should be a central element of the reform of American immigration policy.

COUNTRY–SPECIFIC POLICY PRIORITIES

U.S. priorities must include but not necessarily be limited to the following countries, which are important to our well-being, trade, security, and the quality of our hemispheric neighborhood:

Mexico

The U.S.-Mexican border constitutes a de facto priority because of immigration and trade. Nowhere on earth is there a frontier between two countries of greater economic disparity as that between the United States and Mexico. But it is mutually beneficial to the United States and Mexico that we control our border. Since the cost of an unregulated border has become intolerable, we must be willing effectively to regulate those who cross it. This will require greater effort on our part. The dangers associated with narcotics and the growth of world terrorism compound the necessity.

Recognizing the need for willing Mexican labor by small businesses and farmers, control of the border should be complemented by a program under which temporary Mexican workers would be admitted under a program similar to the Bracero program of the 1960s. This program recognized U.S. needs and protected the rights of the Mexicans as well.

U.S. interests in Mexico must also include efforts to assist the growth of a diversified Mexican private sector. The United States must encourage a Mexican private sector that is market driven, inclusive, and competitive.

The United States must also be prepared to assist Mexico against the growing menace of illegal narcotics through the use of technology and personnel. We must encourage those in Mexico fighting this battle by proper recognition and by indicating our willingness to be more active in combating this problem.

Cuba

Cuba is clearly the second priority for U.S. policy toward Latin America, due to proximity, our large Cuban-American population, and Fidel Castro's historic hatred of America. The Castro regime is now Latin America's last dictatorship, and since the collapse of the Soviet Union and the end of Soviet aid to Cuba, its economy has been collapsing. Communism, not the U.S. embargo, is the cause of Cuban poverty, and the embargo should be maintained until real reforms begin there. A new administration should take all appropriate measures to bring change to Cuba, including aid to opponents of the regime. When Castro seeks to use the lives of would-be refugees as a bargaining chip, two principles should guide our reaction: The United States will welcome individuals fleeing communism but will react vigorously to prevent another Mariel-type maneuver by Castro and will not allow him to exacerbate our own national debate on immigration issues. Cuba desperately cries out for political freedom and a free-market economy, and Castro is the obstacle to both. The real answer to Cuba's problems, and an end to refugee flows, will be Cuba's liberation from communist rule.

Chile

This nation is a success story and a true example of political and economic freedom. Chile should receive NAFTA status as soon as possible. Its agricultural products are counterseasonal and therefore of little concern to most of our producers of fruits and vegetables. Here is a case where virtue deserves to be rewarded and where the American consumer will benefit.

Colombia

Colombia is important to the United States for two reasons. It is the seat of a narcotics empire that is a threat to the integrity of Colombia's government and a menace to the United States. Colombia is also one of three Latin American states with significant and growing petroleum reserves. Its recently discovered on-shore oil fields have been compared to Alaska's Prudhoe Bay, and its off-shore reserves are thought to be greater yet.

U.S. policy toward Colombia must not simply reject this country because of tainted elements in its leadership. The United States must make every effort to help honest Colombians in their struggle for their country. If we do not do so, the corruption that now threatens their government and laps at our Mexican border will surely threaten us.

Panama

This country is important to the United States because the Panama Canal is still strategically valuable to our navy and to our export trade. Although it is of little importance to our merchant marine, it is important to our commodity exporters who use foreign or flag-of-convenience ships. Many friendly states view the canal as vital to their economic survival. For these reasons, and especially the naval one, the United States should arrange for an indefinite security presence in Panama.

Central America

The five countries of Central America—Costa Rica, Nicaragua, Honduras, El Salvador, and Guatemala—are important to the United States because they can either be assets as good trading partners and friends if their economic and political systems work, or sources of illegal immigration, turmoil, and difficulty if they fail. The United States should make every effort to include these nations, and certain others in South America, in NAFTA.

We should encourage the development of political as well as economic democracy in Guatemala, not by punishing that country for minor human rights transgressions, but by building up its civilian-controlled police as an alternative to the military.

In Nicaragua, the struggle for economic growth and real democracy is made even more difficult by the failure to resolve property rights cases and by continuing Sandinista control of the security forces. We should use our influence, and offer technical assistance, to help Nicaragua achieve real civilian control of the military and police, and adopt economic policies that guarantee property rights and attract foreign investment.

Haiti

This island nation is unique in its lack of political and economic structures. We should replace our troops as soon as possible and resist the temptation to build an infrastructure, absent Haiti's ability to use or maintain it. We should encourage NGOs that assist small farm and business enterprises and churches that offer direct aid to the people.

Haiti's small farmers and its economic development are retarded by the vicious tactics of city-based elites who prevent the formation of cooperatives and the construction of storage facilities that might protect the harvests of small farmers and enable them to sell with advantage in the marketplace. Left to the mercies of an unsheltered market, they are reduced to de facto peonage, forced to sell at the time of harvest and overabundance. A Republican administration might encourage the development of agricultural cooperatives in Haiti, and protect them by conditioning our other aid, humanitarian and charitable, on their survival.

Latin America and the Caribbean are important to the United States as part of our contiguous neighborhood, and as friends and trading partners with growing power and potential. This region received deserved special attention from the Reagan administration and should command top priority from any administration. The positives of trade and democratic trend lines and the threats of narcotics and uncontrolled immigration make this region one of critical importance to us in the present and the foreseeable future.

U.S. POLICY IN THE MIDDLE EAST

The tragic assassination of Israeli Prime Minister Yitzhak Rabin, who began his life as a soldier fighting for Israel's very existence and ended his life as a peace for freedom, reminds the world of the fragile balance that must be struck in the Middle East between competing interests, histories, and tragedies on the path to a lasting peace.

The Middle East stands out in American foreign policy for two reasons. First, it appears to be the region least affected by the end of the Cold War; most of the problems of decades past remain in place. Second, the region has particular importance for American interests, principally because of dangers the region poses. From the American point of view, six Middle Eastern issues have outstanding importance: the Arab-Israeli conflict, rogue states, WMD, terrorism, oil and gas, and fundamentalist Islam.

The Arab–Israeli Conflict

Beginning with Richard Nixon, every president has actively engaged in seeking to resolve the Arab-Israeli conflict by working toward two goals: maintaining the security of Israel, and advancing the negotiations between Israel and its Arab enemies. This bipartisan strategy has enjoyed considerable success over the past quarter-century. Americans can claim much credit for Israel's peace treaties with Egypt and Jordan, the several agreements with the Palestinians, and the serious talks now under way with Syria. In fact, the annals of diplomacy know of no comparable diplomatic successes by a mediator. This policy, which enjoys wide congressional and popular backing, should remain in place.

Two particularly controversial aspects of the Arab-Israeli conflict—

Jerusalem and aid to the Palestinians—require special note. The U.S. government has for over forty years withheld recognition of Jerusalem as sovereign Israel territory; the time has come to end this legalistic timidity for it only encourages some enemies of Israel to think they can still claim the whole of Jerusalem. Moving the U.S. embassy to Jerusalem is a good first step toward ending this illusion.

Second, the U.S. government has pledged to help Yasir Arafat's Palestinian Authority with money and other assistance; but such assistance should only be forthcoming if the authority lives up to its many agreements with Israel (and especially the promise to crack down on violence against Israelis).

Rogue States

The Middle East hosts most of the world's subversive states: Libya, Sudan, Syria, Iraq, and Iran. Each of these regimes raises distinct problems for the United States, and every one of them must be dealt with in a tough and consistent manner. Libya under Muammar al-Qaddafi has gone from being a major problem to a minor nuisance, thanks mainly to two events—Ronald Reagan's April 1986 bombing of Tripoli and George Bush's getting UN sanctions applied to Libya in April 1992. Continued firmness should keep Qaddafi relatively quiet.

Sudan is remote and poor; nonetheless, the country has recently emerged as a significant problem. In addition to terrible humanitarian abuses against the non-Muslim southerners and aggressiveness against neighbors (including Egypt), the military regime has adopted a fundamentalist Islamic orientation, joined forces with Iran, and facilitated the export of international terrorism.

The Syrian government of Hafiz al-Asad has slightly improved its behavior over the past five years, both internally and externally, following the collapse of its primary arms supplier, the former Soviet Union. But it remains a totalitarian regime with a huge arsenal that occupies one neighbor (Lebanon), subverts another (Turkey), and threatens a third (Israel). A peace treaty with Israel must be a precondition to improved U.S. relations with Syria.

Weapons of Mass Destruction (WMD)

At a time when other regions are reducing their arsenals, the Middle East continues to militarize. As a region, it spends well over twice the world average on the military. This spending means that the Middle East hosts more tanks, armored personnel carriers, artillery, and aircraft than does non-Russian Europe.

In recent years, a large number of Middle Eastern states have turned to WMD. Missiles have become commonplace and have been found in the arsenals of eight states. The story is the same with chemical and biological capabilities, while several states are attempting to build nuclear weapons.

These weapons can affect the United States in many ways, directly (biological or chemical agents smuggled into American territory) and indirectly (missile attacks on allies). An effective U.S.-led effort is required both to control the development of a proliferation threat through export controls and to deter it through the deployment of theater and national ballistic missile defense.

Terrorism

Innovations in terrorism that come out of the Middle East—the car bomb, attacks on embassies, government support for terrorist groups—have made the region important because of new methods that can affect the course of history. The U.S. response in years past has been weak: ineffective punishment of terrorist groups, a tendency to hunker down, and sometimes even appeasement of the sponsors of terrorism.

The American people need something better than this defeatist approach. A proper approach to terrorism must contain three components: an understanding that most operations have connections to state security services; a principled approach to the use of force, even against fairly powerful states (for example, Iran); and a readiness to accept the short-term costs of applying this more robust policy.

Oil and Gas

The Middle East has huge economic importance for the United States because of the region's immense oil and gas reserves—some two-thirds of the world's total. The United States has throughout the twentieth century worked for the free flow of oil from the Middle East; at the same time, as current restrictions on Libya, Iraq, and Iran indicate, this cannot be our top priority.

Rather, the number one priority should be preventing any single power from gaining hegemonic control over the oil and gas resources of the Persian Gulf. Just as American forces twice fought Germany to prevent any single power from gaining control of Europe, so too they fought Iraq to keep it from dominating the Gulf. They may well be called on again for this purpose.

Fundamentalist Islam

Fundamentalist Islam (or "Islamism") represents the most vibrant anti-American ideology extant anywhere in the world today. Fundamentalists hate the West, and the United States in particular, with a venom that goes beyond political. They see the culture of the United States, both high and low, as the enemy of Islam, and they target Americans, especially those serving abroad. Accordingly, the United States must ensure the safety of all U.S. diplomatic personnel and facilities worldwide by providing adequate levels of security resources.

Policy toward fundamentalist Islam suffers from two main problems. First, it deals individually with each country when it occurs (Algeria, Sudan, Iran, Afghanistan, Pakistan), without looking at the ideology as a whole. As in the case of prior aggressive and totalitarian movements (fascism, communism), this one too needs to be seen as a whole, with a policy toward the whole.

Second, while the Clinton administration's policy toward fundamentalists in power (especially in Sudan and Iran) has been appropriately tough, it has been weak toward the fundamentalist movements trying to get into power (most especially in Algeria). The U.S. government must not urge the inclusion of fundamentalists for they are radical utopians and will both inflict great damage on their own societies and pursue deeply hostile policies toward the United States.

Regional Security

The question of regional security has stimulated the most visible American interest in the region. The region has been the primary focus of American civil and military assistance for two decades. Containing the destabilizing regimes of Iran and Iraq as well as Libya has preoccupied American security policy, and well so, for these nations have encouraged international terrorism and have covertly acquired WMD and their means of delivery. The growing danger of proliferation has been abetted by the failure of the Clinton administration's counterproliferation strategy. The exposure of all of America's friends and allies in the region from the Gulf to the Straits of Gibraltar to WMD requires that America attend to our security concerns on a regional basis.

Gulf Security
The dual containment of Iran and Iraq needs to be managed separately to take into account the different types of foreign policy and threats these nations pose to American interests. The nations in the Gulf that are committed to a constructive security policy should be able to obtain the weapons, training, and linkage to the United States that they require to carry a significant share of the defense burden imposed by their aggressive neighbors through prepositioned stocks of equipment, joint exercises, command and control arrangements, and so on. American policy needs a sustained deterrence of aggression in the region. Or, if deterrence fails, the United States must provide the sophisticated support such as was provided to the allied Coalition Forces in Operation Desert Storm and gave them their decisive edge in the conflict (for example, long-range precision strike systems, missile defense, a sophisticated surveillance system).

Israel
More than four decades of American support for Israel has paid off in promising prospects for peace between Israel and its contiguous neighbors. Egypt and Jordan are both signatories to a peace treaty, and the preliminary signs of long-term peace between Israel and the Palestinians are beginning to emerge. An unwavering commitment to a strong and secure Israel has been the catalyst that has made these crucial gains possible. Continuation of this policy should, in due course, see an Israeli-Syrian agreement as well. In the longer term, Israel's security will continue to be an American commitment and in our interest. The threat

posed to Israel, from states beyond Israel's borders, will come from long-range strike systems such as ballistic and cruise missiles and high performance aircraft. The nature of this threat will justify continuing American support for Israel's acquisition of specialized early warning sensors, ballistic missile defense, and other systems that can help sustain or strengthen deterrence in the region.

Egypt

American support and engagement for Egypt has similarly provided many benefits for the United States. Egypt has become the bulwark of the struggle against radical Islam; it has helped to dilute Iran's aggressive efforts to spread its terrorist doctrine throughout North Africa and the Arab world. Egypt has also been a key player in sustaining the dialogue between Israel and its Arab neighbors. Despite the inevitable disappointments at elements of the peace process, Egypt continues to be a valuable partner in America's broader Middle East regional security strategy. As is the case in several of the important nations of the region, economic reform remains a central factor in the political stability of the area. American efforts to stimulate effective economic policy reform will serve to reinforce our security efforts.

AFRICA

The vital interests of the United States in Africa differ markedly from those in many other areas of the world. First of all, from a strictly strategic sense, Africa is not of the highest importance to this country. The more clearly this fact is stated, the easier it is to define our true interests. As fellow human beings, we who live in one of the richest countries in the world have a moral obligation to assist the millions of people in Africa who are living in abject poverty. The best way to help is by providing an efficient package consisting of trade, aid, and private investment. Too often this country has been content to allow the United Nations and its affiliated agencies, including the World Bank and the International Monetary Fund, to carry the major burden. Their many inefficiencies often have deprived the African continent of proper assistance. The United States should be more forthcoming in taking the lead in assistance projects.

The move to majority rule in South Africa has succeeded well beyond all expectations. Nelson Mandela deserves a great deal of the credit, but not all. Millions of people of good will from all ethnic groups deserve their share. The United States should encourage cooperative ventures with South Africa in all commercial and intellectual areas. A stable, prosperous, and democratic South Africa provides the best hope of a spill-over effect for the rest of the continent. The example of the United States is widely admired in South Africa. We should take advantage of this state of good feeling to encourage free enterprise and to work in harmony with the Mandela government.

The African continent has been the slowest to initiate political and economic reform of any major area of the world. Apart from the singular exception of South Africa, where the fragile process of political and economic reform is now under way, much of the continent is worse off, where human rights and economic prosperity are concerned, than before its independence.

Africa's development has been blighted by its protracted dependence on bilateral and multilateral foreign assistance organizations and state domination of their economies. The extraordinarily diverse resource base and markets available in Africa have been rendered a burden rather than an asset because the international foreign assistance community has built up and reinforced all-powerful centralized economic institutions. Their iron control over the economies of most African states far exceeds that of the former colonial powers.

Tolerance for a succession of antidemocratic and often brutal leaders of African states has sustained the grip of tribal forces and allowed them to prevail over the building of a nation. It has also contributed to Africa's declining growth in national per-capita income and its dictatorial regimes. Africa can and should become part of the international community of democratic and market-oriented states that are able to provide economic growth and personal liberty to their citizens. Changes in American policy can have a major impact in bringing this about, but it will require a fundamental departure from the practices and policies of the Clinton administration.

Economic Growth, Not Handouts

Africa's economic development has been strangled by three decades of good intentions, which have sought to promote economic development through bilateral and multilateral economic assistance. But good intentions cannot make bad policies work. State-run/-regulated institutions, high marginal tax rates, government interference with the price mechanism, property rights violations, and similar development-defeating initiatives have characterized the international aid effort in Africa. It is a record unblemished by success.

America's policy of economic development in Africa needs to shift from aid to trade. Providing markets for African products within existing multilateral trade arrangements, and ending the reinforcement by the state of existing bilateral and multilateral aid, will stimulate the development of market-oriented institutions. Residual aid should be restricted to technical advice on how to eliminate statutory, regulatory, and extralegal obstacles to economic development. Such aid should be provided only to African states that have initiated an economic policy reform agenda.

Political Reform

Africa's escape from colonial rule has been a Pyrrhic victory. Distant dominion from Paris, London, or Brussels has been replaced by a dismal procession of local despots whose rule has placed the entire continent in jeopardy. Affording local African tyrants international legitimacy rewards Africa's kleptocracy while frustrating forces for democratic change. American efforts to delegitimate Africa's nondemocratic leadership while promoting economic reform will accelerate Africa's movement along the path so successfully explored elsewhere in the world.

Regional Political and Economic Rationalization in Africa

Africa's arbitrary geographic division along lines once convenient to colonial administrators has been sustained largely to accommodate Africa's ruling kleptocracy. In many cases, this has frustrated a natural nation-building process. Sustaining colonial boundaries in defiance of political, social, and economic considerations leaves Africa bound to its colonial past. Africa's future political and economic configuration should be determined by local and regional economic and political modernization. The United

States should encourage processes that will help achieve a postcolonial political and economic equilibrium consistent with the continent's development along democratic and market-oriented lines.

THE LIMITS OF MULTILATERALISM

The Clinton administration has done grave damage to the credibility of U.S. foreign policy with its empty rhetoric about "assertive multilateralism." Moreover, by using the United Nations as an excuse for its own ineptitude (as in Haiti) or indecision (as in Bosnia), it has undermined the credibility of the United Nations as well.

The next administration must restore the primacy of American interests and values in all decisions concerning U.S. engagement—whether political, economic, diplomatic, or military—in shaping the course of world affairs.

The United Nations's effectiveness can be measured only in relation to America's national interests. The United Nations is one, but only one, of the available vehicles of U.S. foreign policy. It can be a useful forum for multilateral consultation and negotiation, and for coalition-building for mutual security, as it was in turning back Iraq's aggression against Kuwait. But it is essential to put first things first. United States leadership of the Gulf War coalition was the result of a prior U.S. decision that vital national interests were at stake. The resolutions of the UN Security Council reflected that decision; and the successful outcome was determined by the firmness of America's commitment, the skillful use of its multilateral diplomacy, and the formidable power of the U.S.-led coalition.

This combination of commitment and effective implementation, displayed throughout the Reagan and Bush presidencies, burnished the credibility of U.S. world leadership and gave decisive weight to the prudent engagement of U.S. military force, or the threat of its use. The United Nations has neither the authority nor the competence for nation-building. U.S. acquiescence in open-ended UN "peacekeeping" missions, which are ambiguous in purpose and lacking in precise rules of engagement, invites uncontrollable costs (borne disproportionately by the United States), diversion of the United Nations from its legitimate roles (including traditional peacekeeping, with the consent of the parties to a conflict), the scattering of limited resources, and even the loss of American lives. Somalia is a glaring example of UN overreach. Insofar as the United Nations turns every emergency call into a "threat to international peace and security"—which is the only basis in its charter for the use of force under the UN flag—it tends to trivialize real threats to peace and to dilute whatever capability it may have to resolve real conflicts.

In rare cases, when international peace and U.S. security are truly on the line, the United States must consider intervention by force—unilaterally if need be. In all cases, America's decision has to be grounded explicitly in our vital national interests. The UN Security Council can never substitute for the U.S. constitutional process. And there is no shortcut to a binding national consensus, which must always be a prerequisite to putting American lives at risk. These were core principles of the Weinberger rules, articulated by President Reagan's defense secretary: they made good sense then and will again—with Republican leadership of a U.S. foreign policy clearly and unapologetically rooted in American interests.

The Republican Congress is at present designing an affirmative approach to the United States–United Nations relationship. It puts a reasonable cap on U.S. contributions to UN peacekeeping, requires the president to contain American participation in UN peacekeeping efforts to compelling national interests, and imposes stringent conditions on placing U.S. troops under UN command and control. U.S. contributions to all UN programs, moreover, are made contingent on thoroughgoing UN management reform. Nothing less than this Republican legislative package will put the United States–United Nations relationship back on its proper course.

NATIONAL OCEANS POLICY

In March 1983, in a little-noticed but historic act, President Reagan issued a proclamation confirming American sovereign rights and control over all living and nonliving resources within two hundred miles of U.S. coasts—a staggering addition to our natural patrimony of some 2 million square miles, or about 4 billion acres. The seabeds we now control and the ocean above are an unopened treasure house. Our new offshore domains could become a Louisiana Purchase of the twenty-first century.

Reagan's actions were a sound alternative to the ill-considered 1982 United Nations Convention on the Law of the Sea. This UN proposal would create a socialistic system of control and regulation of the seas. It embodies an outmoded 1970s view of the world. Reagan would not approve the convention. The Clinton administration, however, after some essentially cosmetic tinkering, has now signed the pact. It should not be ratified.

If the nation is to realize the full potential of President Reagan's vision, we must create a forward-looking oceans policy that recognizes our many and complicated interests. Our National Oceans Policy must ensure that we retain robust scientific research capabilities, both in government and in universities. An appropriate oceans policy will replace the current bewilderingly fragmented patchwork of laws and regulations that prevents American firms from fully utilizing the ocean's vast potential.

Conclusion

ANY ATTEMPT TO SUMMARIZE the policy recommendations in this book would amount to a short volume in itself. I haven't tried to tally up the specific proposals in these chapters, but there are hundreds of them. Their number alone guarantees that no one is likely to agree with all of them. (As I mentioned in the introduction, I take exception to a handful of them myself, though I won't divulge which I have in mind.)

At the same time, I am confident the great majority of these policy suggestions can be accepted, and eagerly, by the great majority of Americans. That's not surprising. After all, these recommendations—and the comprehensive blueprint for change that, in their entirety, they compose—came from the people themselves.

That's what we aimed for in creating the National Policy Forum (NPF) three years ago. We didn't intend to add another Capitalcentric think tank to the proliferating ranks of those institutions of both the Right and the Left. They serve an important purpose, but we wanted to do something different. That's why we established, in the NPF, a unique instrument for channeling—and hopefully amplifying—the voice of the rest of the country to official Washington.

This volume, I believe, justifies our unprecedented initiative, which was based on what may have seemed a nostalgic vision in participatory democracy. I can best explain that by referring to something that once was, and may once again become, an icon of our nation's political culture: Norman Rockwell's painting—one of his "Four Freedoms" series—of a town meeting. Think hard, and you'll remember the scene. One of the local residents, a hard-working man to judge from his practical and worn attire, has risen to speak his mind on the issue at hand. (It matters not at all what that was.) He appears neither bold nor intimidated. We assume he has not had a great deal of formal education, but in his face we discern a more important wisdom. And as he speaks, his neighbors, of all stations in life, listen attentively.

In that single scene, the artist captured the best in American democracy: our spirit of community, our egalitarian bent, the mutual respect that transcends superficial differences of class and party.

This was our vision as well as our hope and expectation: that those decent, determined Americans in that half-century-old painting were still out there, still had something important to say, and still had faith that their views could make things better. Indeed, we believed such Americans were resolved to have a voice in what the government was saying and doing.

We were absolutely right—though some important things have changed. The townsfolk Rockwell portrayed now appear in much greater diversity—racial, cultural, and political. Today our town meetings are as likely to be held on the Internet as in a village hall, but they are nonetheless vibrant for all their modernity. In fact, come to I think of it, this volume—along with its predecessor, *Listening to America*—has served somewhat as a town meeting for a national "town" of more than 250 million independent-thinking and blessedly opinionated souls. If you've read it through carefully, you've heard them speak, not always with the same voice, but invariably about the same values.

It is a daunting task to draw a few uniting basic elements from the hundreds of policy proposals that came our way, but here's my attempt at it.

First, change—indeed, accelerating change—is inevitable. As a society we can modulate it, steer it, move through it. But we cannot ignore it or turn it back. Hence the innovative change that enlivens most of these chapters. They are built on an unstated common axiom: When government attempts to protect the status quo—and what better description is there of the liberal agenda of the last two decades?—it contorts the present, distorts the future, and fails to preserve the good in the past. America adapts to and prospers from change more than any other country or culture, and while we are often anxious in the doing, we ultimately flourish.

A second element we can draw from these chapters is that we Americans are more than a random group of people who happen to live within certain boundaries on a map. In a time of international dissolution, there is among us a vibrant sense of nationhood that mocks the prophets of ruin. We are not blind to the contrary forces that, today and tomorrow, challenge our unity. But they are counterbalanced—and in time will be overwhelmed—by the deep-down sense of common purpose that keeps bringing one out of many. Indeed, America is a multiethnic country, but we have one culture—drawn from the best of the multitude of prophets who have become America, and from the morals and values derived from the great religions and traditions of these peoples.

A third element is an unspoken realization that underlies much of this document. The changes our country needs to make in both the structure of the federal government—its size, its relation to individuals and to the states—and in its substance (which is to say, its policies) are so many and so massive that they cannot be accomplished by politics alone. Even the best leadership cannot do the job if it operates only in the context of government. The depth of change envisioned in the foregoing chapters calls for something more like a mass movement, operating both within and outside of a party structure. (Ideally, I could refer to party structures, but the plural is probably too much to hope for.)

In other words, implicit in the recommendations that are the substance of this volume is the need for a rebirth of committed citizenship, so that what government facilitates, the people can implement; what government encourages, the people can accomplish; what government should give up, the people can pick up and carry forward.

A fourth unifying element in these chapters is the interrelatedness of many of their specific proposals. The American renewal of which these proposals form the blueprint is one, an entirety, a whole. It cannot be chopped up into parts, some pursued, others discarded. As we listened our way through all of the NPF's public forums and conferences of the past three years, one theme was constant: the most pressing problems of our society are entangled. Here's just one example. Our international competitiveness is hindered by the failures of our education system and by a host of other behavioral pathologies, all of which are related to family structure—which itself has huge impact on economic circumstances, that have everything to do with the size and shape of government, and so on.

That explains why we have not attempted rigorously to compartmentalize these chapters, or to eliminate their overlapping. Government is pervasive; it overlaps most things—too many things. The way these policy recommendations fit snugly together, however, tells us something important about how we must proceed toward American renewal. We cannot fragment the nation's agenda, for its seemingly separate components—economic, social, cultural, international—in fact, cohere and blend and reinforce one another.

One of the silliest canards in American politics, still sometimes heard among the diminishing advocates of Big Government, is that the Republican party is "the party of the rich." The voices in this volume find the truth hidden in that falsehood. They reveal a party that increasingly speaks for all Americans who are rich in ideas, rich in faith, rich in children, rich in promise.

All those form the true "wealth of nations," if I may borrow Adam Smith's quoting from Scripture. What Americans treasure most are the intangibles not found on the charts and graphs that usually dominate public policy. We can't quantify freedom or security, opportunity or decency, responsibility or a sense of purpose. But we can pursue them, foster them, protect them. And in doing so, we ward off the danger of being a nation rich in things but poor in spirit.

Freedom and personal responsibility emerge as the common goals, the ultimate unifying factors, among the scores of policy proposals presented herein. I cannot help but be proud of all those who have helped to formulate them, starting with the citizens—thousands of them—who accepted our open invitation to meet with us, debate with us, share with us.

What we have learned or, perhaps, relearned from them gives form and direction to what you have read here. It is as simple as this: Politics operates for today. Statesmanship applies to tomorrow. But common sense serves the generations to come.

Notes

Chapter 1

1. Joint Economic Committee, 1995.
2. Ibid.
3. Dan Mitchell, senior fellow, Heritage Foundation, 1995.
4. Gary Robbins, Institute for Policy Innovation, 1995.
5. House Budget Committee, 1995.

Chapter 2

1. Much of the information in this chapter can be found in "A Citizen's Guide to Regulation," ed. Susan M. Eckerly (The Heritage Foundation, September 1994).
2. Clyde Wayne Crews, *Journal of Commerce* (5 July 1995).
3. Mark Isakowitz, legislative representative, National Federation of Independent Businesses, before the House Small Business Committee, 28 July 1993.
4. For an excellent overview of this problem, see David Schoenbrod, *Power Without Responsibility: How Congress Abuses the People Through Delegation* (New Haven: Yale University Press, 1993).
5. Henri A. Termeer, "The Cost of Miracles," *Wall Street Journal*, 16 November 1993.
6. Information in this section is found in Edward L. Hudgins's "Handicapping Freedom: The Americans with Disabilities Act," in *Regulation Magazine*, 1995, 2, published by the Cato Institute.

Chapter 3

1. Information in this chapter was taken from Walter Olson, *The Litigation Explosion: What Happened When America Unleashed the Lawsuit*, (E. P. Dutton, 1991).

2. The "Oprah Winfrey" show, 8 July 1991. Walter Olson, "Make the Loser Pay," *Reader's Digest.*

3. Monroe Freedman, "Access to the Legal System: The Professional Responsibility to Chase Ambulances," ed. Monroe Freedman, *Lawyers' Ethics in an Adversary System* (Bobbs-Merrill, 1975).

4. *Bates v. State Bar of Arizona,* 97 S.Ct. 2691 (1977).

5. "How Lawyers Abuse the Law," *U.S. News & World Report,* 30 January 1995.

6. *Patients, Doctors, and Lawyers: Medical Injury, Malpractice Litigation, and Patient Compensation in New York: The Report of the Harvard Medical Practice Study to the State of New York,* 1990, 7–34.

7. Las Vegas Review Journal, 9 August 1992.

8. Walter Olson, *The Litigation Explosion: What Happened When America Unleashed the Lawsuit* (E. P. Dutton, 1991) 157–160.

9. Jack Weinstein, *Improving Expert Testimony,* University of Richmond Law Review, 20, (1986) 473–482.

10. Wayne E. Green, "Worse Yet, Surgeons Might Start Doing Things with Pizza Cutters," *Wall Street Journal,* 13 September 1990.

11. "Priest at Detroit Crash Suspected as Impostor," *New York Times,* 14 September 1987; Wayne E. Green, "Bar Groups Take on Ambulance Chasers," *Wall Street Journal,* 28 September 1988.

12. Letter from the National Highway Traffic Safety Administration, Office of Defects Investigation Staff, to the Center for Auto Safety, 18 September 1989.

13. Olson, *The Litigation Explosion,* 157–160.

14. Gina Kolata, "Legal System and Science Come to Differing Conclusions on Silicone." *New York Times,* 16 May 1995.

15. Ibid., 224.

16. Ibid., 230.

17. Lester Brickman, "Limiting Lawyers' Unearned Windfall," *New York Law Journal,* 4 August 1994.

18. Stephen Budiansky with Ted Gest and David Fischer, "How Lawyers Abuse the Law," *U.S. New & World Report,* 30 January 1995.

19. California Counts the Cost of Lawsuit Mania," *Wall Street Journal,* 3 June 1992.

20. Walter Olson, *The Litigation Explosion,* 157–160.

21. Dennis Hevesti, "Three Lawyers Accused of Using Bribes and Faked Evidence," *New York Times,* 12 January 1990; Wade Lambert and Wayne Green, "Personal Injury Lawyers Charged with Fraud," *Wall Street Journal,* 12 January 1990.

22. The National Insurance Crime Bureau, "Insurance Fraud: The $20 Billion Disaster."

23. "Of Tobacco, Torts and Tusks," *Newsweek,* 28 November 1994.

24. Kirk Victor, "The Long Hello," *National Journal*, 12 December 1992.

25. George Will, "Lawyers Too Litigious for Their Own Good," *Washington Post*, 11 December 1994.

26. "The Bizarre Results of Punitive Damages," *Wall Street Journal*, 8 March 1995.

Chapter 4

1. Henri A. Termeer, "The Cost of Miracles," *Wall Street Journal*, 16 November 1993.

2. National Center for Policy Analysis, Health Care Briefing Book (Dallas, Texas: NCPA, 1994), 5; "1081 State Mandated Benefits Identified," Health Benefits Letter, vol. 2, no. 2, 31 July 1992.

3. National Center for Policy Analysis, Health Care Briefing Book, 11.

4. 1994 Foster Higgins National Survey of Employer Sponsored Health Plans.

5. Peter J. Ferrara, "More Than a Theory: Medical Savings Accounts at Work," CATO Institute, Washington, D.C., Policy Analysis No. 220, 14 March 1995.

6. Ibid.

7. With MSAs, workers get catastrophic insurance along with savings accounts equal to the deductible on that insurance, providing complete first dollar coverage. The MSA funds can also be used for check-ups, preventive care, dental care, eye exams and glasses, and other health services not covered by the old policy. And, of course, workers can each withdraw remaining MSA funds at the end of each year.

8. 1995 Annual Report of the Social Security and Medicare Board of Trustees, April 1995.

9. Peter J. Ferrara, "Why the Democrats' Medicare Plan Won't Work," National Center for Policy Analysis, NCPA Brief Analysis No. 190, 17 November 1995.

10. U.S. General Accounting Office, "Prescription Drugs and the Elderly," GAO/HEHES-95-152, July 1995.

11. Ibid.

12. Centers for Disease Control/NIHS Advance Data No. 254, 3 August 1994.

13. *American Journal of Public Health*, October 1994.

14. Group Health Association Data.

15. Merrill Mathews, Jr., "A Long-Term Solution to a Medical Problem," National Center for Policy Analysis, NCPA Brief Analysis No. 190, 17 November 1995.

16. Peter J. Ferrara, "Resolving the Medicare Crisis," *Washington Times*, 25 July 1995.

17. Merrill Mathews, Jr., "A Long-Term Solution to a Medical Problem," National Center for Policy Analysis, No. 175, 15 September 1995.

18. National Institutes of Health, National Institute of Neurological Disorders and Stroke, Interagency Head Injury Task Force Reports.

19. Report of the Minority Staff of the Senate Committee on Aging under Senator William Cohen, July 1994.

Chapter 5

1. Kelly Herstad, "The EPA's Bureaucratic Hell," *Washington Times*, 3 October 1995, A17.

2. Testimony of Mr. Yee, U.S. Senate Superfund, Waste Control and Risk Assessment Subcommittee, 29 March 1995, as related by subcommittee chairman Robert C. Smith during the National Policy Forum's 29 March 1995 environment megaconference.

3. Statement by Hutchinson City Manager Joe Palacioz during the National Policy Forum's 29 March 1995 environment megaconference.

4. Peter Brimelow and Leslie Spencer, "You Can't Get There from Here," *Forbes,* 6 July 1992, 59.

5. Keith Schneider, "New View Calls Environmental Policy Misguided," *New York Times,* 28 September 1995.

6. Statement by House Commerce Committee Chairman Thomas J. Bliley, 28 September 1995.

7. *The Cost-Effectiveness of Further Regulation of Mobile Source Emissions*, Sierra Research Report No. SR94-02-04, 28 February 1994.

8. Statement by Nicholas A. Pyle of the International Bakers Association during the National Policy Forum's 29 March 1995 environment megaconference.

Chapter 6

1. Competitive Enterprise Institute.

2. Statement by Margaret Rector during the National Policy Forum's property rights roundtable, Washington, D.C., 6 December 1994.

3. Statement by Ben Cone during the National Policy Forum's Washington forum on the Endangered Species Act, Washington, D.C., 13 June 1995.

4. Energy Information Administration.

5. *Potential Impact of Environmental Regulations on the Oil and Gas Exploration and Production Industry,* American Petroleum Institute, March 1995.

6. Ibid.

7. *Unbuilding the U.S. Electric Power Industry: A Blueprint for Change,* Enron Capital & Trade Resources, March 1995, iv.

Chapter 7

1. Robert Rector, Heritage Foundation, 1995.

2. Ibid.

3. U.S. Bureau of the Census, *Current Population Reports, Series P-60, N-180, Money Income of Households, Families and Persons in the United States,* 1991, 7.

4. Ibid.

5. Dr. June O'Neil, Director, Congressional Budget Office and Anne Hill: *Underclass Behaviors in the United States: Measurement and Analysis of Determinants* (New York, City University of New York, Baruch College, August 1993).

6. U.S. Bureau of the Census, *Current Population Reports, Series P-60, N-180.*

7. House subcommittee on Crime.

8. Michael Garter, "Values? What About Divorce?" Counterpoints: USA Today, 6 June 1995, 13A.

9. Draft Report, Majority Staff, "VA, HUD and Independent Agencies Subcommittee of the Senate Appropriations Committee," November 1994.

10. Ibid.

11. Executive Summary, Fiscal Year 1996 Budget, Department of Housing and Urban Development.

12. Conversations with Staff, Department of Housing and Urban Development, 1995.

13. Cited in Marshall Jay Kendell, "Public Housing: The Ostrich Strategy," Planning, June 1995.

Chapter 9

1. Charles J. Murray, "What's Really Behind the SAT-Score Decline?" *The Public Interest,* 106, winter 1992.

2. U.S. Department of Education, National Center for Education Statistics, "Common Core of Data" and "Financial Statistics of Institutions of Higher Education," Surveys and unpublished data.

3. The Alexis de Tocqueville Institution, "The Budgetary Implications of Eliminating the U.S. Department of Education," John E. Berthoud, Ph.D.

4. National Education Association, "Resolutions Adopted by the 1994 NEA Representative Assembly. B–27. Multicultural Global Education." NEA Handbook 1994–95, 260.

5. Claudice Wallis, "A Class of Their Own," *Time,* 31 October 1994, 61, as reported in Charter Schools: An Irresisible Force, by David W. Kirkpatrick, distinguished fellow of The Blum Center, Marquette University.

6. David W. Kirkpatrick, "Charter Schools: An Irresistible Force," The Blum Center, Marquette University, 11 August 1995.

7. Ibid.

8. Janet R. Beales, "Doing More with Less: Competitive Contracting for School Support Services," Policy Study No. 179, 2 (Los Angeles, Calif.: Reason Foundation).

9. Mike Bowler, "Sylvan Experiment Reaps Results in Student Scores," *The Sun,* (Baltimore, Md.) 28 July 1994.

10. "Sylvan Learning Systems Announces New Partnerships with Two of the Nation's Largest School Districts," Press release, Sylvan Learning Systems, Inc., (Columbia, Md.) 27 July 1995.

11. Janet R. Beales, "Doing More with Less: Competitive Contracting for School Support Services."

12. *Fourteenth Annual Report to Congress on the Implementation of the Individuals with Disabilities Act,* Division of Innovation and Development, Office of Special Education Programs, U.S. Department of Education, Washington, D.C., 1992, A-53.

13. Janet R. Beales, "Doing More With Less."

14. The People's Cause: Mobilizing for Public Education, A Resource Book from the National Education Association (draft), i.

15. For example, the Wilkinsburg Education Association filed for, and won, a preliminary injunction in April 1995 against the school board, barring it from signing a contract with alternative Public Schools. The school board won on appeal.

16. For more information about private practice teaching, see *Teacher, Inc.: A Private-Practice Option for Educators,* Policy Study No. 181, Janet R. Beales, Reason Foundation, Los Angeles, California, October 1994.

17. Information provided by labor relations staff, New York City Board of Education, cited in Lieberman, *Teacher Unions: Is the End Near?,* 12.

18. Information provided by U.S. English, Inc., Washington, D.C.

Chapter 10
1. Bolick, Clint. *Changing Course: Civil Rights at the Crossroads* (Transition Books, 1988), 90.

Chapter 12
1. U.S. Dept. of Commerce, International Trade Administration, *GDP and U.S. International Trade in Goods and Services,* 1970–93.

2. Developed countries have agreed to reduce their tariffs on industrial goods from an average of 6.3 percent to 3.8 percent, a 40 percent reduction. General Agreement on Tariffs and Trade, Results of the Uruguay Round of Multilateral Trade Negotiations, Market Access for Goods and Services: Overview of the Results, GATT Secretariat, Geneva, November 1994, 6. Also see Office of USTR, *Uruguay Round—Jobs for U.S.— Growth for the World,* 7.

3. International Monetary Fund, International Financial Statistics, vol. 48, no. 11, November 1995, 598.

4. U.S. International Trade Comission, *Foreign Protection of Intellectual Property Rights and the Effect on U.S. Industry and Trade,* USITC pub. 2596 at H-3 (February 1988).

5. International Economic Review, USITC pub. 2934, November 1995; *Free Trade Area for the Americas: Chile is Linchpin,* James Stamp, 12.

6. Office of the U.S. Trade Representative, *Report to the President and the Congress on Significant Market Opening,* May 1994, 2.

7. CATO Institute, defense expenditures following WW II (in 1996 dollars). (Note figure does not include foreign assistance, which, if included, would add an additional $1 trillion to the estimate above.)

8. See chart "CEE FY 1990–94 Obligations by Country, as of 30 September 1994 (in U.S. $000s)," *SEED Act Report,* U.S. Department of State, January 1995.

9. U.S. International Trade Commission, Office of Economics, "Foreign Investment in Former Communist Central Europe: U.S. Firms Play a Vital Role," *International Economic Review,* February 1994, 12–15.

10. *World Bank Statistical Handbook 1994, States of the Former USSR.* See also *Concise World Atlas,* GLA Kartor AB, Stockholm, Sweden, 1991.

11. Report to the President, *Op. Cit.* 2.

12. Gordon Piatt, "Investment and Aspiration," *Journal of Commerce,* 8 December 1994, 10A.

13. Report to the President, *Op. Cit.* 3.

14. Ibid., p. 5.

15. See U.S. Office of Technology Assessment, *Advanced Network Technology: A Background Paper* (June, 1993) 68–70; U.S. Department of Commerce, *1994 U.S. Industrial Outlook* (1994) chapters 29-1 (telecommunications services) and 26-1 (computer equipment & services); U.S. National Research Council, Computer Science and Telecommunications Board, *Information Technology in the Service Society* (1994), 2–3, 33.

16. U.S. National Telecommunications and Information Administration, *NTIA Telecom 2000: Charting the Course for a New Century* (1988), 70 et seq.

17. See, for example, U.S. Information Industry Task Force Report, Global Information Infrastructure: Agenda for Cooperation (February 1995) 11 (and citations therein).

18. See, generally, Statement of Federal Communications Commission Chairman, Reed E. Hundt, Before the Subcommittee on Commerce, Justice, State, and the Judiciary, Committee on Appropriations, U.S. House of Representatives (18 April 1994) 3 (reprinted at Hearings Before the House Commerce, Justice, State Appropriations Subcommittee, 103rd Cong., 2nd Sess. 732 (1994); WEFA Group, Economic Impact of Eliminating the Line-of-Business Restrictions on the Bell Companies (July 1993) 31–33; U.S. Office of Technology Assessment, U.S. Telecommunications Services in European Markets (August 1993) 21.

19. See Agenda for Cooperation, supra note 3 at p. 11. See also U.S. Council of Economic Advisors, 1995 Economic Report of the President (February 1995) 159–60.

20. U.S. Department of Agriculture, *Economic Indicators of the Farm Sector,* Economic Research Service, USDA, Washington, D.C.

Chapter 13

1. Deborah Clay-Mendez, Richard L. Fernandez, and Amy Belasco, *Trends in Selected Indicators of Military Readiness, 1980 Through 1993,* Washington, D.C., Congressional Budget Office, 1994, 3.

2. Caspar W. Weinberger, *Annual Report to the Congress, Fiscal Year 1984,* Washington, D.C., Government Printing Office, 1983, 43; and Caspar W. Weinberger, *Report of the Secretary of Defense to the Congress, Fiscal Year 1988,* Washington, D.C., Government Printing Office, 1986, 38.

3. Frank C. Carlucci, *Annual Report to the Congress, Fiscal Year 1990,* Washington, D.C., Government Printing Office, 1989, 143.

4. General Charles A. Gabriel, USAF (Ret.), General Alfred M. Gray, USMC (Ret.), Admiral Carlisle A.H. Trost, USN (Ret.), General Robert W. RisCassi, USA (Ret.), "A Report on Military Capabilities and Readiness for United States Senator John S. McCain" (7 February 1995), 9.

5. Compare Harold Brown, *Department of Defense Annual Report: Fiscal Year 1982* (Washington, D.C., Government Printing Office, 1982), with subsequent Department of Defense *Annual Reports.*

6. The Clinton administration requested a total of only twenty-eight fixed wing combat aircraft for Fiscal Year 1995. See Department of Defense, *Department of Defense Budget for Fiscal Year 1995: Procurement Programs (P-1),* (February 1994).

Chapter 14

1. "Senate Intelligence Committee Releases Unclassified Intelligence Assessments," *News Release,* Senate Select Committee on Intelligence, 1 May 1995.

2. Ferry Gildee, "Former CIA Chief Urges Caution on BMD Cooperation with Russia," *Defense Daily,* 17 May 1995, 239.

3. Talk at recent focus group meetings in South Carolina, Ohio, Pennsylvania, and New Hampshire, conducted by Luntz Research Company with congressmen or senators in attendance, was consistent with numerous previous public opinion polls, including those reported by Keith B. Payne in the Appendix of his *Strategic Defense: "Star Wars": in Perspective,* Hamilton Press, 1986.

4. *Defending America: A Near- and Long-Term Plan to Deploy Missile Defenses,* the Missile Defense Study Team, the Heritage Foundation, 1995.

5. *1994 Annual Report of the U.S. Arms Control and Disarmament Agency,* transmitted to the Congress on 13 July 1995. See section of that report on "Adherence to and Compliance with Arms Control Agreements."

The National Policy Forum:
Board and Policy Councils

Board of Directors

Officers
Haley Barbour, *Chairman*
John R. Bolton, *President*

Members
John Boehner
William E. Brock
W. L. Lyons Brown, Jr.
Jeb Bush
James A. Garner
Gwendolyn S. King
Teresa Lubbers
Robert Michel
Don Nickles
George V. Voinovich

Policy Council Members

**Free Individuals
in a Free Society**
William Bennett, *Co-Chair*
Carol Iannone, *Co-Chair*
William B. Allen
Kenneth W. Anderson
Martin Anderson
David Barton
Peter L. Berger
Mary Ellen Bork
Allan C. Carlson
Henry E. Catto

Linda Chavez
Stanley Crouch
Carol Dawson
Mimi W. Dawson
Edwin J. Delattre
Larry D. Dixon
Don E. Eberly
Carol Ellinger
Arlene Ellis
Tina Flaherty
Martha McBryde Foy
Gary A. Franks
Thad Garrett
Orrin G. Hatch
Miriam Hellreich
Mike Huckabee
Paul Loy Hurd
Lee F. Jackson
Charles R. Kesler
James A. Leach
Mary Elizabeth Lewis
Tex Lezar
Edwin L. Meese
Pat Miller
Mauro E. Mujica
Ted O'Meara
Mitchell Pearlstein
Francois L. Quinson
Grover Joseph Rees
Wayne A. Ross
Mary Rumph
Paula Parker Sawyers

Lisa Schiffren
Frances Scully
Jeremy Shane
Andrea Sheldon
Rosalie Gaull Silberman
Nancy Silvers
Harry M. Singleton
Peter Smith
Merrie Spaeth
Jack Svahn
Michael M. Uhlman
Robert S. Walker
Marlene A. Wohleber
Penny Young

Reforming Health Care
Nancy Johnson, *Co-Chair*
Pete du Pont, *Co-Chair*
Ken Abramowitz
Ann C. Agnew
Beth M. Anderson
Ray C. Anderson
Grace-Marie Arnett
Ken Auchter
Kay F. Barber
John Barrasso
Nelda Barton-Collings
Ramon Batson
David Beal
Brenda Larsen Becker
Don C. Bedell
Joe Bentivoglio

Eugene M. Bishop
Virginia Blankenbaker
Richard L. Blomquist
Gwen Boeke
Robert Boknecht
Enid A. Borden
Beau Boulter
Janice Bradford
Deborah L. Brezina
Nancy Brinker
J. Robert Brouse
Jeffrey T. Buley
Stuart Butler
W. Grimes Byerly
Barbra Calvert
Earl J. Campazzi
Carroll A. Campbell
Frank Cappadora
Robert S. Carter
Winthrop Cashdollar
Arcadio Casillas
Donald A. Clarey
Lois Copeland
Kenneth M. Courey
Charles Crowders
James R. Cunningham
Quentin Dastugue
Carolyne Davis
Donald J. Devine
Sewell H. Dixon
Tom Donnelly
Lynn A. Drake
David Durenberger
Juanita S. Farrow
Marlene L. Faust
Robert W. Feldtman
Peter J. Ferrara
Carol Fraser Fisk
Kellyanne Fitzpatrick
Lois Frels
Donna Galluzzo
Frank Galluzzo
Jeri G. Garner
Kenneth L. Garver
Bruce Gates

John Gibbons
Richard G. Glogau
John C. Goodman
John O. Goodman
Phillip H. Goodwin
Judd Gregg
Larry Griffin
Carl J. Guzzo
Mark E. Hamister
Betty Hanicke
Charles Hardwick
Debby Hardy-Havens
Kathleen M. Harrington
Sarah Hartwig
Dennis Hastert
Spencer Hathaway
Clark C. Havighurst
Bernardine Healy
Philip D. Hellreich
Greg Hook
Margaret Ingraham
Cheri Isett
Chad Jackson
Jana Jones
Grace Jorgensen
Jon L. Kyl
Fred P. Lampropoulos
Lynne C. Layne
Burton J. Lee, III
Alan Levey
Virginia Newman Littell
Bert A. Loftman
W. Bruce Lunsford
Sandra K. Mahkorn
Roy Marden
Wayne S. Margolis
Roy Mason
Dennis Mather
Merrill Matthews
William M. Mayer
S. Anthony McCann
Marty McGeein
John McKay
Sally F. McKenzie
J. Alex McMillan

Paul R. Meyer
Dane A. Miller
Lee Miller
Thomas Miller
Thomas Mills
C. J. Milmoe
Kevin E. Moley
Don Moran
Gerald J. Mossinghoff
Gerhard H. Mundinger
Gerald L. Musgrave
Rick Nelson
Antonia Novello
John J. O'Shaughnessy
Jane Orient
Jacquelyn Paige
Derick Pasternak
Vincent D. Pettinelli
Jeanne Johnson Phillips
John Pinto
Peter Polloni
David Pringle
Chitranjan S. Ranawat
Diane Rath
Judy Dunn Riedlinger
Darrell S. Rigel
J. Patrick Rooney
C. Julian Rosenthal
Joe S. Roth
Max B. Rubin
B. A. Rudolph
Robert A. Rusbuldt
Thomas C. Sadauskas
Martin Sbriglio
Ray Scalettar
Jerry Schenken
Richard Scott
Mark Seklecki
Steven W. Sell
Erwin Small
Chris Smith
Jose Sosa
William Stead
Cliff Stearns
Louis W. Sullivan

Pat Sullivan
Charles W. Swan
Nancy Taylor
Frederick W. Telling
Arnold R. Tompkins
Martha Towler
Clarence Traum
Monroe E. Trout
John Troy
Roy Vagelos
Dirk Van Dongen
Elliott Vernon
Steven Weisman
Colleen Conway Welch
Dianne White-Delisi
Tom Wilder
Gail R. Wilensky
Paul Willging
Deborah Wince-Smith
Cal Winslow
Marshall Wittman
H. Paul Womack
Kenneth P. Yale
Christian G. Zimmerman

Strengthening the Family
Nona Brazier, Co-Chair
Tommy Thompson, Co-Chair
Cathie Adams
Mary Cunningham Agee
Greg Alex
Carl A. Anderson
Michael Antonovich
Kris Ardizzone
Patricia P. Bainbridge
Walter E. Barbee
Jack Barben
Elizabeth P. Barnes
Linda V. Barnett
Gary Bauer
Mariam Bell
Helen Bie
David Blankenhorn
John W. Bode
Fay W. Boozman

James Bopp
Sally S. Campbell
Robert B. Carleson
Michael A. Ciamarra
Betty Gault Cordoba
Gayle Cozens
Bruce A. Craswell
Shirley Curry
Marjorie J. Dannenfelser
R. Mark DeMoss
Thomas DePree
Katie L. Dixon
John T. Doolittle
Scott J. Freitas
Mary Lou Gartner
Phyllis R. Gault
Michael Geer
Deborah G. Hander
Brenda Harrison
Ronald Haskins
Susan Brackin Hirschmann
Peter Hoekstra
Wade F. Horn
Allan B. Hubbard
Peggy Jeffries
Gordon Jones
Mary C. Kasten
Pat Kelley
Jeff Kemp
Cynthia Stevens Kent
Gloria Kirking
William Kristol
Beverly LaHaye
Barbara J. Ledeen
Marilyn Loeffel
Colin Luke
Jane Maroney
Ginny Marschman
Connie Marshner
Bradley J. Mattes
Loyce McCarter
Lawrence M. Mead
Athenia Michel
Elwood Mose
Kay Orr

Michael Pappas
Donald E. Parker
Bonnie Quirke
Dana G. Reed
Ralph Reed
Kay Rieboldt
Lynn Rose
Marge Roukema
Mike Schwartz
Alan Sears
Ann E. W. Stone
Mary Dietrich Strosin
Louis E. Sturns
Mary Potter Summa
Jonathan T. Swain
Marilyn Thayer
Virginia Thomas
Sandra Usher
Daniel D. Van Hoy
Susan Vergeront
Bonnie Weber
Dick Weinhold

**Safe and Prosperous
Neighborhoods**
Deborah Pryce, Co-Chair
William Barr, Co-Chair
Whitney Adams
Jo Ellen Allen
Victor Ashe
Richard Berkley
Morton C. Blackwell
Michael Block
Ronald E. Bogle
Michael D. Carey
John Carlson
Jack Collins
Donna Crandall
Deborah Daniels
Michael DeWine
Steve Dillingham
Charles G. Douglas
Elizabeth Z. Doyle
Aerin Dunkle
Laura Federline

Sarah Flores
John Gillis
Slade Gorton
Reuben M. Greenberg
Martin Growald
Arlene Ham
Robert O. Heck
Bul bol Howard
Stanley Interrante
George Kettle
Richard J. LaRossa
Trent Lott
Dan E. Lungren
Norm Maleng
Carlos Mayans
John McClaughry
Bill McCollum
Paul McNulty
Luther Millsaps
Mary Mohs
Sandra Mortham
J. Mark Mutter
Sue Myers
Cheryl Nolan
Peter K. Nunez
Jack O'Malley
Russell Oberlin
Carl Peed
Steven Plumber
Bob Preston
Morgan Reynolds
Richard Robinson
Bret Schundler
Rider Scott
F. James Sensenbrenner
Gwyn Shea
Joy Silverman
Alan K. Simpson
John Smietanka
Lamar S. Smith
Arlen Specter
Dewey Stokes
Kenneth W. Sukhia
Elizabeth J. Swasey
George J. Terwilliger

John Walters
John C. Weicher
Susan Weiner
Louise R. White
Peggy Wilson
James Wooton

Improving Schools and Education

Lynn Martin, *Chair*
John Agresto
Lamar Alexander
Norma Anderson
John Arledge
David Armor
Leslye Arsht
Roger Baskerville
Ken Bastian
Milton Bins
Marion Blakey
Eleanor Goodfriend Blum
Clint Bolick
Robert R. Botkin
Betsy Brand
Mark J. Bredemeier
David Brennan
Christine Brownlee
Bettye Fine Collins
Lorraine R. Colville
James K. Coyne
T. Kenneth Cribb
Harry Crisp
Dinesh D'Souza
Teresa Damasauskas
Stephen I. Danzansky
Elisabeth DeVos
Edward Donley
Denis P. Doyle
Bobbi B. Dunn
Wade Dyke
Jay Eagen
Thomas N. Edmonds
Mike Farris
Scot M. Faulkner
Tom Feeney

Susan R. Feldtman
Robert Fincher
Chester E. Finn
Jacquelyn A. Fish
William H. G. Fitzgerald
Martin Gerry
Tricia Gibbons
Lanny Griffith
Steve Gunderson
Charlene K. Haar
Joseph H. Hagan
Cheryl Halpern
Donna Hearne
Charles L. Heatherly
Steve Hofman
Stephen Horn
Shirley Hoskins
Chris Jacobs
James Jeffords
Ruth G. Johnson
Roberts T. Jones
Thomas H. Kean
Ray Keating
Dan Kelly
Erica Kenney
Ken Khachigian
Dave Kirkpatrick
Anchi Ku
Bonnie Ladwig
John Leinenweber
Charles G. Lewis
Thomas W. Luce
John MacDonald
Horace Edward "Chip" Mann
Bruno V. Manno
Allen Martin
Jeffrey C. Martin
Howard McKeon
John R. McKernan
James A. Milam
Jim Miles
Guy Millner
George Mims
John Murphy
John Mutz

Lisa Nagle
Jane Nelson
Frances M. Norris
Louise Oliver
Lisa Farringer Parker
Meg Parson
Diane Patrick
Norma Paulus
Malcolm E. Peabody
Paul Peterson
Joseph F. Petros
Dick Posthumus
Larry Pressler
Mary S. Pyle
Terese Raia
Diane Ravitch
Richard Rhone
Annette Rickel
Dennis Rochford
Nancy Risque Rohrbach
Harriet B. Rotter
Linanne Sackett
Ted Sanders
Nathaniel Semple
Florence Shapiro
Ivan A. Somers
Shannon H. Sorzano
Lynn Sparkman
Charles Sykes
Joyce Lyons Terhes
Allyson Tucker
Josephine Wang
Robert L. Wehling
Anne Wortham
Elaine Wynn

Stimulating Economic Growth and Entrepreneurship
Jack Kemp, *Co-Chair*
Michele Dyson, *Co-Chair*
Dwight Adams
Kenneth Adelman
David G. Albert
John M. Albertine

Annelise Anderson
Faye M. Anderson
Patrick L. Anderson
Dick K. Armey
Ruthann Aron
Bill Baker
Jim Baker
Bruce Bartlett
Raymond Basey
Erika Lee Baum
Paul Beckner
James F. Bednar
Robert F. Bennett
Barry Beringer
Michelle D. Bernard
Fred K. Biebel
Anita K. Blair
Richard H. Bornemann
Debra Bowland
Melanie W. Bradford
Alan Brink
Richard Burr
Denise Caldeira
James A. Calderwood
Michael F. Camardo
W. Glenn Campbell
Michael N. Castle
William C. Cleveland
John F. Cogan
Paul H. Cooksey
Ben Cooper
Joanna B. Cooper
John W. Cooper
Kevin Cramer
Eugene R. Croissant
C. Hines Cronin
Alfonse M. D'Amato
Michael R. Darby
Hal Daub
Gail M. Davis
J. Morton Davis
Roderick A. DeArment
Shirley Dennis
Remedios Diaz-Oliver
Teresa Dogget

John Doggett
Dorene C. Dominguez
Richard B. Dressner
Marillia A. Duffles
Robert M. Duncan
Michelle Engler
Larry Epstein
Eddie Faith
Byron L. Farrell
James E. Ferrell
William E. Flaherty
Michael Forbes
Barbara Hackman Franklin
Tim French
John Gartland
Karen L. Gillmor
Keith Gleasman
Ricardo A. Gonzalez
Steve J. Gonzalez
Phil Gramm
Harry G. Greenleaf
W. W. Gresham
John Griffin
Michael J. Grigsby
Clifford J. Groh
Paul J. Haire
Bill Hall
John R. Hall
Alam Hammad
Ed Harrison
Ed Haugland
Patricia de Stacy Harrison
Charles Hawkins
Doug Hendrickson
Robert Hiler
J. French Hill
Edith E. Holiday
Henry Holley
Mark Holmes
Linwood Holton
Constance Horner
Rob Hurtt
Kay Bailey Hutchison
Andy Ireland
Dennis R. Israel

John Jefferson
Louis F. Joachim
Jennifer R. Johnson
Lindsey Lee Johnson
Barbara Keating-Edh
Michael Keck
Richard R. Kelley
Karen Kerrigan
Thomas A. Kershaw
Jay Kim
Brent Kincaid
Robert L. King
John T. Korsmo
Gerald Kosmensky
Alan M. Kranowitz
Thomas F. Kranz
Robert B. Kronman
Richard J. LaRossa
Tom Latham
Chuck Leach
Howard Leach
Michael Leavitt
Daniel A. Lehner
Catherine J. Liebl
Marc C. Little
Dennis E. Logue
Lawrence Lorber
Thomas E. Lorentzen
John R. Lott
Jean C. Lu
Yvonne Lucero
Sioban Macguire
Connie Mack
Fred Malek
John J. Marchi
Ronny Margason
Bruno J. Mauer
James B. McGregor
Sara K. McGregor
Jeffrey C. McGuiness
Carolyn McKecuen
James D. "Mike" McKevitt
R. Tim McNamara
Gene McNary
Gerald T. McPhee

John K. Meagher
Gary Mendoza
James C. Miller
James F. Miller
Margie Shaw Miller
Charles V. Montalbano
Todd A. Moore
Rita L. Mullins
Robert Mumma
Deroy Murdock
Fernando Niebla
Robert Nolan
Grover Norquist
Richard D. Novik
Mark Olson
Burgess Owens
John N. Palmer
Wendy Pangburn
James L. Pate
Joseph Petrilli
Robert Philibosian
Alice E. Phillips
Willard (Bill) Phillips
Earl N. Phillips
Peyton E. Pitts
Roger B. Porter
John Post
Todd A. Pride
James B. Rapp
Rebecca J. Ravine
John E. Reed
Thomas Reilly
Brenda Reneau
Delia Reyes
Craig E. Richardson
Davis M. Richardson
Ken Rietz
Steve Roach
Roger Roberson
John E. Robson
Donald F. Rodgers
Ed Rogers
Barry Rogstad
Cynthia Roselle
William V. Roth

Ellen Sauerbrey
Jim Saxton
Terrrence Scanlon
Mark S. Schweiker
Jeannette Reddish Scollard
George Scott
Hillard F. Selck
Bernard J. Simbole
Alex Sinclair
Judy Singleton
Gene Snyder
John D. Sorell
Kenin M. Spivak
Frank D. Stella
Susan Stokes
Ken Stribling
Mark Sullivan
Kevin Swift
Augustus Tagliaferri
Dennis B. Tenney
Michael ter Maat
W. Dennis Thomas
David L. Thompson
Mary A. Toman
Gloria E. A. Toote
Thomas Topuzes
Mark Treesh
Victor N. Tucci
Norman B. Ture
Demos Vardiabasis
Sally Jo Vasicko
Rachel Wachs
C. Everett Wallace
Joseph P. Watkins
Vin Weber
Thomas W. Weisel
G. Theodore Wolf
Robert L. Wright
Bruce Young

Reducing the Size and Scope of Government
William Weld, *Co-Chair*
Cheryl Lau, *Co-Chair*
Jim Alexander

Thomas B. Andrews
Nancy Brown
James H. Burnley
Andrew H. Card
Susan M. Collins
William Craycraft
George Deukmejian
Richard Dion
Joseph P. Duggan
Bill Eggers
William D. Eggers
Ken Eikenberry
Bert Ely
Janice O. Faiks-Jones
Douglas Fearing
Dorothy Felton
Julie Finley
Sheila Frahm
Bob Franks
Howard M. Fry
Stephen Goldsmith
William F. Goodling
Rod Grams
Janet Hale
William Hansen
Bill Hardiman
Dorcas Hardy
Mary Hawkins
Paul Helmke
Scott A. Hodge
Judith L. Hofmann
Perry O. Hooper
Tim Hutchinson
James M. Inhofe
John R. Kasich
James F. Kelley
Dirk Kempthorne
Sally Klein
Charles Lancaster
Hubert E. Lillis
Robert E. Littell
Michael Long
Paul Mannweiler
John McCain
Natalie Meyer

Laurie L. Michel
Clyde Middleton
Susan Molinari
Kate L. Moore
Thomas F. Needles
Robert L. Olden
George Omas
Bob Packwood
Kurt Pfotenhauer
Gregg A. Phillips
George S. Pillsbury
George P. Radanovich
Jan Rasch
Stephen W. Roberts
Hal Rogers
Clint Rotenberry
Janet Rzewnicki
Christopher Shays
Deborah M. Skinner
Nick Smith
Barbara Snelling
Courtney A. Stadd
Charles Steele
Nancy Harvey Steorts
Candace L. Straight
Nat Swanson
Eugene F. Swanzey
William M. Tidwell
Frank Vandersloot
William von Raab
John Watt
Gary White
Steve Wilson

**Natural Resources,
Agriculture & Energy**
Malcolm Wallop, *Chair*
Rick Agnew
Eugene L. Ames
Neil Amondson
James V. Anderson
John A. Anderson
Vicky A. Bailey
Mary Ann Baron
Harry E. Barsh

Anthony G. Bennett
Sean D. Bersell
John R. Block
Charles Boddy
Michael Boland
Thomas M. Bresnahan
Pam Bronson
Conrad Burns
Greg Cawley
Paul N. Cicio
John Clark
Candace J. Conger
Tom Corcoran
Tom Craddick
Wendell M. Cramer
Michael Crapo
Frank M. Cushing
Randy Davis
Warren Dean
Tom DeLay
Ken Dickerson
Pete Domenici
George S. Dunlop
Macon T. Edwards
Bill Emerson
Allan K. Fitzsimmons
Ted Garrish
Loydee S. Grainger
Carol Hamilton
Russell L. Hanlin
Mark O. Hatfield
Arnold I. Havens
Taylor Haynes
John R. Hays
Pam Hendrickson
Basil Hercules
Donald Paul Hodel
Guy Hurlbutt
Cy Jamison
Michael H. Kappaz
Stan Kiser
Richard Knight
Melanie E. Kowalski
Thomas Kuhn
James J. Lack

Vince Limmex
Jim Magagna
William F. Martin
Margaret N. Maxey
Alby Modiano
W. Henson Moore
William Moshofsky
John T. Myers
William Northrop
William F. O'Keefe
Hugh O'Riordan
James C. Oberwetter
Tom Parker
Gail Phillips
Billy R. Powell
John F. Rasor
Charles Resnick
James E. Rich
Randle Richardson
Pat Roberts
Rick Robitaille
Tom Sansonnetti
Mark C. Schroeder
Thomas P. Sheahen
C. J. Silas
Linda Skladany
Edward S. Smida
R. J. Smith
James F. Spagnole
Jay Stone
Linda Stuntz
C. William Swank
Paul M. Temple
Diemer True
Chandler L. Van Orman
Joe Vasapoli
Ann M. Veneman
Gregg Ward
Harlan L. Watson
Myles Watts
R. Thomas Weimer
Margaret A. Welsh
Mark Whitenton
Barry Williamson
Bruce Yandle

Harry M. Zachem
James W. Ziglar

Environment
Gale A. Norton, *Co-Chair*
Robert W. Kasten, *Co-Chair*
Gary H. Baise
Alex Beehler
James Boland
Thomas Borelli
James F. Bostic
Ted R. Brown
Tim Burns
Carolyn T. Burridge
Ed Cassidy
Don R. Clay
Ben Cohen
Cesar V. Conda
Larry E. Craig
Lewis S. W. Crampton
Robert Dawson
Kenneth Derr
Becky Norton Dunlop
Paula Pence Easley
Alex Echols
R. A. Edwards
Lauch Faircloth
Joseph Findaro
Mary A. Gade
Teresa Gorman
Charles L. Grizzle
Henry Habicht
Daryl Harms
Barry Hartman
Marc Himmelstein
Robert Horn
Edward R. Ingle
Catherine Killian
Charles Kolb
Jan Larimer
Thomas R. Long
Howard Marguleas
Chad McIntosh
G. Tracy Mehan
Randy Miller

William J. Mulligan
Gordon L. Ness
Michael J. Norton
Richard D. Otis
J. Winston Porter
James D. Range
Alan Charles Raul
Clarke Reed
James E. Rich
Don Ritter
Ernie Rosenberg
William D. Ruckelshaus
William H. Satterfield
John Schrote
Mark K. Seifert
John C. Shanahan
Carol S. Singer
Fred Singer
Fred L. Smith
Robert E. Steinberg
Wallace E. Stickney
Richard Stroup
Craig Thomas
LaJuana S. Wilcher
Robert B. Wilkins
Lyn Withey
Roy G. Wuchitech
Buck J. Wynne

Competing in the Global Marketplace
Noel Irwin-Hentschel, *Chair*
Jeanne Archibald
Judith H. Bello
Oren L. Benton
Tristan Beplat
Doug Bereuter
Robert A. Best
Everett E. Bierman
John A. Bohn
Donald Bollinger
Ali Riza Bozkurt
Susan Braden
Reginald J. Brown
Sam Brownback

Anne E. Brunsdale
Joseph A. Cannon
Dan Caprio
James J. Carey
Edward C. Chow
Charles E. Cobb
Michelle M. Conner
Jack L. Copeland
Frederic W. Corle
R. Lawrence Coughlin
Carol Crawford
Charles H. Dallara
John C. Danforth
Michael R. Darby
Carol Dawson
James L. Denson
Joseph L. Dillon
David Dreier
Thomas J. Duesterberg
Alan M. Dunn
Thomas "Mike" Dyer
Woods Eastland
Gary Edson
Troy A. Eid
Richard D. English
Frank J. Fahrenkopf
Edwin J. Feulner
Eugene V. Fife
George Folsome
Tom Fowler
Mark A. Franz
Craig L. Fuller
Christopher J. Fussner
Eric Garfinkel
James Gattuso
Julian H. Gingold
Claud L. Gingrich
Martin Gruss
D. George Harris
Joseph W. Harrison
Cornelius Higgins
Carla A. Hills
Alan F. Holmer
Samuel M. Hoskinson
Roy M. Huffington

James D. Jameson
Charles R. Johnston
Tirso del Junco
Gilbert B. Kaplan
Christopher B. Kearney
John G. Keller
J. Darrell Kelley
Michael T. Kelley
Robert W. Kelly
James L. Kenworthy
Jeffrey G. Kupper
Alan Lenz
Robert E. Lighthizer
W. Kenneth Lindhorst
Marilyn Loewy
Jennifer Macdonald
Michael C. Maibach
Todd Malan
Dan Mariaschin
Herbert E. Marks
Dan Mattoon
Eugene J. McAllister
Tim McBride
Shellyn McCaffrey
Richard McCormack
Paul W. McCracken
Frank Mermoud
Fred Meyer
Johnathan Miller
Lane F. Miller
William A. Mogel
Antonio Monroig
Randall B. Moorhead
Robert A. Mosbacher
Sol Mosher
Michael H. Moskow
Robert Mottice
Frank Murkowski
Robert Neimeth
Connie Nicholas
Robert D. Orr
C. R. "Bobby" Ortiz
John E. Osborn
Eric C. Peterson
Gwen Pharo

David J. Posek
Jerome H. Powell
R. Sean Randolph
Jack Ranson
James B. Rapp
John M. Rau
Holland L. Redfield
Julie Reese
Thomas H. Reynolds
Edwina Rogers
Joseph E. Rogers
Theodore Rosen
Fred Rowe
Gloria Cataneo Rudman
Charlotte Rush
Leonard E. Santos
Bill Sauey
William B. Schuck
Susan Schwab
Doug Seay
Jeffrey L. Seltzer
Mark Serrano
Therese Shaheen
Philip Shapiro
Judy Shelton
Sichan Siv
Michael P. Skarzynski
Josh Smith
Mary Louise Smith
Ronald J. Sorini
Carey Stacy
John E. Stiner
James M. Strock
Chris Swonger
Dennis B. Tenney
Margaret G. Thompson
Robert L. Thompson
Pam Turner
Paula Unruh
Herb D. Vest
M. Christine Vick
Jackelyn Viera-Iloff
J. Antonio Villamil
Fred Volcansek
June Langston Walton

Russ Wapensky
Peter S. Watson
Olin L. Wethington
Dennis E. Whitfield
Edwin D. Williamson
Richard S. Williamson
Ewen M. Wilson
Deborah Wince-Smith
James L. Wolbarsht
Esther Lee Yao

**U.S. Leadership in a
Changing World**
Olympia Snowe, *Chair*
Elliott Abrams
Richard V. Allen
Richard Armitage
Elliott Auchter
James A. Baker
Doug Bandow
David H. Barron
Jeffrey Bergner
Robert Blackwill
Richard R. Burt
R. Ian Butterfield
Gerald Carmen
Peter Tali Coleman
Thomas Crocker
J. D. Crouch
Peter H. Dailey
Brian A. Davenport
Thomas C. Dawson
J. Michael Deault
Vincent DeCain
Kenneth E. deGraffenreid
David B. H. Denoon
Chuck DeVore
Lawrence T. Di Rita
Walter Herbert Dixon
James W. Dyer
Nancy Bearg Dyke
Lois L. Evans
Blanche Hill Fawell
Max Fisher
James D. FitzPatrick

Henrietta Holsman Fore
Randy Fort
Matthew C. Freedman
Frank J. Gaffney
Christopher Gersten
Patrick Glynn
Jeffrey J. Grieco
Richard N. Haass
Alexander Haig
Stefan A. Halper
Morris B. Hansen
Peter J. Hickman
Robert C. Hill
Jack Holmes
Richard N. Holwill
Charles Horner
G. Philip Hughes
William B. Inglee
Karl D. Jackson
Robert Jenkins
Whittle Johnston
Elliott Jones
Richard Joseph
Walter Kansteiner
Nancy Landon Kassebaum
Henry A. Kissinger
Linas Kojelis
Jim Kolbe
Michael V. Kostiw
Sven F. Kraemer
Edward J. Lacey
Jewel Lafontant-Mankarious
John F. Lehman
Ronald F. Lehman
Welquiz Ray Lopez
Carnes Lord
Richard G. Lugar
Marlin Maddoux
Dan Mariaschin
Susan Marone
Jorge Mas-Canosa
Shawn H. McCormick
Robert McCreight
Edward J. Melanson
Constantine C. Menges

Dean Metropoulos
J. William Middendorf
Adib Mikhail
G. Cranwell Montgomery
Steven Mosher
Henry R. Nau
John R. New
David Norcross
William J. Olson
Douglas Paal
R. N. Palarino
Frank J. Parker
Gerald Parsky
Gardner G. Peckham
Kenneth Peel
Daniel Pipes
Alec Poitevint
John Price
Janos Radvanyi
Jay S. Reibel
Peter Rodman
Stephen L. Rosen
Lonnie Rowell
Derik Schmidt
William Schneider
Suzanne Scholte
Brent Scowcroft
Andy Semmel
Frederick F. Shaheen
Robert M. Smalley
Jed C. Snyder
Rob Sobhani
Michael E. Sotirhos
Jacob Stein
Andy Taggart
Sheldon Tajerstein
Paul M. Temple
Margaret DeB. Tutwiler
James Webb
Caspar W. Weinberger
Curtin Winsor
Ann B. Wrobleski
Robert Zoellick

Defense

Dick Cheney, *Co-Chair*
Jeane Kirkpatrick, *Co-Chair*
David Addington
Wendy Safford Allen
Stanton D. Anderson
Ernest Angelo
John R. Apel
Anne L. Armstrong
Walter A. Baker
Douglas A. Brook
Hayden G. Bryan
Gregory B. Butler
Stephen Buyer
Margo D. B. Carlisle
Ron Carlson
Philip Cherry
Angelo Codevilla
William E. Conner
Henry F. Cooper
Thomas Crocker
Jeremiah A. Denton
William L. Dickinson
Paula J. Dobriansky
Elaine Donnelly
Nancy Dorn
Raymond F. DuBois
Judy Dunaway
Wil Ebel
Stanley Ebner
Andrea Fischer-Newman
S. Robert Foley
Anne Foreman
Frank J. Gaffney
Ruth Eileen Ganister
H. Lawrence Garrett
Margaret B. Graham
William R. Graham
Martin Gruss
Stephen J. Hadley
Stefan A. Halper
Mike Hellon
Michael Herson
Amoretta Hoeber
Marjorie Holt

Mildred Homan
Mary L. Howell
Edwin L. Hullander
Duncan Hunter
Fred C. Ikle
Bruce Jackson
P. X. Kelley
Robert W. Kelly
Sven F. Kraemer
Thomas F. Kranz
Edward J. Lacey
Christopher M. Lehman
I. Lewis Libby
Susan Morrisey Livingstone
Sandy Martel
Theodor C. Mataxis
Mack F. Mattingly
Edward J. Melanson
Dale L. Moody
Diane Morales
David R. Nicholas
Terrence O'Donnell
Sean O'Keefe
Ann C. Petersen
Kien Pham
H. McGuire Riley
Will Roosma
Phyllis Schlafly
John P. Schmitz
John D. Selby
Perry T. Sikes
David J. Smith
Thomas H. Snitch
Floyd Spence
Herbert Baker Spring
Delbert L. Spurlock
Ruth Steinberg
Ted Stevens
William H. Taft
Jacqueline Tillman
Victoria Toensing
Michelle Van Cleave
Barbara Vucanovich
Harry Walters
Erwin C. Ward

John W. Warner
W. Bruce Weinrod
Heather A. Wilson
Paul D. Wolfowitz
John W. Wood
Dov S. Zakheim

Reforming the Legal & Regulatory Systems

Marilyn Quayle, *Co-Chair*
Robert Bork, *Co-Chair*
Susan Allen
Joseph A. Artabane
Bob Auchter
Thorne Auchter
Charles Bailey
Don Bain
Barbara Barrett
Christopher Bond
Diana Culp Bork
Phil Brady
Marshall Breger
Patty Cafferata
Timothy R. Campbell
Gerald Caplan
A. Thomas Carroccio
Roger Clegg
Joe Cobb
Nielsen Cochran
Thad Cochran
Charles J. Cooper
Paul Coverdell
Andrew Cowin
Woody Cozad
LeGree S. Daniels
Miguel De Grandy
Susan Eckerly
Gary D. Engebretson
Peter Ferrara
David Flory
Charles Fried
Stuart M. Gerson
Donald Goff
Patricia Gormley
C. Boyden Gray

Eugene W. Hickok
Peter Hoffman
Perry O. Hooper
John L. Howard
Asa Hutchinson
Sally Reed Impastato
J. Barrington Jackson
Jared E. Jossem
John C. Kalavritinos
James F. Kelley
R. E. Kincaid
David M. Laney
Richard G. Larsen
Will Lauber

Bill Ludwig
Robert MacKichan
William Wade Matchneer
C. V. McClellan
Edward R. McGlynn
Michael Miller
Mike Mills
Daniel Oliver
Walter Olson
William Perry Pendley
Shirley D. Peterson
Daniel J. Popeo
George Priest
Daniel P. Ryan

Gene Schaerr
Randal P. Schumacher
Warren S. Shulman
Mary Sophos
Chris Swonger
Gerald J. Todaro
Everett M. Upshaw
John W. Vardaman
Carolyn L. Weaver
Elizabeth Whelan
Carolyn Wright
Geoff Ziebart

Index

A

ABA. *See* American Bar Association
ABM Treaty, 219, 221-222, 225, 233
Abortion issues, 161
Acid rain, 75
Acquisition streamlining, 226
Acreage Reduction Program, 199
ADA. *See* Americans with Disabilities Act
Adams, John, 154
Adoption, 161
Advertising by lawyers, 39-40
AEGIS air defense system, 223
Affirmative action, 32, 147, 150-151
AFL-CIO, 17
Africa: Clinton administration foreign policy, 174-175; emerging trade markets, 193; U.S. policy, 273-276
AFT. *See* American Federation of Teachers
Agriculture: trade policy, 198-200
Aid to Families with Dependent Children, 103-104
Air defense system, 223
Air traffic control, 32
Allen, George, 124
Alternative sentencing, 124-125
American Academy of Matrimonial Lawyers, 41
American Bar Association, 37
American Bar Foundation, 40

American Federation of Teachers, 129-130, 145
American Medical Association, 57
American Petroleum Institute, 91
Americans with Disabilities Act, 20, 25-26
Amtrak subsidies, 31-32
Andean Act, 192
ANWR. *See* Arctic National Wildlife Refuge
APEC. *See* Asia Pacific Economic Cooperation
Arab-Israeli conflict, 268-269
Arafat, Yasir, 269
Archer, Bill, 14
Arctic National Wildlife Refuge, 94
Armey, Dick, 14
Arms control, 232-234
Arms Export Control Act, 228
Asean. *See* Association of Southeast Asian Nations
Asia: Clinton administration foreign policy, 173; emerging trade markets, 190-191; U.S. foreign policy, 258-264
Asia Pacific Economic Cooperation, 191
Assault weapons, 126
Assertive multilateralism, 169
Association of Southeast Asian Nations, 231; U.S. policy, 262
Association of Trial Lawyers of America, 43
ATLA. *See* Association of Trial Lawyers of America

P

Palestinian Authority, 269
Panama: U.S. policy, 266
Parents' rights, 153-154
Parole policies, 124
Partnership for Peace, 170
Payroll taxes, 8
Peace. *See* Foreign policy
Peacekeeping missions, 205-206, 231, 276-277
Pell Grant Program, 143, 144
People's Republic of China: U.S. policy, 260-261
Perry, William, 148, 255
Pinckney (Mich.) Board of Education, 135-136
Plan 3, 60
Point-of-service plans, 64
Poland: emerging trade markets, 188
Political assistance: for Russia, 256; U.S. foreign policy, 247
Political leadership, 166
Politically Incorrect, 159
POS. *See* Point-of-service plans
Poverty. *See* Welfare
Powell, Lewis, 45
PPOs. *See* Preferred provider organizations
Prayer in schools, 159-160
PRC. *See* People's Republic of China
Preferred provider organizations, 64
Prescription drugs, 64
Preventive health care, 64
Private attorney general statutes, 39
Private-practice teaching, 138
Private property rights, 77, 154
Procedural reforms for litigation, 47-48
Product liability, 44, 49
Project SEED, 137
Property rights. *See* Private property rights
Provider-sponsored networks, 64
PSNs. *See* Provider-sponsored networks
Public education system. *See* Education

Public housing, 118. *See* Federal housing policy
Public Utility Holding Company Act of 1935, 96
Public Utility Regulatory Policies Act of 1978, 96
PUHCA. *See* Public Utility Holding Company Act of 1935
Punitive damages, 45, 49

Q

Quota system, 147-150

R

Rabin, Yitzhak, 268
Racial quotas. *See* Quota system
Rand Corporation, 150
R&D. *See* Research and development
Reagan, Ronald: National Oceans Policy, 277-278; prodemocracy policy, 245; results of Reagan tax cuts, 4-5; vision for America, ix
Reagan administration: free trade reforms, 184; international trade policy, 177-178; military buildup, 203-204; tenant-based subsidy program, 113. *See also* Uruguay Round
Reconstruction Finance Corporation, 110
Rector, Margaret, 82
Reed, Ralph, 159
Reformers, 156, 158-159
Regulatory policy: building support for reform, 21-23; case examples of excessiveness, 17-18; costs of regulation, 19-21; effect on health care costs, 53-54; empowerment approach, 27-28; environmental regulations, 22-23; impartiality of, 28; incentives, 28-29; returning power to state and local governments, 24; transportation, 29-33; wetlands